# International Banking Deregulation

# International Banking Deregulation

## The Great Banking Experiment

RICHARD DALE

First published 1992
Reprinted 1994

Blackwell Publishers
108 Cowley Road
Oxford OX4 1JF
UK

238 Main Street
Cambridge, Massachusetts 02142
USA

*British Library Cataloguing in Publication Data*
A CIP catalogue record for this book is available from the British Library.

*Library of Congress Cataloging-in-Publication Data*
A CIP catalogue record for this book is available from the Library of Congress.

ISBN 0–631–16057–4
Typeset in 11 on 13pt Ehrhardt by Alden Multimedia Ltd.
Printed in Great Britain by Athenaeum Press Ltd, Newcastle upon Tyne.

This book is printed on acid-free paper.

# Contents

# List of Tables

# List of Figures

# Acknowledgements

I wish to thank the publishers of the *Journal of International Banking Law* for allowing me to draw on material contained in 'The new financial regulatory framework in Canada', 3, 3 (1988); 'Japan's "Glass–Steagall" Act', 2, 3 (1987); and 'Glass–Steagall and US banks' securities activities' 5, 8 (1990). I would also like to thank the publishers of the *Journal of International Securities Markets* for permission to use material contained in 'The EEC's approach to capital adequacy for investment firms', 4 autumn (1990) and 'Repealing Glass–Steagall', 5, summer (1991).

Research undertaken for this book was funded by the Economic and Social Research Council (ESRC) to whom I would like to express my appreciation. This funding relates to a project on the regulation of financial conglomerates and also to work undertaken as part of the ESRC's single European market initiative.

Finally I would like to thank Siobhan Nelson for her patience and tireless dedication in preparing the typescript for publication.

# Introduction

Seventy years ago US banks were becoming heavily involved in securities markets, as their traditional lending business showed signs of drying up. Learned articles were written with such titles as 'The decline of the commercial loan',[1] as more and more companies went directly to the capital markets to raise funds, thereby by-passing the banking system altogether. In other words, the process of 'securitization' that we hear so much about today was also a characteristic of US financial markets in the 1920s. Furthermore, the response of the banking industry was the same then as it is now — namely a determination to find ways round regulatory barriers standing in the way of banks' entry into the securities business.

As US banks circumvented statutory restrictions on their activities by setting up securities affiliates, some observers became increasingly uneasy. For instance, the US Comptroller of the Currency reported in 1920 that the securities affiliates of banks 'have become an element of increasing peril to the banks with which they are associated'. He went on to say:

> The business of legitimate banking is entirely separate and distinct from the kind of business conducted by many of the 'securities corporations', and it would be difficult if not impossible for the same set of officers to conduct safely, soundly, and successfully the conservative business of the national bank and at the same time direct and manage the speculative returns and promotions of the ancillary institutions. These varying institutions demand a different kind of ability and experience on the part of those who manage them, and the two types of business when combined with one management are likely to be operated to the advantage of neither.[2]

The entry of US banks into the securities industry was followed in 1929–33 by the most dramatic banking collapse in financial history. During this period 9,000 institutions failed, representing one-fifth of US commercial banks holding nearly one-tenth of the volume of deposits. The contemporary view was that banks' involvement in securities business had played a major part in the disaster. A subcommittee of the Senate Committee on Banking and Currency reported in 1931 that 'the experience of the past ten years lends spectacular confirmation to the view that the more intensive participation by commercial banks in the capital market exaggerates financial and business fluctuations in the economy and undermines the stability of the economic organisation of the country'.[3] This interpretation of events was subsequently reflected in the US Glass–Steagall Act of 1933 which formally separated banking from securities business and, in particular, prevented banks from setting up securities affiliates.

Today the same market pressure that propelled US banks into stock market business in the 1920s — namely the 'securitization' of lending — is engulfing the banking industry worldwide and eroding the residual barriers between commercial and investment banking. In continental Europe where there is a long tradition of universal banking, banks are rapidly increasing the scale of their securities activities; in the UK, banking and securities business is being merged in a revolutionary upheaval of the whole financial system; and in those countries where banking and securities business is still separated by law, notably the US and Japan, banks are free to combine both activities in third markets and are increasingly finding ways round the law in their home markets. Against this background the Glass–Steagall Act is itself under critical review and may soon be amended to accommodate the current trend towards financial conglomeration.

The question that has to be considered is whether banks' growing involvement in securities activities could have destabilizing consequences of the kind which contemporary observers attributed to US banks' securities affiliates in the 1920s and early 1930s. Put another way, can the mixing of banking and securities business be regulated in such a way as to avoid the danger of catastrophic destabilization of financial markets? This study addresses the policy implications behind the banking industry's move into securities markets, drawing on the regulatory experience of the USA, UK, Canada, Japan, West Germany and Switzerland. Chapter 1 examines the problem of bank failures and the role of the lender of last resort; chapter 2 reviews the US banking crisis of 1929–33 which is central to the whole debate about mixing banking and securities business. Chapter 3 considers the arguments for and against allowing banks to underwrite and deal in securities; chapters 4–8 describe and assess the regulatory approach adopted by major financial centre countries towards banks' securities operations; chapter 9 examines EEC policy initiatives in this area; chapter 10 compares national regulatory regimes in the light of theoretical policy alternatives; and chapter 11 draws together the conclusions from the

preceding analysis. Chapter 12 has been added as a postscript to incorporate the regulatory lessons of the collapse of Bank of Credit and
Commerce International.

## Notes

1 Lauchlin Currie, 'The decline of the commercial loan', *Quarterly Journal of Economics*, 45 (1931), pp. 698–709.
2 'Report of the Comptroller of the Currency' (1920), pp. 55–6.
3 Cited in Edward Kelly, 'Legislative history of the Glass–Steagall Act', in Ingo Walter, ed., *Deregulating Wall Street* (John Wiley, New York, 1985), p. 46.

# 1

# Bank Failures and the Official Safety Net

The purpose of the present study is to examine the safety and soundness implications of banks' increasing involvement in securities markets. In order to assess the risks involved in this extension of banks' non-bank activities it is necessary first of all to understand the innate fragility of deposit-taking institutions, their propensity to contagious collapse and the consequent need for official safeguards in the form of deposit insurance, the lender of last resort and other protective mechanisms.

## The Fragility of Banks

It has long been recognized that banks are, within a free market setting, prone to failure. It is also well understood that the failure of one bank can have damaging knock-on effects as confidence is shaken, leading to precautionary deposit withdrawals and generalized financial turbulence. The US banking collapse of 1929–33 was triggered by large-scale conversions of bank deposits into cash, but other forms of transfer can also be destabilizing. For instance, following the failure of Herstatt Bank in June 1974 there was a flight from Eurodollar deposits into domestic US deposits; the UK in 1973–5 experienced a massive run on small or 'secondary' banks that eventually threatened the entire domestic banking system; the collapse of Continental Illinois in the spring of 1984 was followed by a 'flight to quality' as investors switched their funds from US bank deposits to government paper, thereby driving up the cost of bank funds; and, most recently, the USA has had to cope with a precautionary shift of deposits out of the troubled savings and loan industry.

Banks possess a number of characteristics that can, taken together, give rise to contagious financial disorders of the kind described. First, there is the question of gearing. Banks, in fulfilling their intermediary function, operate on a relatively low capital base which, depending on the definition of capital used, will typically be in the region of 4–8 per cent of total assets. Any diminution in asset value can therefore have a correspondingly large impact on net worth.

A second characteristic of banks is that a large proportion of their assets are not readily marketable and can be disposed of promptly (if at all) only at a significant discount on their book value. Therefore rapid asset contraction of the kind that might be necessary in the face of severe liquidity pressures can typically only be accomplished at heavy cost.

A third feature of banks is their dependence on a precarious deposit/ funding base which can be relied upon to sustain operations only so long as the bank concerned commands the confidence of financial markets. Once confidence is lost funds cannot be attracted by raising the return to depositors, since a risk premium is often interpreted as evidence of a deteriorating financial position.

Finally, the financial condition of a bank cannot be determined from its published statements. This is because key risk parameters such as the quality of the loan portfolio are not captured in the accounts and also because such information as may be available can be quickly out-dated by subsequent transactions (for instance, in the foreign exchange, futures and options markets). The lack of transparency means that sound banks can fall victim to market rumour and unsound banks may go undetected until it is too late.

Various regulatory initiatives have been taken from time to time to limit the above potential sources of instability. Banks have been required to raise their capital ratios; maturity-mismatching − the extent to which the maturity of assets exceeds that of liabilities − has been subject to supervisory review; more comprehensive disclosure of banks' financial condition has been required; and the regulatory environment has also favoured the 'securitization' (or repackaging in marketable form) of an increasing proportion of bank assets.

Nevertheless, the underlying fragility of banks remains and the possibility of contagious disorders sparked off by some unexpected event continues to be a source of anxiety to regulatory authorities. Accordingly, most national banking systems have in place extensive protective mechanisms, embracing deposit insurance, access to official liquidity support and even recapitalization and nationalization schemes, designed either to support troubled banks or to safeguard depositors in the event of failure.

Paradoxically, the presence of this official safety net has the effect of subsidizing risk-taking because banks are no longer subject to the discipline of the marketplace — in particular their cost of borrowing does not accurately reflect the risks they incur because depositors believe they are protected. Therefore, in order to prevent risks being transferred to the deposit insurance fund or the lender of last resort, regulatory authorities have felt obliged to introduce a panoply of controls designed to curb risk-taking by banks. For their part, banks are forever trying to break free of these bonds, for instance by introducing innovative off-balance-sheet transactions, so that regulators must constantly be on their guard to ensure that they are controlling *all* and not merely *some* of the risky activities that go to make up a bank's overall risk profile. Quite simply, if an aggressively managed bank is prevented by regulatory constraints from adopting its preferred high-risk/high-return policy in one business area, it will be inclined to seek out lesser regulated activities where it is free to pursue whatever risk strategy it chooses.

For all these reasons banks and other depository institutions are vulnerable to contagious financial disorders even at the best of times. However, these are not the best of times for the banking industry. On the contrary, worldwide the competitive position of banks has been deteriorating in response to several adverse developments.

In the first place, banks have faced increasing competition on the assets side of their balance sheet as commercial paper, corporate bonds and other forms of direct financing have displaced conventional bank lending. Simultaneously, they have faced a squeeze on the liabilities side. The dismantling of deposit interest rate controls in the USA and Japan, and the introduction of interest-paying current accounts elsewhere (depriving banks of a major proportion of their traditional free funding) has pushed up banks' own borrowing costs. This trend has been further aggravated by a marked decline in banks' credit standing over the last decade and an associated rise in the cost of wholesale funds.

More generally, the revolution in communications technology has reduced the value of the banking franchise. As the cost of recording, transmitting and processing information has fallen, it has become more possible for borrowers and lenders to deal with each other directly, thereby by-passing the banking system. The shift in the competitive environment, which has eroded the economic role of banks while enhancing the function of securities firms, is viewed by some as a reason for allowing banks greater participation in securities markets.[1] However, this kind of reasoning — which was used in a slightly different context to support US banks' involvement in securities markets in the 1920s — is surely flawed. The fact that traditional banking business is under pressure on a number of fronts should make one more and not less cautious about extending the range of banks' permissible activities to include potentially high-risk securities business.

## The Official Safety Net

It is a paradoxical fact that as national banking systems have been deregulated in deference to market forces, regulatory authorities, in their role as lender of last resort, have become more inclined to intervene in support of troubled banks and/or their depositors. The following survey of national practice in this area points to a growing official commitment in most countries to safeguard depositors and avoid market disruptions — although, in a major departure from this trend, the US Administration is proposing financial reforms that would leave depositors more exposed to the risk of bank failures.

In the *United States* the Federal Deposit Insurance Corporation (FDIC) handles bank insolvencies, while the Federal Reserve exercises the traditional lender of last resort role by providing liquidity support where appropriate. The FDIC offers two kinds of protection to depositors. First, all deposits under the statutory cut-off point (currently $100,000) are formally insured. Second, and just as important, there is de facto protection for *uninsured* deposits arising from the FDIC's favoured method of dealing with failed banks — the so-called 'Purchase and Assumption' transaction. Under a P and A transaction the FDIC replaces bad assets with cash while deposits and other non-subordinated liabilities are assumed by another bank. In such assisted mergers *all* depositors, insured and uninsured, are made whole. Thus in the 620 bank failures recorded in 1933–82, 99.8 per cent of all *depositors* had their deposits paid in full and 98.9 per cent of all *deposits* were recovered.[2]

Against this background, the FDIC came round to the view that the extent of de facto deposit insurance cover was tending to undermine financial discipline. An FDIC policy study published in 1983 argued this case on a number of grounds. It noted that because of increased volatility of earnings, intensified competition, higher loan losses and greater financial instability, the US banking system was becoming more risky. It further argued that this risk would increase as the process of bank deregulation proceeded ('the responsibilities of the deposit insurance system are expanding at a time when regulation is contracting, setting up a potentially dangerous situation'). The study also concluded that banks' increased reliance on uninsured money-market liabilities was not, as might have been hoped, strengthening market discipline since 'the suppliers of these funds, who have the potential to provide some discipline, also appear somewhat indifferent to risk in larger banks because of the conviction that the FDIC or some other arm of the Federal Government will intervene to prevent them from suffering any loss'.[3] Finally, the FDIC study observed that because the P and A approach was almost invariably adopted for large bank failures,[4] it had 'effectively provided large depositors in large banks with a much greater degree of insurance protection against loss than has been provided to large depositors in relatively small banks'.[5] The overall policy conclusion was as follows:

> The FDIC recommends adoption of procedures that would result in reduction in the de facto level of insurance protection for 'uninsured' depositors and general creditors. By introducing an element of loss-sharing, large creditors and investors would be more risk-sensitive and more selective in their choice of banks; therefore, market discipline could be increased significantly.[6]

In line with this reasoning the FDIC developed a 'modified pay-off' experiment. In lieu of its usual P and A approach to failed banks, the FDIC proposed to combine a pay-off of insured depositors and other general creditors based on the present value of anticipated collections by the receivership. In other words, uninsured depositors would be exposed to losses arising out of the receivership in a way that did not happen when the FDIC organized assisted mergers. The procedure was used in 9 out of 17 bank failures between March and May 1984 but the experiment was then cut short by the Continental Illinois crisis.

Continental Illinois was then the seventh-largest US bank with assets of over $41bn. Following the revelation of serious problems with non-performing loans the bank suffered a catastrophic withdrawal of deposits, amounting at one point to well over $12bn. The implications of a bank failure of this size were subsequently spelled out by the then FDIC Chairman, Mr William Isaac, in congressional testimony:

> closing the bank and paying off insured depositors could have had catastrophic consequences for other banks and the entire economy. Insured accounts totalled only slightly more than $3bn. This meant that depositors and other private creditors with over $30bn in claims would have had their funds tied up for years in a bankruptcy proceeding awaiting the liquidation of assets and the settlement of litigation. Hundreds of small banks would have been particularly hard hit. Almost 2,300 small banks had nearly $6bn at risk in Continental; 66 of them had more than their capital on the line and another 113 had between 50 and 100 per cent. More generally, closure of a bank, whose solvency was apparently not impaired, in response to its

liquidity and confidence problems would have raised concerns about other, soundly managed banks.[7]

In an attempt to stabilize the situation the FDIC announced on 17 May a temporary capital infusion to Continental while massive liquidity support was provided both by a consortium of 24 banks and the Federal Reserve Bank of Chicago. At the same time the FDIC gave an unprecedented undertaking that 'in any arrangements that may be necessary to achieve a permanent solution, all depositors and other general creditors of the bank will be fully protected, and service to the bank's customers will not be interrupted'.[8] When the funding crisis persisted the FDIC announced on 26 July that in consideration for a permanent capital infusion it was acquiring 80 per cent ownership of the parent company, Continental Illinois Corporation. The biggest rescue operation in financial history had ended with the effective nationalization of the victim bank, albeit the US authorities preferred to use the term 'conservatorship'.

The Continental episode not only terminated the experiment of exposing depositors to greater risk of loss through the modified pay-off, it also brought to the fore the perception that there were some banks which were quite simply too big to be allowed to fail.

As Mr William Seidman, Chairman of the FDIC put it in 1988, 'it was assumed, though never made official government policy, that there were 10 to 12 banks that were too-big-to-fail in the sense that all creditors would be protected',[9] and Mr Seidman went on to lend further credence to this perception when he stated:

> The bottom line in this discussion is that *nobody really knows what might happen if a major bank were allowed to default*, and the opportunity to find out is not one likely to be appealing to those in authority or to the public. Combining cost factors with unacceptable risk, most large banks likely are going to be handled in a manner that protects all depositors and other general creditors.[10] (Italics added.)

If some banks are indeed too-large-to-fail, then smaller banks clearly operate at a competitive disadvantage. In recognition of the dangers arising from preferential treatment of larger banks. Mr Seidman stated that 'we are endeavouring to reduce that problem by using failure resolution methods that protect all depositors and bank creditors whenever feasible'.[11] Consistent with this approach, over 99 per cent of uninsured deposits were fully protected in bank failures from 1985 through 1990 — a period covering the highest number of US bank failures since the 1930s.[12] Attempts to harness market discipline by allowing non-insured depositors to incur losses were therefore abandoned in favour of a policy of de facto deposit insurance for all.[13]

In a remarkable about-turn the US Administration, in early 1991, proposed as part of its broader financial reforms a curtailment of deposit protection and abandonment of the too-big-to-fail doctrine. The reasons behind this move were similar to those which prompted the FDIC to introduce its ill-fated 'modified pay-off' experiment in the early 1980s. The central idea is to 'return the system to a level of coverage that preserves stability, while obtaining an important level of market discipline from ... sophisticated investors'.[14] Accordingly, it is proposed (inter alia) that insurance coverage should be reduced for multiple insured accounts, that protection for non-deposit creditors should be eliminated and that uninsured depositors should only be protected where this represents the least costly resolution method or where the Federal Reserve Board and the Treasury Department jointly determine that there is a broader threat to financial stability.

This last qualification may prove crucial if the proposals are implemented, since it could lead to a reinstatement of the too-big-to-fail doctrine in a somewhat different form. In the meantime the mere *possibility* that large depositors could be exposed to greater risks may have destabilizing consequences.

In the *United Kingdom* the Bank of England has also adopted a highly cautious approach to bank failures and deposit losses. The Bank's present policy has been influenced by the UK secondary banking crisis of 1973–5 which was characterized by contagious deposit withdrawals from virtually the entire secondary banking sector. A Bank of England director who helped to set up an emergency lender of last resort facility (the 'lifeboat') to deal with this crisis has commented on the experience as follows:

> In the first eight months of 1974 about thirty secondary banks had to be taken into communal support by the Lifeboat ... and outside the Lifeboat at least as many required support under individual arrangements from their clearing bankers or from the Bank of England itself or from parent companies and other large shareholders. Without these supporting operations virtually all of them would have collapsed and the cumulative effect of those collapses would have spread much more widely through the banking system. Undoubtedly many of the primary banks would have been swept away in the maelstrom.[15]

The Bank's rescue operation included not only large-scale liquidity support, but the guaranteeing of a troubled bank's loan portfolio, the acquisition of another problem loan portfolio and the takeover of one institution as a subsidiary of the Bank.

The events of 1973–5 undoubtedly shaped the Bank of England's response to the next major UK banking crisis which was the collapse of Johnson Matthey Bankers (JMB) in September 1984. JMB was a modest-sized British bank with only £2bn worth of assets but its operations penetrated to the heart of the domestic banking system, in that, as a member of the London Gold Market, it had close interbank dealings with other, more prestigious, institutions. Rather than allow JMB to fail the Bank of England put together a rescue package that involved a takeover of JMB by the Bank for a nominal sum. In subsequently explaining its decision to act in this way the Bank referred specifically to the danger of a contagious loss of confidence centring on, but not confined to, members of the London Gold Market — citing as evidence the fact that, while the rescue operation was still being discussed, 'some major foreign banks were refusing to deal with first-class British banks'.[16]

The implication is that if the failure of a bank the size of JMB can have dangerously destabilizing knock-on effects, other, larger, banks would also have to be supported. On the other hand, the Bank of England declined to support British and Commonwealth Merchant Bank, a small but well capitalized institution with some £300mn of deposits, when it was forced to close its doors in June 1990 as a result of problems originating within a non-bank affiliate.

*Germany's* policy on bank failures has similarly moved in a more protective direction.[17] In June 1974 Bankhaus Herstatt, with total assets of around $800mn, was ordered by the West German authorities to close its doors, after suffering foreign exchange losses which were eventually put at over $450mn. The timing of Herstatt's closure disrupted the clearing mechanism for spot foreign exchange transactions and imposed heavy losses on counterpart banks. This in turn had damaging effects on the international inter-bank market, where Japanese and Italian banks, in particular, experienced funding problems. Furthermore, within West Germany there were heavy deposit withdrawals from smaller banks, some of which received official support.

The turmoil that followed the collapse of Herstatt clearly had an impact on the Deutsche Bundesbank's subsequent attitude to bank failures. Accordingly, when it became apparent in November 1983 that Schröder, Münchmeyer, Hengst (SMH), a private bank with assets of DM 2.2bn, was insolvent, the Bundesbank orchestrated an elaborate rescue operation involving the support of the domestic banking industry. The inference to be drawn is that West Germany is no longer prepared to contemplate major bank failures or deposit losses.

*France,* too, has adopted a protective policy towards bank failures.

Under Article 52 of the 1984 Bank Law the Governor of the Bank of France may 'call on all credit institutions to participate in the necessary measures to protect the interests of depositors and third parties, ensure the continued proper operation of the banking system and protect the reputation of the financial community'. This controversial power to *demand* financial support from commercial banks was exercised in October 1988 when a rescue package was put together for Al Saudi Banque which had incurred losses of over FF 2bn. As part of this package, all banks operating in France were required to provide loans on concessionary terms to Al Saudi, or, alternatively to make a one-off lump sum payment equivalent to just over 30 per cent of their share of the total loan facility. In contrast, all non-resident depositors were repaid in full.[18]

This operation was designed primarily to protect Paris's reputation as an international financial centre, but the French authorities were no doubt aware that the liquidation of a bank of even Al Saudi's moderate size (approximately FF 8bn or $1.25bn in assets) could have had powerful ripple effects (there having been no bank failure in France since 1980). However, when a smaller institution, Banque de Participations et de Placements, became insolvent after incurring losses of FF 200mn on a balance sheet total of FF 900mn, the French authorities decided to accept its closure and liquidation in the knowledge that the ensuing losses (most deposits were fully insured) would have little impact on financial markets.[19]

*Canada* experienced its first bank failures in 60 years when in September 1985 Canadian Commercial Bank (CCB) and Northland Bank were forced to close their doors after receiving some C$1.8bn of official liquidity support. The earlier publicized troubles of CCB had caused a large-scale shift by uninsured wholesale depositors out of Canada's regional banks into the large chartered banks. In their attempts to sustain confidence in CCB (the tenth largest of Canada's 14 domestic banks, with stated assets of some C$3bn) Ministers and public officials had made reassuring statements about the bank's financial condition which might have founded compensation claims by uninsured depositors. Accordingly, special legislation was enacted to compensate all depositors fully, regardless of the C$60,000 statutory cut-off point for insured deposits.

The Estey Report on the collapse of CCB and Northland Bank, commented as follows on the lender of last resort role:

> what has developed from this crisis is not so much a policy of universal compensation of creditors caught up in a bank failure, but the recognition that a decision to save a bank carries with it, almost inevitably, the obligation to either see the bank through the crisis one way or another, or to pay off

in full all persons at loss in the failure, other than capital investors broadly defined.[20]

In all, the financial contagion originating with CCB's troubles had a major impact on five other banks. Northland Bank failed; Mercantile Bank and Morguard Bank were found merger partners; and Continental Bank survived a funding crisis. During this upheaval the federal government paid out C$430mn to uninsured depositors and incurred total losses of C$900mn.

The events of 1985 have certainly brought home to the Canadian authorities the destabilizing potential of contagious deposit withdrawals by uninsured depositors. Furthermore, the lengths to which the authorities were prepared to go in safeguarding depositors with CCB suggest that deposit losses will not be readily countenanced in future.

*Japan* experienced a major banking panic in 1927 during which 32 banks were forced to close their doors and 8 per cent of domestic deposits were lost. The Bank of Japan was then hampered in its rescue efforts because it had no legal authority to grant unsecured loans — a deficiency subsequently remedied by the Bank of Japan Law of 1942.

In 1965 the Bank of Japan used its new powers to save Yamaichi Securities, one of the big four securities firms, from collapse. The Bank's total lending (mainly unsecured) to Yamaichi and to Oi Securities — a smaller firm that had also defaulted — amounted to the equivalent of $93mn at one time.[21]

There have been no bank failures in Japan during the post-World War Two period, other than the forced merger of Haiwa Sogo Bank in December 1985, and no deposit losses whatsoever. Indeed, Japan's deposit insurance fund has not once been drawn upon since its inception in 1971. Even so the Bank of Japan takes the view that in the context of domestic financial deregulation 'prevention of the domino-effect of bank failures has become the key issue'.[22] Accordingly, the deposit insurance fund has been considerably strengthened with passage of the Deposit Insurance Act in July, 1986. At the same time the Deposit Insurance Corporation's powers have been enlarged to include the provision of financial assistance to an institution which is assisting a problem bank through merger. In the light of both the post-war historical record and these recent precautionary initiatives it would appear that the Japanese authorities are determined to avoid destabilizing bank liquidations and deposit losses.[23]

## New challenges for safety net

The above survey of lender of last resort policies suggests that the major financial centre countries have developed a strong aversion to bank failures. This attitude is rooted in the fear of contagious deposit runs and destabilization of the domestic financial system of the kind that several countries have experienced in various forms. Yet while national authorities' *willingness* to provide lender of last resort (and recapitalization) assistance appears to have increased, their *ability* to deal effectively with major banking crises may be diminishing. The reasons for this apparent erosion of the lender of last resort's ability to influence events are outlined below.

In the first place, the effectiveness of the lender of last resort function may be limited by the sheer volume of global financial transactions measured against central banks' ability to lend. During the Continental Illinois banking crisis in 1984 the then Vice-Chairman of the Federal Reserve Board, Mr Preston Martin, invoked the old central bankers' adage: 'Lend, lend boldly and keep on lending.' Within the confines of domestic financial markets as we have traditionally known them that may indeed be an excellent precept. But in today's global financial marketplace, it is more difficult to envisage a commitment to open-ended liquidity support.

It has been estimated that due to major technological improvements the cost of many financial transactions has fallen by more than 90 per cent over the past two decades.[24] The lowering of transaction costs has contributed to explosive growth in the volume of trading in securities, futures and foreign exchange markets and this in turn has been reflected in the soaring volume of business routed through the various payments or settlements systems that clear transactions between banks. For instance, the daily volume of transactions on the two major dollar payment systems currently averages around $1 trillion, total intraday overdrafts on accounts with the Federal Reserve exceed $100bn and many institutions build up debit positions during the course of a trading day well in excess of their capital base. As the Federal Reserve Bank of New York has recently warned, a settlement failure stemming from a default could play havoc throughout the financial system. Indeed towards the end of 1985 the Federal Reserve was obliged to lend a record $22.6bn overnight to the Bank of New York when it faced a settlement problem due to the failure of its computer systems.[25] The rapidly increasing volume of transactions in all major financial centres increases the danger of an interruption to settlement systems while also magnifying the lender of last resort's task should a major default occur.

A second difficulty for the lender of last resort is the volatility of banks' funding. Banks and other deposit-taking institutions are becoming increasingly dependent on wholesale money markets and less able to rely on a captive retail deposit base. In addition the spread of money-market funds in the US and elsewhere has further eroded the traditional relationship between the depositor and his or her bank. Unpublished research by the US Office of the Comptroller of the Currency indicates that when banks get into difficulties the first depositors to run are the money-market funds (presumably because they do not wish to publish holdings in a troubled bank), then other holders of bank certificates of deposit and last of all the retail depositors. Just as 'relationship banking' appears to be eroding on the lending side so it is on the liabilities side, and as the proportion of captive retail deposits in total deposits falls the whole deposit base is loosened and banks in general become more vulnerable to confidence-induced deposit withdrawals.

An alarming example of the fickleness, speed and power of wholesale financial markets was provided by Continental Illinois which lost 20 per cent of its deposit base in the two weeks ending 18 May 1984. Admittedly, Continental had been funding its operations in a particularly dangerous manner, relying heavily on overnight borrowings to fund its loan portfolio: specifically, the bank had to purchase each day around $8bn from the money markets, representing around 20 per cent of its total funding.

A third factor which has greatly complicated the task of the lender of last resort is the internationalization of banking. There are several problematical consequences here. Most importantly, in a regime of self-contained national banking systems, borders act as natural firebreaks in the sense that contagious financial disturbances are unlikely to spread beyond national frontiers. However, the internationalization of banking has removed this safeguard. For instance, as a direct consequence of the Herstatt Bank collapse in West Germany in 1974, Japanese and Italian banks found that they were unable to fund themselves in the Eurodollar market. A more recent example was the regionalization of the financial disturbances associated with the failure of Hong Kong's Overseas Trust Bank in June 1985, when a number of financial institutions in Malaysia, Singapore and Thailand were adversely affected.

The internationalization of banking also raises awkward questions about who should act as lender of last resort in cases where foreign subsidiaries are involved. The Basle Concordat has already established rules for allocating bank regulatory responsibilities between national authorities but there is no formal declaration relating to lender of last resort responsibilities. Similarly, a large foreign banking presence may make it much more difficult to secure a cohesive response from the domestic banking industry. In recent banking crises involving Continental Illinois in the USA, Canadian Commercial Bank in Canada, Schröder Munchmeyer Hengst in West Germany, and Johnson Matthey Bankers in the UK, an important contribution to the financial stabilization package has been provided by a consortium of domestic banks. But with increasing penetration of domestic banking markets by foreign institutions there may be less scope in the future for this kind of combined support operation.

Finally, the creation of financial conglomerates, and in particular banks' increasing involvement in securities business, adds considerably to the problem of ensuring a cooperative, prompt and adequately funded response to stresses within the financial system. In part, this is because the difficulties of allocating lender of last resort responsibilities become even more daunting when distinctions between banks and non-bank financial entities become blurred. For instance, a central bank may well be unwilling to support a financial conglomerate whose survival is threatened by problems in a securities subsidiary operating in a weakly regulated foreign jurisdiction. There is, after all, a natural reluctance on the part of central banks to extend financial assistance to institutions whose activities are beyond their control. Similarly, domestic banks may be disinclined to cooperate in providing financial support to one of their number which has suffered losses in its securities operations.

But, above all, the involvement of banks in securities activities increases the potential for contagious financial disorders. The available evidence points strongly to the fact that the market itself does not distinguish neatly between the credit standing of different members of the same financial group. Debt holders appear to be largely indifferent to the location of debt within such a group and look to the strongest component of the group for ultimate protection.[26] The corollary is that if one part of a financial conglomerate gets into difficulties this would be viewed as a threat to the whole enterprise. More generally, the integration of banking and securities markets — even in financial systems such as the USA which separate banking and securities firms — may create conditions in which a shock originating in the securities markets may spread through the banking system and feed back again to the securities markets.

An example of this occurred in the USA in 1985 with the failure of two relatively obscure trading firms in government securities markets, ESM Securities in Florida and Bevill Bresler and Schulman in New Jersey. A number of savings and loan institutions or 'thrifts' were counterparties to repurchase deals with these two firms and had failed to secure their underlying collateral. The result was large publicized losses by thrifts in Ohio and Maryland, a perceived threat to the integrity of the state-sponsored deposit insurance funds and large-scale deposit runs leading to the temporary closure of thrifts in the two states. There was then a feedback to the securities markets when a subsidiary of one of the

Maryland thrifts defaulted on over $1bn in mortgages and mortgage-backed securities, resulting in heavy losses for certain mortgage insurance firms.

In the light of this experience the Federal Reserve Bank of New York commented as follows in its 1985 Annual Report:

> The interconnections among institutions and markets in the new environment get more and more complex. A shock that starts in one market may spread quickly along this network of linkages until it finds a weakness in some seemingly unrelated place. In fact there is a growing tendency to build financial links along regulatory fault lines where the responsibility for supervisory oversight is weak, divided or clouded.[27]

It should be added that if financial disturbances can spread from securities to banking markets under a US regime which purports to separate these businesses, the scope for contagious disorders when banking and securities activities are combined is much greater. Put another way, financial distress can be more readily contained if, like the bulkheads of a ship, the risks incurred within one sector of the financial services industry can be prevented from overflowing into other sectors. But with the trend towards global integration of the financial services industry, shock waves can be transmitted not only from bank to bank and from country to country but from the securities markets to banks and vice versa. Therefore, as banking groups diversify and expand across borders there is increasing potential for a self-feeding and large-scale crisis engulfing both banks and the securities markets internationally.

## Notes

1   See, for instance, Testimony by Alan Greenspan, Chairman of the Federal Reserve Board, before the Committee on Banking, Housing and Urban Affairs, US Senate, 1 December 1987, pp. 7–10.
2   *Deposit Insurance in a Changing Environment* (Federal Deposit Insurance Corporation, Washington DC, 15 April 1983), Appendix F, p. 1.
3   Ibid., p. II-4.
4   Until Penn Square Bank failed in mid 1982, no bank with assets of $100bn or more had been dissolved by way of a pay-off of insured deposits.
5   *Deposit Insurance in a Changing Environment*, p. III-2.
6   Ibid., p. III-3.
7   Statement on Federal Assistance to Continental Illinois Corporation and Continental Illinois National Bank, presented to Subcommittee of Financial Institutions Supervision, Regulation and Insurance of the Committee on

Banking Finance and Urban Affairs, House of Representatives, 4 October 1984, pp. 2–3.

8  Joint press release by the Federal Deposit Insurance Corporation, the Federal Reserve Board and Office of the Comptroller of the Currency, Washington DC, 17 May 1984.

9  Remarks Before the Garn Institute Deposit Insurance Forum, 14 November 1988, p. 6.

10  Ibid., p. 9. On the too-big-to-fail issue see also *Deposit Insurance for the Nineties* (FDIC, Washington DC, January 1989), pp. 254–84. This study concludes:

> the too large to pay off doctrine in all probability is here to stay. There always will be certain situations where an individual bank will be perceived to be too important to macroeconomic or international stability to allow to be handled in a way that would inflict losses on bank creditors. This becomes increasingly true as other countries provide *de jure* or *de facto* 100 percent coverage to their banks and as banking and finance become more international in scope. Thus, it would be counter-productive to design a system that does not accommodate this reality (p. 280).

11  Remarks before the Garn Institute Deposit Insurance Forum, p. 14.

12  See *FDIC Statement of Policy and Criteria on Assistance to Operating Insured Banks* (FDIC, Washington DC, 1986).

13  The only class of lenders excluded from this highly protective regime are creditors of bank holding companies. Under new FDIC guidelines such creditors can no longer expect to benefit from the official safety net (although they were protected in the Continental Illinois rescue). Thus, when the FDIC was forced in 1988 to rescue First Republic Bank of Dallas — the largest bank in Texas, with $35bn of assets — all depositors and creditors of the bank were immediately assured that they would be fully protected, but the bank holding company was allowed to default on $1.2bn of debt and preferred stock. Similarly, when the Bank of New England collapsed in January 1991 — the third biggest failure in US history involving total banking assets of some $23bn — all uninsured depositors were protected but holding company creditors were not. However, since bank holding companies have no deposit liabilities they can neither be the subject of nor can they easily transmit deposit runs.

14  *Modernizing the Financial System* (US Treasury Department, Washington DC, February 1991), p. 17.

15  Cited in Margaret Reid, *Secondary Banking Crisis, 1973–75* (Macmillan, London, 1982), p. 90.

16  The Bank of England and Johnson Matthey Bankers Ltd, Bank of England, *Annual Report* (1985), p. 29.

17  For a more detailed discussion of the German approach to handling bank

failures see Richard Dale, *The Regulation of International Banking* (Woodhead-Faulkner, Cambridge and Englewood Cliffs, New Jersey, 1984), pp. 156–9.

18  For details of this remarkable episode, see: 'Al Saudi Banque bailout raises questions' *Financial Times Financial regulation report*, October 1988, p. 18; and 'Consequences of Al Saudi affair' *Financial Times Financial regulation report*, November 1988, p. 23.

19  George Graham, 'Paris applies banking pragmatism' *Financial Times*, 29 March 1989, p. 37.

20  'Report of the inquiry into the collapse of the CCB and Northland Bank' ('Estey Report') Minister of Supply and Services, August (1986), p. 267.

21  For a detailed account of this episode, see Statement by Gerald Corrigan, President of the Federal Reserve Bank of New York, before the US Senate Committee on Banking, Housing and Urban Affairs, 3 May 1990, Appendix I, pp. 3–8.

22  Shijuro Ogata, 'Maintaining a sound financial system in Japan', speech prepared for a conference on 'Risk, international financial markets and public policy', Geneva, 11–13 September 1986, p. 4.

23  An indication of the Japanese authorities' determination to avoid bank failures was given in a speech by the Minister of Finance, Mr Hashimoto, in June 1991. Referring to the fall in Japanese land prices Mr Hashimoto insisted that the government would stand behind its banks. See David Lascelles, 'Government assures Japanese banks over land price fall' *Financial Times*, 4 June 1991.

24  See 'Recent innovations in international banking' ('Cross Report') Bank for International Settlements, April (1986), p. 4.

25  The technical details of this remarkable episode are described by Gerald Corrigan, President, Federal Reserve Bank of New York, in his evidence before the Subcommittee on Domestic Monetary Policy of the Committee on Banking, Finance and Urban Affairs, US House of Representatives, 12 December, 1985.

26  See 'An analysis of the concept of corporate separateness in bank holding company regulation from an economic perspective', in appendices to the Statement by Paul Volcker, Chairman Board of Governors of the Federal Reserve System before the Subcommittee on Commerce, Consumer and Monetary Affairs, of the Committee on Government Operations of the US House of Representatives, June, 1986, p. c-6.

27  Edward Frydl, 'The challenge of financial change', Federal Reserve Bank of New York, *Annual Report* (1985), p. 26.

# 2

# Lessons of the Great Crash

The US banking crisis of 1929–33 is central to the debate about the risks of financial diversification and, more particularly, banks' involvement in securities activities. It was the experience of those years that led to the legal separation of banking and securities business in the USA and the subsequent importation of the US model of segmentation into Japan after World War Two. Those who oppose the current global trend towards integration of banking and securities markets invoke the US financial crash which was blamed by contemporary opinion on the expansion of banks' securities activities during the 1920s. On the other hand, the advocates of financial conglomeration argue that the causes of the US crash have been misconstrued and had nothing to do with the mixing of banking and securities business. Any policy analysis in this area must therefore begin with an examination of US financial developments in the inter-war period.

## Financial Diversification and the Banking Crisis

The separation of banking and securities business was established very early on in England. The theory that the assets of a commercial bank should be capable of ready liquidation and not invested in property or corporate stock was generally applied as a matter of practice and also reflected in the terms of the charter granted by Parliament to the Bank of England in 1694.[1] The early bank charters in the USA were modelled along English lines and, in effect, confined banks to the acquisition of short-term liquid assets.[2] The abandonment of this practice in the so-called 'wildcat' banking era in the second quarter of the nineteenth century was followed by the financial panic of 1837 and the failure of one quarter of all US banks in the following six years. This experience resulted in passage of the National Banking Act of 1864 which confined banks to issuing currency, accepting deposits and making short-term commercial loans. The underlying theory behind the statute was the 'real-bills doctrine' which asserted that if banks limited their assets to short-term, self-liquidating commercial loans or 'real bills', liquidity within the banking system would be assured.

From the early twentieth century, however, US banks were under increasing pressure to by-pass the restrictions of the National Banking Act. In the first place, there was a general movement towards 'department store' banking, with banks competing with insurance and trust companies to provide customers with a wide range of financial services including deposit, credit, fiduciary, investment and insurance services. As one study put it in 1909:

> It is a distinct convenience to most people to have all of their financial business attended to under one roof. The trust company will not only care for their banking business, but will also receive their valuables for safekeeping, care for their property, manage their estates temporarily or permanently, make investments for them, give financial and legal advice.[3]

Further pressure in favour of financial diversification arose from the weakening demand for bank loans. High levels of corporate profitability during the boom years of the 1920s reduced reliance on short-term bank credit, while larger companies found that they were able to raise long-term finance on advantageous terms by issuing securities directly to the public. One contemporary study reported that the ratio of national banks' commercial loans to total earning assets declined from 57.5 per cent in 1920 to 37 per cent in 1929 and concluded that 'if economic progress continues to be associated with the growing relative importance of the larger corporations having access to the stock and bond markets, there is a strong probability that the commercial loan will continue to decline relatively to other bank assets'.[4] In other words, a firm trend towards what we today would call 'securitization' was under way during the 1920s and played a major part in US banks' efforts to extend their activities into the securities markets.

There were, broadly speaking, two ways in which banks were able to circumvent the statutory restrictions on their securities operations incorporated in the National Banking Act. First, the McFadden Act of 1927 provided the legal basis for national banks to invest in bonds. This statute contained the provision 'that the business of buying and selling investment securities ... shall hereafter be limited to buying and selling ... marketable obligations evidencing indebtedness of any person, copartnership, association or corporation, in the form of bonds, notes and/or debentures, commonly known as "investment securities" as may by regulation be prescribed by the Comptroller of the Currency'. Even before this enactment, however, the Comptroller's permissive interpretation of banks' statutory powers to negotiate promissory notes and other evidence of debt had allowed national banks to invest in securities. After 1927 the only restriction on the types of bonds which national banks could purchase was the requirement of 'marketability' but this term was interpreted very liberally by the Comptroller.[5] Because of the difficulty of distinguishing between investing and underwriting, the Comptroller also allowed banks to underwrite bonds to the extent they were permitted to invest in them, although the courts prevented national banks from underwriting equities or engaging in securities brokerage. Meanwhile state-chartered banks were often authorized to invest in equities as well as bonds.

During the 1920s, then, the way was open for commercial banks to make investments in long-term bonds and other securities, in a manner which was in clear breach of the real-bills doctrine and which had never been contemplated by the National Banking Act. According to contemporary writers, the shift of banks' business away from commercial lending and in favour of securities purchases in the period 1921–31 played a major part in the failure of many institutions, particularly smaller and country banks, as the value of their assets became increasingly exposed to stock market fluctuations.

In addition to acquiring the power to purchase investment securities for their own portfolios, national banks were also able to undertake general investment banking business (underwriting and distribution of corporate securities) by the simple device of establishing state-chartered securities affiliates. In a 1902 ruling the Comptroller of the Currency had determined that under the National Banking Act national banks were prohibited from engaging in investment banking. The banks' response was to move their investment banking business out of their bond departments and into newly organized securities affiliates which were chartered under permissive state laws. In addition, banks which opted for state charters were often able to secure broad securities powers. Subsequently, the Federal Reserve Board lent its own weight to the erosion of the distinction between commercial and investment banking in order to encourage state banks to enter the still experimental Federal Reserve System. Specifically, state banks were allowed to become members of the System without having to give up any of the corporate privileges granted to them by state law, the result being 'to recognize formally the right of at least one class of member banks to engage in investment banking'.[6]

By 1930 the English model of banking had, in practice, been abandoned in the USA and commercial banks had become the dominant force in the distribution and underwriting of securities. By that date there were 105 securities affiliates of national banks, nearly every large urban bank had one or several such affiliates (usually with a name slightly altered from that of the parent) and the percentage of the total volume of bonds, in the distribution of which banks and their affiliates participated, had risen to over 60 per cent. In the words of Nelson Peach, a leading authority on this period of US financial history, by the end of the 1920s: 'commercial banks and their security affiliates occupied a position in the field of long-term financing equal to that of private investment bankers, both from the standpoint of investment banking machinery and from the standpoint of the volume of securities underwritten and distributed by the two groups of institutions'.[7]

The role of the Comptroller of the Currency in this process of financial integration is particularly noteworthy. In 1920 the Comptroller had warned in the clearest possible terms of the dangers of allowing banks to engage in securities business through the affiliate system (see p. 1 above). Yet during the 1920s the Comptroller was instrumental in extending banks' securities powers. Evidently, this was an example of what today might be called competition in regulatory laxity. According to Nelson Peach: 'because of competition with state banks and trust companies and the fear of driving banks out of the National Banking System, the Comptroller did not enforce the existing restrictions on the powers of national banks and suggested greater leniency in the national banking laws'.[8]

The growing involvement of banks in securities business was followed in 1929–33 by the collapse of the US banking system. During the collapse, more than one-fifth of the commercial banks in the USA, holding nearly one-tenth of the volume of bank deposits, suspended operations because of financial difficulties. In total, the number of commercial banks declined by about one-third, culminating in the suspension by President Roosevelt of all banking transactions nationwide on 6 March 1933.

The banking crisis was characterized by three intense phases.[9] First there was the crisis beginning in October 1930 when a contagious collapse of confidence afflicted many small banks, mainly in agricultural areas. In December 1930 the Bank of the United States in New York City failed and this was particularly significant in two respects. First, the Bank of the United States had deposits in excess of $200mn, more than the combined deposits of the 551 banks that had failed during the year ending 30 June 1929. Second, this was a bank with no less than 59 affiliates, including securities affiliates. Alleged abuse of the affiliate system by the Bank of the

Table 2.1.  US bank failures, 1921–1933

| | Number of failed banks | Deposits of failed banks ($ thousands) | Number of failed banks (% of all banks) | Deposits of failed banks (% of all bank deposits) |
|---|---|---|---|---|
| 1921 | 506 | 172,806 | 1.16 | 0.619 |
| 1922 | 366 | 91,182 | 1.15 | 0.300 |
| 1923 | 646 | 149,601 | 2.10 | 0.462 |
| 1924 | 775 | 210,150 | 2.58 | 0.609 |
| 1925 | 617 | 166,937 | 2.08 | 0.440 |
| 1926 | 975 | 260,153 | 3.28 | 0.661 |
| 1927 | 669 | 199,332 | 2.39 | 0.491 |
| 1928 | 498 | 142,386 | 1.84 | 0.338 |
| 1929 | 659 | 230,643 | 2.47 | 0.543 |
| 1930 | 1350 | 837,096 | 5.29 | 2.01 |
| 1931 | 2293 | 1,690,232 | 9.87 | 4.42 |
| 1932 | 1453 | 706,187 | 6.94 | 2.43 |
| 1933 | 4000 | 3,596,708 | 20.53 | 14.23 |

*Source*: Mark Flannery, 'An economic evaluation of bank securities activities before 1933', in Ingo Walter, ed., *Deregulating Wall Street* (John Wiley, New York, 1985), p. 77.

United States was a major factor turning both congressional and public opinion against securities affiliates. Notwithstanding the biggest bank failure in US financial history, there were signs in early 1931 of some easing in financial tensions, as the bank failure rate fell and the scramble for liquidity abated.

The second intense phase of the banking crisis developed in the second quarter of 1931 and was accompanied by a sudden rise in domestic interest rates, associated with an outflow of gold from the USA. Government bond prices fell sharply, thereby weakening the capital position of many banks. However, the epidemic of bank failures ended in January 1932.

Finally, a renewed spate of bank failures occurred in the last quarter of 1932, to be followed by the banking panic of 1933 (see table 2.1). As the panic spread, a succession of statewide bank holidays were declared, leading eventually to the nationwide bank holiday that came into effect on 6 March.

A key feature of the later stages of the banking collapse was the depression of bond values, which had started as far back as 1929 but gathered pace in 1931–2. From mid 1931 to mid 1932 railroad bonds lost nearly 36 per cent of their market value, public utility bonds 27 per cent, industrial bonds 22 per cent, foreign bonds 45 per cent and even US Government securities 10 per cent.[10] As Friedman and Schwartz put it: 'the impairment in the market value of assets held by banks, particularly in their bond portfolios, was the most important source of impairment of capital leading to bank suspensions, rather than the default of specific loans or of specific bond issues'.[11] Paradoxically, too, it was banks' holdings of marketable bonds, which were marked to market for valuation purposes, rather than their portfolio of unmarketable loans, which posed the most serious threat to solvency.

## The Role of Banks' Securities Affiliates

The contemporary view of the events leading up to the banking debacle of 1929–33 was that banks' securities activities had played a crucial role in undermining confidence in the financial system. A subcommittee of the Senate Committee on Banking and Currency, which conducted hearings in 1931 under the chairmanship of Senator Glass, reported that 'the experience of the past ten years lends spectacular confirmation to the view that the more intensive participation by commercial banks in the capital market exaggerates financial and business fluctuations'.[12] The subcommittee analysed the financial performance of 14 bank securities affiliates and listed a number of ways in which the operations of a securities affiliate could affect (and in several instances had so affected) the position of the affiliated bank. These have been summarized as follows:[13]

(1) 'Very prevalent' borrowing by the affiliate from the bank;

(2) The selling of securities by an affiliate to its bank or other affiliates under repurchase agreements, or their purchase by the affiliate from the bank in the same manner;

(3) The purchase of securities by the bank to relieve the affiliate of excess holdings;

(4) More liberal lending by the bank to customers on issues sponsored by the securities affiliate in order to support their distribution. The Subcommittee report stated '... it may prove more difficult to insist upon the maintenance of adequate margins on these security loans than on other such advances, in view of the fact that customers are encouraged to make the loans by the bank's own affiliate';

(5) Injury to the good will of the bank if depositors suffered substantial losses on securities purchased from the bank;

(6) Causing undesirably wide fluctuations in the price of the affiliated bank's stock as a result of purchases and sales of the stock by the securities affiliate. The report noted that '... efforts made in some cases to push the sale of the bank's stock through the affiliate to depositors of the institution hurts

the position of the bank when its shares suffer a major market decline subsequently';

(7) Making of unwise commitments by the bank, in the knowledge that in case of need they could be shifted to affiliates and thus removed from the bank's condition statement;

(8) In reliance upon the resources of the parent bank in case of need, the tendency of securities affiliates to assume commitments less cautiously than private investment bankers; and

(9) In the case of banks with both a trust department and a securities affiliate, adverse effects upon the independence with which fiduciary activities were exercised.

In addition to these congressional concerns, some leading bankers also came to the conclusion in the immediate aftermath of the 1933 banking panic that the securities affiliate system posed a threat to financial stability and took steps to liquidate their own securities affiliates. In March 1933 both National City Bank and Chase National Bank announced that they were disposing of their securities affiliates. When these announcements were made, Mr Winthrop Aldrich, the chairman of Chase National Bank, issued the following statement:

> I heartily commend the action of National City Bank in taking steps to divorce its security affiliate... It is impossible to consider the events which took place during the past ten years without being forced to the conclusion that intimate connection between commercial banking and investment banking almost inevitably leads to abuses.[14]

Indeed by the spring of 1933 banks' securities operations had fallen into such disrepute and the investment banking business in general was in such decline that many bank securities affiliates had been, or were in the process of being, dissolved. Against this background Senator Glass's proposal to formally separate banking from securities activities met with little opposition and the Glass–Steagall Act was signed into law on 16 June 1933. The Act, which is considered in greater detail in chapter 4, prohibited banks from underwriting or purchasing securities for their own account, with exceptions for government securities and certain investment securities, and banned affiliations and interlocks between banks and companies primarily engaged in securities activities.

Nearly sixty years later, the view is now gaining ground that passage of the Glass–Steagall Act was a rushed response to the events of 1929–33, based on inadequate analysis of the causes of the US banking collapse. Indeed, the Comptroller of the Currency stated recently that 'studies have consistently demonstrated that the securities activities of banks had little, if anything, to do with the collapse of the banking system in 1933'.[15]

Similarly, a 1987 staff study by the Federal Deposit Insurance Corporation concluded that 'there is little or no evidence that the investment banking activities of commercial bank affiliates were a factor impacting bank failures in the banking collapse of 1929–33'.[16] Finally, George Benston, a leading US banking academic, has concluded that 'the evidence from the pre-Glass–Steagall period is totally inconsistent with the belief that banks' securities activities or investments caused them to fail or caused the financial system to collapse'.[17]

The new interpretation of the inter-war US banking crisis focuses on two distinct aspects of banks' securities activities — the operation of banks' securities affiliates and banks' own holdings of securities.

So far as banks' securities affiliates are concerned, one of the main objections to the contemporary congressional view is that only a very few banks could have failed due to abuses involving these affiliates. As one writer has put it: 'failures due to this cause could not have accounted for more than a handful of total bank failures. There were a total of 9,096 bank failures in the years 1930–34, involving depositor losses of $1.3bn, but relatively few banks had securities affiliates — probably less than 200'.[18]

Indeed, the Senate subcommittee that investigated securities affiliates in 1931 was able to identify only the Bank of the United States as an example of a failure caused by the relationship of the bank and its securities affiliate. In contrast, most banks that had securities affiliates survived the collapse and the principal, large New York banks engaged in securities underwriting remained in business.[19] Furthermore, a statistical analysis of bank failures during this period concludes that: (1) the presence of a securities affiliate reduced the probability of bank failure; (2) affiliates did not cause wider fluctuations in combined bank/affiliate earnings; (3) capital ratios did not decline, the larger were affiliates relative to their parent banks; and (4) banks' liquidity was evidently not weakened by the presence of an affiliate.[20]

The corollary of the above line of argument is that the great mass of bank failures in the 1920s and early 1930s involved small unit banks with concentrated loan portfolios. Many of these were rural banks hit by the agricultural difficulties of the 1920s. During the entire period 1921–33 there were around 11,000 bank failures in the USA, more than 80 per cent of which were small institutions with a capitalization of under $25,000.[21] These figures lend support to the view that one of the major weaknesses of the US financial system at this time was the fragmented nature of the banking industry and in particular the denial of the potential for asset diversification afforded by branch banking (in contrast Canada, which allowed branch banking, experienced no bank failures during the period).

A second, and related, objection to the idea that securities affiliates were a major factor in the US banking collapse is based on the kinds of abuse to which such affiliate relationships gave rise. That there were abuses cannot be doubted, given the evidence that emerged before the Senate investigation into stock exchange abuses (which included the so-called Pecora Hearings of 1933). However, most of this evidence relates to the securities affiliates (National City Company and Chase Securities Corporation) of the country's two largest banks — National City Bank and Chase National Bank.

The abuses that came to light can be divided into three categories: those common to the entire investment banking industry; abuses arising from the use of affiliates for the personal profit of bank officers and directors; and abuses involving conflicts of interest resulting from the mixing of commercial and investment banking.[22]

The main abuses common to the investment banking business during this period were underwriting and distributing speculative securities, conveying misleading information in the prospectuses accompanying new issues and manipulating the market for securities while they were being issued. Both National City Company and Chase Securities Corporation engaged in such activities. For instance, in 1927 and 1928 National City Company participated in the underwriting of three bond issues by the government of Peru, knowing that the issuer was an extremely poor credit risk but failing to disclose relevant information. The public were persuaded to purchase all $90mn of the bonds which went into default in 1931 and sold for less than 5 per cent of their face value in 1933.[23]

It has been argued that abuses of this kind were not a consequence of the bank/securities affiliate relationship, and that the appropriate legislative response was more stringent regulation of the securities markets (as subsequently provided by the Securities Act of 1933 and the Securities Exchange Act of 1934) rather than the prohibition of banks' securities business.

The second category of abuse arose from the use of affiliates for the personal profit of bank officers and directors. Elaborate schemes were devised to enable officers and directors to receive earnings from affiliates far in excess of the remuneration paid to them by their banks. Such schemes included special management funds and investment pools which traded in the stock of the parent bank, evidently on the basis of inside information. Revelations of self-dealing of this kind tended to inflame public opinion against the securities affiliate system, but the abuses did not directly jeopardize the safety or soundness of affiliated banks and could in any event have been prohibited without severing banks' securities activities.

Finally, there were abuses directly attributable to the mixing of banking and securities business. Under this heading, Peach identified three ways in particular in which the investment banking activities of affiliates might lead to undesirable loans and investments on the part of the parent bank. First, if an affiliate were unsuccessful in distributing an issue of securities the parent bank might feel obliged to take a part or all of the issue into its own portfolio, in order to relieve the affiliate of its underwriting commitment. For instance, Chase National Bank, in order to protect its affiliate, took into its own portfolio more than $10bn of undesirable loans during the period 1927–33.[24]

Second, if the price of securities sold by the affiliate to the general public declined, the bank might feel obliged to make large purchases to support the price and protect its reputation. Third, a bank might feel obliged to lend to a borrower that would otherwise default on an issue underwritten by the securities affiliate.

Although abuses of this type did occur, it is not clear that they were undertaken on a sufficient scale to threaten the survival of more than a handful of institutions. Furthermore, the incentive to concentrate credit risks in the bank or its securities affiliate would only exist if either: (1) the stock of the affiliate were not owned rateably by the stockholders who owned the parent bank; or (2) one of the institutions were more leveraged than the other (the incentive here being to shift bad assets into the most leveraged entity). As one authority has commented: 'An important reason for the historical view that securities activities represent a danger to bank soundness stems from the widespread practice of banks in the 1920s of doing this business through separate affiliates having different ownership and capital structures.'[25] According to this view, securities activities could be more safely conducted by the bank itself and it was the affiliate system of the 1920s, rather than securities operations per se, which endangered bank stability.

An alternative criticism of the affiliate system is that the security affiliates themselves were virtually unregulated: 'There was no legal distinction between a separately capitalized securities affiliate and any other bank customer, leaving bankers free to undertake virtually any desired trans-action with their own affiliates regardless of the potential effect on the bank's welfare.'[26] However, excessive lending to an affiliate could have been prohibited by the simple device of placing a limit, as a percentage of bank capital or assets, on transactions between banks and their affiliates. Indeed, Section 23A of the Federal Reserve Act, which was introduced in 1933, imposes such a limit while also prohibiting transactions with the affiliate which are detrimental to the bank.

In summary, then, modern writers have tended to downplay the importance of abuses connected with banks' securities affiliates, on the grounds that there is little evidence that such practices were responsible for more than a small number of bank failures, that many of the abuses were of a kind that did not directly threaten bank safety and soundness, and that legislative reforms, falling well short of the severance provisions of Glass–Steagall, could have eliminated potentially destabilizing transactions between banks and their related entities.

Nevertheless, while recognizing that contemporary opinion was too quick to attribute the 1929–33 banking collapse to the activities of banks' securities affiliates, there is a risk of moving too far in the opposite direction. In particular, confidence is the most crucial ingredient of financial stability, and circumstances which could harm the reputation of a securities affiliate could equally damage confidence in its parent bank. The last word on this aspect of the debate, which is taken up again in chapter 3, may for the moment be given to Nelson Peach:

> There are certain dangers arising from these [bank/affiliate] relationships and it is not possible to avoid these by legislation. If affiliates sell securities on the good name of the parent bank, then the good will of parent bank and affiliate rise and fall together. Since the stock of the affiliate must be tied to that of the parent bank and since the nature of the business conducted by affiliates is such that their earning power is subject to wide variations, fluctuations in the price of the stock of parent banks would be greater than if the stock of the affiliate was separate from that of the parent bank. Fluctuation in the price of bank stock leads easily to a lack of confidence in the bank and may precipitate a run on it even though the bank is in a sound condition.[27]

# The Role of Banks' Securities Holdings

While the alleged role played by banks' securities affiliates in the US banking collapse is open to serious doubt, what cannot be easily denied is that banks' own holdings of long-term securities contributed in a major way to the spate of insolvencies. There remains, however, a vital question of interpretation: were banks to blame for acquiring an excessive volume of illiquid, high-risk assets? Or was a flawed macroeconomic policy responsible for producing a catastrophic decline in financial asset values which no prudent banker could reasonably have foreseen? Put another way, was there an ex ante, or only an ex post, decline in the quality of bank assets?

Between 1921 and 1930 banks shifted a significant proportion of their assets from commercial loans to the securities markets. During this period the balance sheet total of all commercial banks rose by 45 per cent, but investments increased by 63 per cent whereas loans and discounts rose by 31 per cent and all 'other loans' by 12 per cent. Furthermore, there appears to have been a deterioration between these two dates in the quality of securities held by banks, with the proportion of US government bonds falling from 35 per cent to 26 per cent of total securities held, and the proportion of bank investments outside the US government, state, municipal, railroad and public utility groups rising from 39 per cent to 49 per cent of the total. It is significant, too, that the smaller state-chartered and country banks, where failures were concentrated, held the highest proportion of lower-grade securities.[28]

Bond prices began to decline in 1929, and, as described above, fell precipitously between mid 1931 and mid 1932. More importantly, there was a 'flight to quality', with yields on higher-risk corporate bonds rising much more sharply than yields on US government securities. The widening spread between higher- and lower-grade securities was reflected in the yield differential between BAA-rated and AAA-rated bonds which rose from 117 basis points in June 1929 to 300 basis points two years later.[29] Most contemporary and modern writers are agreed that the decline in bond values during this period had a devastating impact on bank's balance sheets and accounted for a large number of insolvencies.

An important exception is George Benston who, in his study of the events leading up to Glass–Steagall, concludes that 'the data reviewed do not support the contention that many banks failed as a result of losses on their bond portfolios'.[30] However, Benston's analysis is based largely on evidence made available during the 1931 and 1932 Congressional hearings on the banking crisis which does not fully incorporate the bond market collapse of 1931–2 and the associated spate of bank failures in the two years 1932–3 (over 5,400 failures, representing nearly 60 per cent of total failures recorded during the 1929–33 crisis).[31]

In any event, very different explanations have been offered for the severity of banks' bond losses at this time. The predominant contemporary view was that banks had behaved imprudently in acquiring a large volume of relatively high-risk and potentially illiquid corporate securities, thereby exposing themselves to the vagaries of the stock market. In contrast, modern writers tend to exonerate the banks, and argue instead that the failure of economic policy created conditions in which banks were forced to dump their bonds on an unreceptive market, while corporate default rates rose to unforeseeable levels thereby forcing up risk premiums on corporate bond yields.

For instance, Friedman and Schwartz, while recognizing that some deterioration in the quality of banks' loans may have contributed to the initial bank failures in 1929–30, insist that 'any ex ante deterioration in the quality of loans and investments in the later twenties or simply the acquisition of low quality loans and investments in that period, even if no different in quality than in earlier periods, was a minor factor in the subsequent bank failures'.[32] They focus instead on the unrelieved squeeze on bank liquidity arising from the conversion of deposits into cash and the resulting distress selling of bonds. In similar vein, the Federal Deposit Insurance Corporation has more recently summarized its own reading of the historical evidence in the following terms:

> Many banks did suffer losses on their securities portfolio but this was because they were illiquid in the face of massive withdrawals and were forced to sell their assets at deep discounts. Thus it could be argued that bank security holdings contributed to a liquidity problem, but unless a bank is holding only cash almost any other asset will not be sufficiently liquid in the face of a run on deposits and no back-up source of liquidity.[33]

According to this interpretation, what was lacking was an active counter-cyclical monetary policy, and an effective lender of last resort. Yet, as with the debate over banks' securities affiliates, the reassessment of the part played by banks' securities holdings in the 1929–33 banking crisis may have gone too far. For one thing, it is simply not true that banks would have faced similar portfolio losses if they had held almost any asset other than cash. Short-term government securities and commercial paper clearly would have been less vulnerable to price fluctuations than long-term bonds. The key here is the extent to which banks engaged in interest rate mismatching (i.e. funding long-term fixed interest securities with short-term variable rate borrowings) and the ex ante vulnerability of individual banks' balance sheets to interest rate fluctuations. Any final conclusions on the role played by banks' securities holdings would similarly have to take account of the historical pattern of interest rate volatility (on the basis of which banks might reasonably assess their exposure to interest rate changes) including variations in the spread between high-grade and lower-grade bond issues. In the absence of such detailed statistical analysis there must still be a question mark against banks' enlarged role in securities markets in the pre-crisis period.

# Addendum: the 1987 Stock Market Crash

As an addendum to the above discussion of the 1929–33 banking crisis it is worth considering briefly the impact on financial markets of the 1987 global stock market crash — focusing in particular on the USA and UK.

In comparing events with those of the 1920s and 1930s several points of difference should be borne in mind. First, the Glass–Steagall Act was, of course, in place in the USA in 1987, whereas paradoxically the UK, on whose separation model of financial markets Glass–Steagall was based, had just experienced a sudden fusion of banking and securities markets in the wake of Big Bang (see chapter 6). Second, the 1987 crash was confined to equities: bond markets, in contrast, were positively stimulated by national monetary authorities' efforts to inject liquidity into the financial system. Finally, there was no decline in real output in 1987 or 1988, corporate default rates did not therefore rise as they had done in the 1930s and there was no sustained flight to quality or any corresponding increase in the spread between high- and lower-grade bond issues.

On Monday 19 October 1987 the Dow Jones Industrial Average fell by 508 points, or 22 per cent from the previous Friday's close and a 36 per cent decline from its peak in August. The day's absolute price decline in the Dow Jones Industrial Average was four times the record set the previous Friday; and the percentage decline was twice the previous record which was set on 29 October 1929. The *average* daily price movement from 16 October through 30 October was 121 points or more than the previous single-day record.[34] There were correspondingly large price movements during this period on stock exchanges worldwide.

Under the very different circumstances then prevailing, the US national banking system was not adversely affected by the events of October 1987. On the contrary, to the extent that there were credit problems they arose from banks curbing their lending to other non-bank institutions rather than vice versa. In particular, some broker-dealers experienced problems obtaining credit during the week of 19 October — to the point where the Federal Reserve Bank of New York felt obliged to encourage certain City banks to support the securities industry.[35] Of course, had securities houses been starved of credit, the resulting defaults could have had major implications for the banking sector.

In the UK, too, the financial system withstood well the pressures of October 1987, despite banks' direct involvement in securities markets. On the other hand, it needs to be emphasized that the UK securities business had just been enjoying a period of almost unprecedented prosperity, and that banking/securities conglomerates were very strongly capitalized in the run-up to the crash. Furthermore, there was one important incident at this time which recalls some of the abuses that occurred in the USA during the 1920s, and which seriously damaged the reputation of one leading UK financial institution.

In September 1987 National Westminster Bank's investment banking subsidiary, County NatWest, arranged a rights issue for Blue Arrow, a British manpower services group. The £837mn rights issue was a failure, with a take-up of only 49 per cent, but rather than let the market know the true position[36] County NatWest stated publicly that the remaining shares had been placed successfully. In fact County NatWest had acquired over 13 per cent of Blue Arrow in order to support the issue; and as a means of avoiding disclosure (which under the Companies Act becomes mandatory for holdings of 5 per cent or more) it had split its holding into three tranches of less than 5–4.9 per cent with the corporate advisory department, 4.4 per cent with County NatWest Securities (the bank's market-making arm) and 3.9 per cent with stockbrokers Phillips and Drew under a profit and loss sharing arrangement. Subsequently, the stock market crash that began on October 19 wiped more than half off the Blue Arrow share price, reducing the value of County NatWest's holding at one point by over £80mn. County NatWest reported a loss of £116mn for the year and had to be provided with an emergency capital injection of £80mn from its parent bank.

The UK Department of Trade and Industry carried out an investigation into the affair, most of which focused on County NatWest's failure to disclose its Blue Arrow stake and the way in which the market was thereby misled.[37] However, there were also safety and soundness considerations, given the scale of County Natwest's exposure to a single share issue and the parent bank's moral obligation to support its securities subsidiary.

What is clear from this unfortunate episode is that the competitive pressures which led to US banks' securities affiliate abuses of the 1920s and 1930s, can cause similar problems for combined banking/securities businesses even in a tightly regulated financial market regime such as prevailed in the UK in 1987.

# Notes

1  See Bernard Shull, 'The separation of banking and commerce: origin, development and implications for antitrust', *Antitrust Bulletin*, spring (1983).
2  For the historical background to the US Glass–Steagall Act, see Edwin Perkins, 'The divorce of commercial and investment banking', *Banking Law Journal*, June (1971); and Edward Kelly, 'Legislative history of the Glass–Steagall Act', in Ingo Walter, ed., *Deregulating Wall Street* (John Wiley, New York, 1985).
3  Perkins, 'The divorce of commercial and investment banking', p. 487.
4  Lauchlin Currie, 'The decline of the commercial loan', *Quarterly Journal of Economics*, 45 (1931), p. 709.

5  C. D. Bremer, *American Bank Failures* (Columbia University Press, New York, 1935), pp. 111–12.
6  Perkins, 'The divorce of commercial and investment banking', p. 491.
7  Nelson Peach, *The Security Affiliates of National Banks* (Johns Hopkins University Press, Baltimore, 1941), p. 20.
8  Ibid., p. 150.
9  See Milton Friedman and Anna Schwartz, *A Monetary History of the United States, 1857–1960* (Princeton University Press, Princeton NJ, 1963), pp. 312–25.
10  R. W. Goldsmith, *The Changing Structure of American Banking* (Routledge, London, 1933), p. 106.
11  Friedman and Schwartz, *A Monetary History*, p. 355.
12  Cited in Kelly, 'Legislative history of the Glass–Steagall Act', in Ingo Walter, ed., *Deregulating Wall Street* (John Wiley, New York, 1985), p. 46.
13  See William Upshaw, 'Bank affiliates and their regulation', Part I, Federal Reserve Bank of Richmond, *Monthly Review*, March (1973), p. 17.
14  Cited in Perkins, 'The divorce of commercial and investment banking', p. 523.
15  Statement of Robert L. Clarke, Comptroller of the Currency, before the Committee on Banking, Housing, and Urban Affairs, US Senate, 21 January 1987, p. 13.
16  *Mandate for Change: Restructuring the Banking Industry* (FDIC, Washington DC, August 1987), p. 68.
17  George Benston, *The Separation of Commercial and Investment Banking* (Macmillan, London, 1990), p. 41.
18  Upshaw, 'Bank affiliates', p. 17.
19  See Remarks by Martha Seger, Member, Board of Governors of the Federal Reserve System, before 23rd Annual Conference on Bank Structure and Competition, Chicago, 7 May 1987, p. 9.
20  Eugene Nelson White, 'Before the Glass–Steagall Act: an analysis of the investment banking', *Explorations in Economic History*, 23, 1, (1986), pp. 33–55.
21  See Susan Kennedy, *The Banking Crisis of 1933* (University Press of Kentucky, Lexington, 1973), chapter 9.
22  This categorization follows that adopted by the FDIC in *Mandate for Change*, p. 60.
23  Ibid., p. 61.
24  Peach, *The Security Affiliates*, pp. 133–9. It is somewhat paradoxical that banks have been criticized for both acquiring bad assets from their securities affiliates and for shifting their own bad assets onto the books of their securities affiliates. Both practices are open to objection from a prudential standpoint if they encourage banks and/or their securities affiliates to engage in riskier activities than they otherwise would in the belief that they can off-load or hide their bad assets.

25  Franklin Edwards, 'Banks and securities activities: legal and economic perspectives on the Glass–Steagall Act' in Lawrence Goldberg and Lawrence White, eds, *The Deregulation of the Banking and Securities Industries* (Lexington, D. C. Heath, 1979).

26  Mark Flannery, 'An economic evaluation of bank securities activities before 1933', in Ingo Walter, ed., *Deregulating Wall Street*, p. 69.

27  Peach, *The Security Affiliates*, p. 175.

28  For data on banks' securities holdings see Bremer, *American Bank Failures*, chapter 7, and especially pp. 116 and 121.

29  Flannery, 'An economic evaluation', p. 77.

30  Benston, *The Separation of Commercial and Investment Banking*, p. 41.

31  Benston does refer to a 1934 study showing losses realized from bonds sold (relative to original cost) in the liquidation of 34 New York State-chartered banks between 1929 and 1933. For these banks the losses were equivalent to 4.6 per cent of their total assets − large enough, one would have thought to represent a solvency threat. Furthermore, of these 34 banks, 6 experienced losses of over 20 per cent of total assets. Ibid., p. 39.

32  Friedman and Schwartz, *A Monetary History*, p. 355.

33  FDIC, *Mandate for Change*, pp. 56–7.

34  See Statement of David Ruder, SEC Chairman, before the Senate Committee on Banking, Housing and Urban Affairs, 4 November 1987.

35  See 'The October 1987 market break' US Securities and Exchange Commission, February (1988), pp. 5-24 to 5-30.

36  Apart from protecting its own reputation, County NatWest's interest in ensuring that the issue went ahead was the fee structure, which was heavily tilted towards success. See *Financial Times*, Friday 21 July 1989, p. 8.

37  *County NatWest Limited/County NatWest Securities Limited* (HMSO, London, July 1989).

# 3

# Banking and Securities Business: the Separation Issue

The recent reinterpretation of events leading up to the US banking collapse of 1929–33 has coincided with a reappraisal of the arguments for and against allowing banks to engage in securities business. Undoubtedly, the predominant view today among policymakers, practitioners and academics is that the continuing separation of banking and securities activities in two of the world's big three financial centres (New York and Tokyo) is a hangover from the past based on a misreading of history, which can only hamper the development of an efficient financial services industry in the countries concerned.[1] From this standpoint the fusion of commercial and investment banking is seen as an unmixed blessing to users of financial services. However, the argument presented here is that proponents of the universal banking model are inclined to overlook or at least underplay, significant risks attaching to the mixing of these business-risks which could, in the extreme, lead to a dangerous destabilization of the global financial system.

## Benefits of Securities Business

The arguments in favour of banks' freedom to undertake securities business are clear enough. In the first place, it is reasonable to suppose that the effect of banks' participation in securities business, as market-makers, fund managers, underwriters and distributors, is to increase competition and thereby lower securities underwriting and transaction costs. For instance, one US study suggests that underwriting spreads are lower for those (general obligation) state and local government bonds which US banks are authorized to underwrite as compared to those which they are forbidden to issue.[2] The implication is that banks' involvement in corporate securities business would increase access to capital markets and lower the cost of capital. The same argument might be applied even more strongly to Japan, where the big four securities houses have been able to enforce a regime of cartel pricing for their services. On the other hand, it has to be said that universal banking and competitive pricing of financial services do not necessarily go hand in hand: Switzerland provides a notable example of a universal banking system characterized by price cartels.[3] Even so, barriers to entry must be considered anti-competitive and any move to dismantle such restrictions is likely to promote price competition.

In addition to strengthening competition, banks' involvement in securities business may result in greater efficiency in the provision of financial services through economies of scope. Such economies are of two kinds: banks may realize *internal* scope economies through joint production and marketing; and consumers may realize *external* scope economies through joint use of banking and securities services.[4]

So far as internal scope economies are concerned, it is possible to identify three possible categories of cost saving. First, universal banks are able to use their customer base to match issuers and buyers of corporate securities more efficiently than can specialist securities firms. Second, computer facilities that are used to process information for the delivery of banking services may also be used to provide other financial services, including securities broking. Third, the marketing and delivery of financial services can be undertaken more efficiently when these services are combined. For instance banking and securities services can be jointly promoted through advertising and mailing, and jointly delivered through banks' branch networks.

There is another potential benefit to be gained from allowing banks to expand into securities activities that may be considered under this heading. It may be that the returns from banking and securities business are not highly correlated. Accordingly, such diversification may permit banking conglomerates to earn higher returns for a given level of risk, or alternatively to reduce risk without adversely affecting profitability. In other words, the 'portfolio' effect of combining banking and securities business may yield benefits in terms of risk spreading. This argument is, however, best considered in the broader context of the relative riskiness of banking and securities activities, discussed below.

On the consumption side, economies of scope exist where consumers can more conveniently purchase several financial services at a single location or from a single firm. For example, one recent US survey shows that consumers would value the opportunity to purchase mutual funds through their bank, while a study by the US Federal Reserve suggests that many consumers would like to obtain the full range of financial services from their bank.

Finally, it has been suggested that where banks simultaneously lend to and own the equity of a company, so-called 'agency' problems, arising from conflicting interests of shareholders, bondholders and managers, can be avoided. Specifically: 'because the debtholder is also the equity holder, there are no conflicts between holders of debt and equity securities to impede a needed reorganization. The result would be fewer agency problems, lower costs in "work-outs" of financial problems, and a resultant increase in organizational efficiency'.[5]

The UK's experience in recent years can, perhaps, be taken as further confirmation that the benefits of diversification can confer important competitive advantages on universal banks. Following the removal of restrictions on membership of the UK Stock Exchange in 1986 UK-based banks linked up with securities firms to provide combined banking and securities services. If the market is to be taken as the best judge of whether there are economies of scope this episode might be interpreted as evidence of the benefits of conglomeration. However, such a view would have to be qualified by events since the global stock market crash of October 1987, when, faced with an intensely competitive business environment, several UK financial conglomerates have disposed of their unprofitable securities subsidiaries.[6]

It is hardly necessary to add that if banks can strengthen their market position by undertaking securities activities, then any financial centre which prohibits such diversification will itself be placed at a competitive disadvantage. The coexistence of national jurisdictions simultaneously upholding and rejecting the principle of separation must then lead to serious competitive distortions as banks seek to route their securities activities through more permissive regimes. Those countries retaining separation laws are then placed under great pressure to relax their regulatory policies.

This was made clear by the US Federal Reserve Board when in 1989 it authorized subsidiaries of US bank holding companies to undertake limited securities activities:

> A potentially important benefit that may be expected from authorization for US banking organizations to engage in the proposed activities would be the improvement in their overall competitiveness as the world's capital markets become increasingly integrated and as their foreign bank competitors solidify and expand their activities in these areas. In particular, it will enable them to compete more effectively with banks located in the European Economic Community where it is proposed that effective in 1993 banks in

those countries would have a common banking license available to them that would encourage further the combination of commercial banking with securities underwriting and dealing activities.[7]

There are parallels here with the rivalry between US federal and state regulatory authorities that resulted in the separation provisions of the US National Bank Act of 1864 being by-passed in the 1920s. Today, regulatory competition, this time between national banking systems, is again contributing to pressures in favour of accommodating the universal banking model.

## Conflicts of Interest

The case against allowing banks to undertake securities activities is based on two kinds of objection: that the combination of these businesses results in unacceptable conflicts of interest; and that banking/securities conglomerates may incur excessive risks and thereby destabilize the financial system. The present study focuses on the stability issue, but it is appropriate first of all to summarize the arguments about conflicts of interest.

The US Congressional hearings that preceded passage of the Glass–Steagall Act, and the Gessler Commission on universal banking which was appointed in 1974 by the West German Minister of Finance and published its report in 1979, provide numerous examples of potential conflicts of interest. Saunders has suggested the following list:[8]

- *The conflict between the promotional role of the investment banker and the commercial banker's obligation to provide disinterested advice to depositors.*[9] The argument here is that banks will be inclined to promote the securities that they or their affiliates underwrite.
- *Using the bank's securities arm to issue new securities to repay unprofitable loans.* In this case a bank may be able to transfer risk from itself to the client firm's equity holders, or to new or existing bondholders.
- *Economic tie-ins of different bank products.* Banks might, for instance, use the threat of credit rationing to pressure corporate customers into using the banks' underwriting services.
- *Placing unsold securities in the banks' trust accounts.* The suggestion here is that key corporate finance decisions involving the possible use of a bank's underwriting or lending services, might be influenced by the presence on the board of the bank's directors.
- *Bank loans to support the price of a security.* A bank may lend to third-party investors so that they may purchase securities underwritten by its securities arm. Such action may distort the market price of securities while also jeopardizing the safety and soundness of the bank.

- *Imprudent loans to issuers of securities underwritten by the affiliate.* Where a bank has underwritten a securities issue and the issuer subsequently encounters financial difficulties, the bank may be tempted to make high-risk loans to the firm.
- *Bank loans to a securities affiliate to keep it in business.* A bank may be tempted to make high-risk loans to a separately capitalized securities affiliate that has encountered financial difficulties.
- *Informational advantages.* Banks may gain inside information about their corporate clientele which they then use for their own competitive advantage in lending, underwriting and the provision of other financial services.

Saunders notes that the above list involves either conflicts among different customers, conflicts that threaten the safety and soundness of the bank (that is, conflicts vis-à-vis depositors) and conflicts involving insider information. The safety and soundness issue is considered separately below, but so far as other conflicts are concerned most observers today take the view that these constitute insufficient grounds for legally separating banking and securities business.

To begin with, it has been pointed out that conflicts of interest are a feature of all business transactions where advice is sought from those who also act as principals in the proposed transaction(s). For instance, investment firms that deal on their own behalf while also giving investment advice are clearly in this position. The question, therefore is not whether conflicts of interest situations exist but whether they are abused. Here, there are several lines of argument. First, it is difficult to see how it can be in the interests of a bank to exploit certain kinds of conflict. In some cases the bank's shareholders would risk direct financial loss, as in the example of banks making imprudent loans to issuers of securities it has underwritten. In other cases, as the Gessler Commission and others have pointed out, a bank's commercial reputation could be seriously damaged if the abuse became known. More importantly, perhaps, where potential conflicts are identified, regulatory arrangements — whether statutory or in the form of 'Chinese walls' — can, in principle, be devised which would prevent or discourage abuses. So long as the costs of such regulation do not outweigh the economies of scope gained from banks' diversification into securities business, it may make little sense formally to separate the two activities. Furthermore, even if the regulatory costs are high the market is presumably the best judge of whether or not it still 'pays' to undertake banking and securities services within the same organization. The overall conclusion would appear to be that Glass–Steagall type prohibitions on banks' securities activities cannot be justified by concerns over conflicts of interest.

Quite apart from these theoretical considerations, there is considerable controversy as to whether or not allegations about conflict of interest abuses in the USA in the pre-Glass–Steagall period have been overstated. Benston, for instance, reaches the following conclusion after reviewing the relevant contemporary documentation:

> Thus, the record does not support the belief that the pre-Glass–Steagall period was one of abuses and conflicts of interest on the part of banks involved with securities transactions, either directly or through affiliates. Indeed, very little evidence exists of such abuses, and those abuses that the record does describe seem far more prevalent among non-banks. This finding is consistent with the observation that regulated depository institutions benefit from maintaining reputations for integrity and prudence.[10]

While several other authors would no doubt disagree with this statement, the fact remains that on both theoretical and empirical grounds the *non-prudential* case for prohibiting banks from engaging in securities activities is unpersuasive. This, too, was the main finding of the West German Gessler Commission which argued that many of the alleged conflicts of interest arising from universal banking would exist also in a regime of specialized banks and that the economic benefits of the universal banking model outweighed any conflicts that might be uniquely associated with financial conglomerates.[11]

# Risks in Securities Activities

While non-prudential conflicts of interest cannot be regarded as a sufficient rationale for the legal separation of banking and securities business, there remains the contentious issue of safety and soundness. The problem here is that because banks and their depositors are protected by the lender of last resort and deposit insurance, the ordinary market constraints on excessive risk-taking are removed. Accordingly, the risks banks incur must be limited by regulation, in order to protect the taxpayer and the deposit insurance fund. Viewed in this way, allowing banks to engage in risky non-bank activities could either destabilize the financial system by triggering a wave of contagious bank failures — or alternatively impose potentially enormous costs on taxpayers by obliging governments and/or their agencies to undertake open-ended support operations.

The first question that arises in this context is whether securities business in the broadest sense (embracing market-making, underwriting and securities distribution) is inherently riskier than banking. So far as underwriting is concerned Giddy has argued that although the assets purchased in equity underwritings are much riskier than those purchased in bank lending, investment bankers can and typically do limit the magnitude of any loss to a small percentage by reducing the holding period to a very short time interval.[12] Furthermore, even this risk can be hedged, if the underwriter so chooses, by buying an appropriate put option.

As with underwriting, market-making or dealing in securities is as risky as the securities firm chooses to make it — being determined by the size of the position taken, the length of time it is held and the volatility of the underlying security.

The conclusion must be that securities business, at least in the under-writing and market-making areas, is not *inherently* riskier than bank lending. It does, however, present undoubted *opportunity*, for those securities firms which are so minded, to adopt a high-risk/high-return strategy. This being so, it is necessary to examine the performance of securities firms to see how in practice their risk characteristics compare with those of banks.

A number of US studies have investigated this question with a view to assessing the risks to US bank holding companies from expanding their non-bank activities.[13] The variability of returns is generally taken as the measure of risk, although the returns may be calculated on the basis of either stock market data or an accounting measure of profitability. If a new activity is characterized by a greater variability of returns in isolation than does banking it may be said to be more risky. However, this is not the end of the matter, for if the returns from a high-risk activity, such as securities business, are imperfectly correlated with the returns from banking, the overall returns from the combined activities may be less variable than the returns of each activity taken separately. In this case a bank could lower its risk by diversifying into the new activity so long as the size of the invest-ment is not too large relative to the original banking firm. It is necessary to add that even where the returns from the two activities have a close positive correlation, it may still be possible for a combination of the businesses to be risk-reducing if there are economies of scope which increase operating efficiency. In such a case the *average* level of returns may be raised sufficiently to offset the impact of higher earnings variability on the bank's probability of insolvency.

Defining risk as the variance of the average daily stock market returns, Brewer, Fortier and Pavel examined 13 non-bank activities in order to determine which are likely to reduce risk and which are likely to increase it when the activities are undertaken by US bank holding companies.[14] Three time periods were chosen (1980, 1982 and 1986) to represent

**Table 3.1.** Riskiness of banking vs non-bank activities, 1980, 1982 and 1986

| | Variances of average daily returns | Correlations of average daily returns |
|---|---|---|
| Banking | 0.220 | 1.000 |
| Permissible non-bank activities | | |
| Consumer finance | 2.068 | 0.345 |
| Commercial finance | 1.510 | 0.380 |
| Mortgage banking | 4.575 | 0.245 |
| Consumer credit reporting | 1.918 | 0.379 |
| Leasing | 1.367 | 0.457 |
| Impermissible non-bank activities | | |
| Savings and loan associations | 1.409 | 0.647 |
| Securities brokers and dealers | 9.449 | 0.296 |
| Insurance agents and brokers | 0.654 | 0.419 |
| Life insurance underwriters | 1.392 | 0.274 |
| Health and accident insurance underwriters | 3.671 | 0.284 |
| Property/casualty insurance underwriters | 0.659 | 0.668 |
| Real estate | 1.515 | 0.477 |
| Management consulting | 1.711 | 0.445 |

*Source*: Elijah Brewer, Diana Fortier and Christine Pavel, 'Bank risk from non-bank activities', *Journal of International Securities Markets*, summer (1989), pp. 206–7.

different phases of the business cycle. As well as calculating the variance of market returns, and the correlations of those returns with banking returns, the authors also assessed the impact of hypothetical mergers on bank holding company risk. The results of this exercise are shown in tables 3.1, 3.2 and 3.3.

So far as securities business is concerned, the following conclusions can be drawn. First, this activity is by far the riskiest, taken in isolation, of those covered by the study. On the other hand, the returns from securities and banking business have a relatively low correlation. Even so, an investment in securities activities accounting for 10 per cent of the equity of the combined business would increase the bank holding company risk significantly and an investment of 25 per cent or more would increase the risk dramatically.

A US study by Boyd and Graham, using both annual accounting data

**Table 3.2.**   Ranks of non-bank activities according to risk and correlation with banking, 1980, 1982 and 1986

|  | Risk | Correlation |
|---|---|---|
| Permissible non-bank activities |  |  |
| Consumer finance | 4 | 9 |
| Commercial finance | 8 | 7 |
| Mortgage banking | 2 | 13 |
| Consumer credit reporting | 5 | 8 |
| Leasing | 11 | 4 |
| Impermissible non-bank activities |  |  |
| Savings and loan associations | 9 | 2 |
| Securities brokers and dealers | 1 | 10 |
| Insurance agents and brokers | 12 | 6 |
| Life insurance underwriters | 10 | 12 |
| Health and accident insurance underwriters | 3 | 11 |
| Property/casualty insurance underwriters | 13 | 1 |
| Real estate | 7 | 3 |
| Management consulting | 6 | 5 |

*Source*: Brewer, Fortier and Pavel, 'Bank risk', pp. 206–7.

and market data for the period 1971–84, reaches a similar conclusion.[15] The authors found that mergers between bank holding companies and securities firms were likely to increase the profitability of the former, but were also likely to increase risk. Furthermore, due to methodological problems (e.g. the exclusion of any non-bank firms that failed during the sample period) the authors felt that the results understated the risks resulting from expanded powers for bank holding companies.

Even if, as some other studies suggest, there may be *potential* for some risk reduction from banks' diversification into non-bank financial services (including securities business) this does not mean that banks will manage their operations so as to achieve lower levels of risk. On the contrary, there is evidence from the behaviour of US bank holding companies that management will not always voluntarily diversify non-bank assets so as to reduce risk — but instead look for opportunities for increased risk-taking.[16] Similarly many commercially aggressive US savings and loan institutions ('thrifts') appear to have used the new investment powers they acquired in 1982 in a risk-enhancing manner.[17]

**Table 3.3.** The risk effects of hypothetical non-bank acquisitions

|  | Variance w/5% non-bank | Variance w/10% non-bank | Variance w/25% non-bank |
|---|---|---|---|
| Permissible non-bank activities | | | |
| Consumer finance | 0.226 | 0.241 | 0.340 |
| Commercial finance | 0.223 | 0.233 | 0.300 |
| Mortgage banking | 0.233 | 0.268 | 0.502 |
| Consumer credit reporting | 0.227 | 0.242 | 0.336 |
| Leasing | 0.226 | 0.237 | 0.303 |
| Impermissible non-bank activities | | | |
| Savings and loan associations | 0.236 | 0.257 | 0.347 |
| Securities brokers and dealers | 0.263 | 0.350 | 0.874 |
| Insurance agents and brokers | 0.217 | 0.217 | 0.231 |
| Life insurance underwriters | 0.216 | 0.219 | 0.268 |
| Health and accident insurance underwriters | 0.232 | 0.261 | 0.449 |
| Property/casualty insurance underwriters | 0.224 | 0.231 | 0.260 |
| Real estate | 0.227 | 0.240 | 0.315 |
| Management consulting | 0.229 | 0.244 | 0.333 |

*Source*: Brewer, Fortier and Pavel, 'Bank risk', pp. 206–7.

The key point here is that where banks are already risk-constrained by regulation, some institutions may be tempted to adopt a higher-risk profile by diversifying into non-bank activities that are less heavily (or effectively) regulated. As one author puts it: 'if additional risk seeking were concentrated among banks and thrifts already taking the greatest risks, then financial product deregulation could adversely affect the safety and soundness of the banking system, even if other banks and thrifts were able to reduce their risks of failure'.[18] In short, given its potential for risk-taking, securities business could serve as a convenient outlet for risk-seeking institutions.

It needs to be stressed again that the issue here is not one of whether banks' diversification into securities activities *can* reduce overall risk (which, on the evidence cited above, seems unlikely in any event) but whether a sufficient number of banks may conduct their securities operations in a manner that increases risk and thereby undermines financial stability as a whole. In a free-market setting banks that were known to have adopted this approach would presumably be penalized by their depositors and other creditors who would demand an appropriate risk premium; but in a situation where banks are backed by deposit insurance and other official safeguards, the risks that banks incur are not typically reflected in their funding costs. That being so, an aggressive bank management has every incentive to exploit whatever opportunities may arise to achieve its preferred risk profile. Disturbingly, both a priori reasoning, and the evidence from the behaviour of US bank holding companies and thrifts, suggests that banks' move into securities markets could encourage excessive risk-taking and thereby increase the incidence of bank failures.

Finally, mention should be made here of Benston's argument to the effect that since US banks are already permitted to make high-risk loans to (inter alia) property developers, oil and gas explorers and developing countries — activities which in many cases have caused or threatened insolvencies — 'it is difficult to understand how securities activities could increase the amount of risk that a bank is now legally permitted to take'.[19] This line of reasoning is, however, unpersuasive: just because banks have been able to engage in excessive *banking* risks, this is no reason to give them further and additional opportunities for excessive risk-taking in *securities* markets. On the contrary, the evidence that some banks will use whatever powers they have to engage in solvency threatening behaviour should be viewed as a reason for constraining rather than broadening banks' permissible non-bank activities.

# Risk Segregation

If banks' risky securities activities do indeed threaten their solvency, the question that needs to be asked is whether there is any way of segregating those risks in a subsidiary or affiliate of the bank. In other words, can a 'firewall' be constructed between the bank proper and its securities business so that the bank is effectively insulated from the risks incurred by the latter? This question, which has been the subject of intense controversy in the USA and elsewhere, can be de-composed into three distinct albeit related problem areas, namely legal separation, economic separation and market perception.[20]

The problem for those who wish to ensure legal separation between a bank and its securities arm is that the courts can pierce the 'corporate veil' and decide that a bank is liable for the debts of its subsidiary or affiliate. On this point the former Chairman of the US Federal Reserve Board, Mr Paul Volcker, has drawn attention to the case of the *Amoco Cadiz*, the oil tanker that spilled its cargo on the beaches of France after breaking up in a storm.[21] The tanker's owner had been careful to incorporate the ship's operation and separate its corporate structure. In the ensuing litigation, the court held the parent fully liable for its subsidiary's environmental disaster, the management of the parent company having been found to have directed all the operations of the ship-owning subsidiary during the relevant crisis period. As Mr Volcker was at pains to emphasize, it is not unreasonable to suppose that, faced with a major disaster in a securities subsidiary, a parent bank or bank holding company would become similarly embroiled and therefore legally liable for its subsidiary's losses.

Of course, bank regulators may seek to ensure that the bank and securities entities are separate in fact as well as in appearance. For instance, the two businesses may be required to have separate management, separate record keeping, separate premises and non-identical boards of directors. Nevertheless, as the *Amoco Cadiz* example shows, such formal barriers can disintegrate in times of stress.

Quite apart from problems associated with crisis management, the US General Accounting Office has pointed out that joint marketing of banking and securities services could leave the bank exposed to risks incurred by its securities subsidiary or affiliate. This could result from potential estoppel claims by creditors of a failed subsidiary/affiliate who might argue that they had been misled into believing that they were dealing with the bank rather than the securities entity.[22]

Assuming, nevertheless, that such legal pitfalls are overcome, the most that legal separation can achieve is a situation where a bank is relieved from any formal obligation to support a troubled securities subsidiary or affiliate. There remains, however, the possibility that a bank will be so exposed to its related securities entity through its previous normal course of funding that default by that entity will threaten the bank's solvency; *or* that the risk to its reputation will induce a bank to provide open-ended emergency support to its securities subsidiary/affiliate should the latter encounter financial difficulties. Such potential for cross-infection is considered here under the headings of economic separation and market perception.

As explained above, because of the official safety net which protects their depositors, banks have privileged access to credit markets. A banking conglomerate will therefore have an economic incentive to use the bank's low-cost borrowings to fund its risky securities activities — whether or not these be conducted through a separate legal entity. A bank may therefore not only become heavily exposed to the risks undertaken by its securities arm; it may also be viewed as subsidizing high risk activities through its (protected) deposit base. The result is that the official safety net will de facto be extended to banks' securities operations. In other words, the legal separation of a bank and its related securities entity is of no avail if there is economic integration between the two businesses such that the bank is allowed to become a major source of unsecured funding for securities activities. One way of handling this problem would be to impose restrictions on intra-group financial flows, but there are serious practical difficulties here, some of which are considered below.

Even if banks can be separated both legally and economically from their securities operations, there is still the danger that financial markets will fail to distinguish between the credit standing of a bank and that of its related securities entity. If this were so any problems encountered by the securities entity would quickly infect the bank through adverse consequence effects and an associated withdrawal of deposits.

A study undertaken by the staff of the US Federal Reserve Board has examined this question of market perceptions in relation to US bank holding companies' non-bank subsidiaries. The authors suggest that 'it is reasonable to assume that if a non-bank unit of the holding company is so mismanaged that it fails, the affiliated bank may also be mismanaged and could be in unsatisfactory condition'.[23] Furthermore, even where there are legal restrictions on banks' support for a non-bank affiliate 'bank liability holders might still be concerned because the holding company might violate these statutes in a time of crisis'.[24] The conclusion is that the market conceives of a bank holding company as an integrated entity, meaning that problems in one part of the group will inevitably be transmitted to other parts. Furthermore, recent events involving the failure of Drexel Burnham Lambert in the USA, and the collapse of British and Commonwealth Merchant Bank in the UK (see chapter 10) lend powerful support to this assessment of the markets' response to problems arising within a financial conglomerate.

It follows from the above that banks will seek to protect their own reputation and credit standing by coming to the assistance of a troubled non-bank subsidiary or affiliate, even where the two entities are legally and economically separated. Numerous instances of such emergency support have been cited by the US regulatory authorities.[25] Some of the more notable examples are cited below:

- *REITs.* In the mid-1970s a number of real estate investment trusts (REITs) sponsored by bank holding companies ran into trouble during a downturn in the real estate market. In the words of a Federal Reserve Board staff study:

  bank sponsors provided financial support to their REITs on a non-arms length basis to avoid the adverse publicity which a related REIT bankruptcy would bring. As a result, the real estate investment problems were transferred to the sponsoring bank. This support was provided even though the banks were under no legal obligation to do so.[26]

• *United California Bank (UCB)*. In 1970 UCB voluntarily assumed responsibility for the debts of its Swiss bank subsidiary, which failed after incurring losses of nearly $40mn from unauthorized speculation in cocoa futures. There was no legal obligation on the part of UCB to provide such support.

• *Banco Denasa*. In 1985 First Chicago Corporation felt obliged to support Banco Denasa, a Brazilian investment bank in which it held a 44.5 per cent ownership interest. The result was a $131mn loss on the original $15mn investment.

• *Drysdale Securities*. In 1982 Chase Manhattan Bank and Manufacturers Hanover, who had merely acted as intermediaries between Drysdale, a government securities dealer, and a number of participants in the government securities market, agreed to meet interest obligations that Drysdale had defaulted on. However, it seems that in this case the Federal Reserve put pressure on Chase to make the payments.

• *Hamilton Bank of Chattanooga*. In the mid 1970s Hamilton Bank was forced by the parent holding company to buy a large volume of low-quality mortgages from a troubled mortgage banking affiliate of the holding company. These purchases, which were in breach of the law, resulted in the subsequent failure of the bank.

The well documented predisposition of banks to support their non-bank subsidiaries or affiliates suggests that legal separation alone would do little to protect banks from the risks incurred by their securities operations. The US FDIC has objected that 'many of the examples cited as cases where banking organizations have gone to great lengths to preserve their reputation in the marketplace are cases where preserving that reputation came at a relatively low cost to the parent institution'.[27] However, this is surely not the point. If the size of the bail-out costs could threaten the solvency of the bank, then the bank might indeed refrain from providing emergency assistance. But in that event, the non-bank entity would fail, with potentially disastrous confidence effects on the related bank entity. That is the unmistakable message from the failure of Drexel Burnham Lambert — although in this case it was a well capitalized and conservatively managed government securities dealer that was threatened by the bankruptcy of its parent.

The problems outlined above relating to legal separation, economic separation and market perceptions might, in principle, be addressed through appropriate legal and regulatory safeguards. Legal separation could, for instance, be secured by requiring banks and their related securities businesses to be operated as independent entities with separate management and marketing. As recently proposed by the US Comptroller of the Currency any remaining doubts about legal separateness could be removed by amending the banking laws to prohibit banks from being held liable for the obligations of their subsidiaries or affiliates, unless specifically assumed by prior contractual arrangement.[28]

Similarly, economic separation could in theory be achieved by imposing legal constraints on financial dealings between a bank and its related securities business. These restrictions would also be aimed at overcoming the difficulties arising from perceptions of the market. Indeed, US banking laws already apply such restrictions to banks' transactions with their non-bank affiliates.

Section 23A of the Federal Reserve Act generally limits loans to, and guarantees or purchases of obligations of non-bank affiliates by the bank, to 10 per cent of bank capital for any one affiliate, and to 20 per cent in the aggregate. Furthermore, most extensions of credit or guarantees involving a non-bank affiliate must be fully collateralized; the sale of subquality assets to the bank is prohibited; and transactions with affiliates must be undertaken on terms and conditions that are consistent with safe and sound banking practices.[29]

The Competitive Equality Banking Act of 1987 introduced a new Section 23B of the Federal Reserve Act which strengthens these restrictions. Specifically, the new section requires that transactions with affiliates should be on terms and conditions substantially the same as those undertaken with non-affiliated companies, and generally prohibits bank trust departments from purchasing the securities of an affiliate. The new provision also places severe restrictions on the acquisition of securities by the bank during the time any affiliate is acting as an underwriter or member of a selling syndicate of such securities. Finally, Section 23B prohibits any bank or non-bank affiliate from taking any action — including advertising — that would suggest that the bank is responsible for any obligation of the affiliate.

While it might appear that legal and regulatory safeguards of this kind can insulate a bank from the risks incurred by its securities subsidiary or affiliate, there are nevertheless serious flaws in the firewall approach.

In the first place, the imposition of firewalls between the bank and its related securities entity may largely neutralize the economies of scope associated with the fusion of the two businesses. Quite simply, firewalls may have the effect of *internalizing* within the financial conglomerate those same Glass–Steagall type prohibitions to which banks object so strongly. Furthermore, regulators are faced with the onerous task of ensuring that firewalls are maintained in good order and not by-passed or breached.

Therefore, firewalls may involve costly constraints on financial activity similar to those associated with formal separation laws such as the Glass–Steagall Act.

Secondly, it may be argued that laws which prevent banks from supporting their subsidiaries/affiliates could in certain circumstances have destabilizing consequences. For instance, it has been argued that a prohibition on banks making loans to their securities affiliates could weaken the financial system during a liquidity crisis such as occurred in October 1987.[30] In that situation solvent securities affiliates might be cut off from their funding base with no alternative source of credit. More generally, the President of the Federal Reserve Bank of New York, Mr Gerald Corrigan, has warned that firewalls which strictly limit or prevent the mobility of funds and capital among affiliates may promote systemic risk: 'taken to an extreme, absolute firewalls can aggravate problems and instabilities rather than contain or limit them'.[31]

A third and perhaps insuperable difficulty with the firewall approach is that in times of stress the rules may be broken. For instance, in the above-cited case of Hamilton National Bank the purchases of mortgages from its distressed mortgage banking affiliate far exceeded the amount permitted by law. Yet regulatory authorities have tended to overlook this problem. A notable example of such regulatory over-optimism was provided recently by the US Comptroller of the Currency, Mr Robert Clarke. In a speech delivered in January 1987 Mr Clarke explained a new regulatory decision by his office (OCC) which, he claimed, could be used as a model for permitting banks to diversify their activities without jeopardizing the position of depositors:

> A regulatory decision made by the OCC at the end of the year illustrates how this structural isolation could work. Indeed, I think the decision could be seen as a prototype, a trial model of decisions that would regulate banking expansion into other activities in the future.
>
> Several months ago, Continental Illinois National Bank sought regulatory approval to purchase First Options of Chicago, Inc., a leading registered securities broker-dealer and futures commission merchant. Under the proposal, First Options would become a wholly-owned subsidiary of the bank.
>
> Because First Options engages in activities that Continental Illinois itself could engage in under the law if it chose to do so, the OCC approved the acquisition of First Options as an operating subsidiary of the bank. However, as a matter of risk management, we believed that the bank should be insulated from the First Options subsidiary, principally to protect the insured deposits of Continental Illinois from any operating risks arising from

its ownership of the subsidiary. We considered such protection as part of the social goal of providing a safe vehicle for savings to the public.

Therefore, we limited the bank's investment in — and loans to — First Options to an amount equal to the bank's legal lending limit — the latter being essentially the same limitation that would apply to the bank's dealings with an unaffiliated business. Continental Illinois agreed that it would not make any additional investments of equity capital in First Options without prior written consent from the OCC.

In other words, should the occasion arise, the bank could not use its capital to bail out the subsidiary without the OCC's approval.

I think that you would agree with me that this is a logical, practical and reasonable way to protect the insured deposits of the bank while allowing it to expand its business. I hope that you would also agree with me that this is a logical, practical and reasonable approach to protect the insured deposits of any bank while allowing it to diversify.[32]

Unfortunately, this new regulatory model was almost immediately found wanting. On the basis of the OCC limits, Continental Bank could invest in or lend to First Options $381mn unsecured and a further $254mn secured. However, during the week of 19 October 1987 when First Options experienced financial strains, Continental Bank made unsecured advances to First Options which exceeded the agreed limit by $128mn. This occurred, moreover, despite the fact that the OCC was in almost continuous contact with the bank during the week in order to monitor potential problems associated with First Options.[33]

The clear lesson of First Options is that whatever legal barriers may be interposed between a bank and its securities subsidiaries/affiliates these are liable to be ignored under the pressure of events such as those of October 1987.

Finally, even if there were effective legal and economic separation, and banks could somehow be prevented from supporting their troubled securities subsidiaries/affiliates, the confidence problem would remain. That is, the banking arm of a financial conglomerate would still be vulnerable to panic deposit withdrawals in the event that *any* part of the group encountered financial difficulties.

The overall policy conclusion is that the firewall approach to regulating the intersection of banking and securities markets may achieve the worst of all possible worlds. On the one hand, the regulatory constraints on a bank's dealings with its securities arm may erode the economic benefits of conglomeration. On the other hand, the bank will remain vulnerable to cross-infection from the high-risk activities of its related securities entity. All the regulatory authorities would then have achieved is an expensive exercise in self-delusion, while leaving the banking system dangerously exposed to securities-market risks.

## Notes

1  In the academic literature see, for instance, George J. Benston, *The Separation of Commercial and Investment Banking* (Macmillan, London, 1990); Ingo Walter, ed., *Deregulating Wall Street: commercial bank penetration of the corporate securities market* (John Wiley, New York, 1985); and (for a more cautious view of bank diversification) Robert Litan, *What Should Banks Do?* (Brookings Institution, Washington DC, 1987). For the views of US policymakers see, for example, *Mandate for Change: restructuring the banking industry* (Federal Deposit Insurance Corporation, Washington DC, 1987) and Statement (with appendices) by Gerald Corrigan, President, Federal Reserve Bank of New York, before the US Senate Committee on Banking, Housing and Urban Affairs, 3 May 1990.

2  For a review of this issue see Thomas Pugel and Lawrence White, 'An analysis of the competitive effects of allowing commercial bank affiliates to underwrite corporate securities', in Ingo Walter, ed., *Deregulating Wall Street*, pp. 93–139.

3  In April 1989 the Swiss Cartel Commission published a report on bank cartels. It identified 16 out of 22 reported agreements which significantly limited competition, including underwriting syndicates for domestic and foreign bond issues.

4  This classification of economies of scope is based on Litan, *What Should Banks Do?*, pp.74–81. See also Jeffrey Clark, 'Economies of scale and scope at depository financial institutions: a review of the literature', *Federal Reserve Bank of Kansas City Economic Review*, September/October (1988), pp. 16–33. Clark finds little empirical support for economies of scope, although the evidence is acknowledged to be insufficiently strong to support any strong conclusions on the matter.

5  Randall Pozdena, 'Commerce and banking: the German case', *Federal Reserve Bank of San Francisco Weekly Letter*, 18 December (1987).

6  See David Lascelles, 'Universal banking: a relic of the past', *Financial Times*, 3 July 1989, p. 40.

7  Order Conditionally Approving Applications by J. P. Morgan and Co. Inc., The Chase Manhattan Corporation, Bankers Trust New York Corporation, Citicorp and Security Pacific Corporation to Engage to a Limited Extent in Underwriting and Dealing in Certain Securities, 18 January 1989, pp. 31–2. In another example of competitive relaxation of regulatory policy the New York State Superintendent of Banks stated that 'in light of the liberalization of global capital markets, the United States is now at a distinct competitive disadvantage due to the Glass–Steagall Act'. See New York State Banking

Department News Release, 30 December 1986. In response to this concern New York State expanded the permissible securities activities that state banks can conduct.

8    See Anthony Saunders, 'Conflicts of interest: an economic view', in Ingo Walter, ed., *Deregulating Wall Street*, pp. 207–30.

9    Paradoxically, the Gessler Commission was more concerned with the opposite conflict — namely the possibility that universal banks might be biased in favour of bank lending as against securities market financing. Accordingly, such banks might not be interested in recommending their customers to purchase securities, thereby inhibiting the growth of domestic securities markets. See 'Basic banking questions', Summary of the Report of the Commission of Enquiry, Bonn (1979), p. 2.

10   George Benston, *The Separation of Commercial and Investment Banking*, p. 107.

11   See 'Basic banking questions', pp. 17–18.

12   See Ian Giddy, 'Is equity underwriting risky for commercial bank affiliates?' in Ingo Walter, ed., *Deregulating Wall Street*, pp. 145–69.

13   See John Boyd and Stanley Graham, 'Risk, regulation and bank holding company expansion into nonbanking', *Federal Reserve Bank of Minneapolis Quarterly Review*, spring (1986), pp. 2–17; John Boyd and Stanley Graham, 'The profitability and risk effects of allowing bank holding companies to merge with other financial firms: a simulation study', *Federal Reserve Bank of Minneapolis Quarterly Review*, spring (1988), pp. 3–20; Elijah Brewer, Diana Fortier and Christine Pavel, 'Bank risk from nonbank activities', *Journal of International Securities Markets*, summer (1989), pp. 199–210; Larry Wall, 'Nonbank activities and risk', *Federal Reserve Bank of Atlanta Economic Review*, October (1986), pp. 19–34; and Robert Eisenbeis and Larry Wall, 'Risk considerations in deregulating bank activities', *Federal Reserve Bank of Atlanta Economic Review*, May (1984), pp. 6–18. For a critique of the methodology used in some of these studies see Benston, *The Separation of Commercial and Investment Banking*, pp. 149–59. In particular banks' historic earnings may appear to be less volatile than that of securities firms because of differing accounting treatment, especially in relation to mark-to-market valuation of assets. Ibid., p. 151.

14   Elijah Brewer, Diana Fortier and Christine Pavel, 'Bank risk', pp. 205–8.

15   John Boyd and Stanley Graham, 'The profitability and risk effects of allowing bank holding companies to merge with other financial firms', p. 12.

16   See John Boyd and Stanley Graham, 'Risk, regulation'. The authors conclude (p. 3) that 'when BHC nonbank subsidiaries are largely left to their own devices (rather than stringently regulated) higher levels of nonbank activity may be associated with a higher, not a lower, risk of failure'. This conclusion applies even though such nonbank activities offer *theoretical* potential for risk reduction. It is also interesting to note that a Federal Reserve Board staff study shows that non-bank subsidiaries of US bank holding companies are

typically riskier than bank subsidiaries, concluding that the growth in the relative share of non-bank activities 'could have important implications for the safety and soundness of banking organisations'. See Nellie Liang and Donald Savage, 'The nonbank activities of bank holding companies', *Federal Reserve Bulletin*, May (1990), p. 292.

17 See evidence cited in Robert Litan, *What Should Banks Do?*, pp. 109–11.
18 Ibid., p. 105.
19 Benston, *The Separation of Commercial and Investment Banking*, p. 147.
20 This follows the classification in FDIC, *Mandate for Change*, pp. 105–22.
21 See Statement before the Subcommittee on Commerce, Consumer and Monetary Affairs of the Committee on Government Operations, US House of Representatives, 11 June 1986, p. 23.
22 See *Bank Powers: Issues Related to the Repeal of the Glass–Steagall Act* US General Accounting Office, Washington DC, January (1988), pp. 55–6.
23 See 'An analysis of the concept of corporate separateness in BHC regulation from an economic perspective', in Appendices to the Statement by Paul Volcker, Chairman of Governors of the Federal Reserve System, before the Subcommittee on Commerce, Consumer and Monetary Affairs of the Committee on Government Operations of the US House of Representatives, June 1986, p. C-6.
24 Id.
25 Ibid. See also FDIC, *Mandate for Change*, pp. 110–19.
26 'An analysis of the concept of corporate separateness', p. C-7.
27 FDIC, *Mandate for Change*, p. 114.
28 See Statement of Robert Clarke before the Subcommittee on Telecommunications and Finance of the Committee of Energy and Commerce, US House of Representatives, 14 October 1987, p. 17.
29 The stated rationale for the Section 23A restrictions is that the free flow of funds between a bank and its affiliates 'could expose some banks to considerable abuse for the benefit of affiliates, result in a significant increase in bank failures, and thus reduce confidence in the banking system'. John Rose and Samuel Tally, 'The Banking Affiliates Act of 1982: amendments to Section 23A', *Federal Reserve Bulletin*, November (1982), p. 699.
30 One official spokesman has described the danger as follows:

> During the market crash of October 1987, commercial banks were important suppliers of liquidity to market participants, augmented by general support from the Federal Reserve. If a total prohibition is placed on this type of lending between a bank and its affiliated securities firm, we are not sure that the liquidity needs of market participants could be as well met in the event that the October events are repeated....... We recognize that the current 23A and 23B limitations on interaffiliate lending might prevent the bank from meeting its securities affiliate's total funding needs in a market crisis. But such limitations at least allow some room for flexibility in such a situation.

Using Firewalls in a Post Glass–Steagall Banking Environment, Statement of Richard Fogel, Assistant Comptroller General, General Government Programs, before the Subcommittee on Telecommunications and Finance, Committee on Energy and Commerce, US House of Representatives, 13 April 1988, p. 8.

31   Statement before the US Senate Committee on Banking, Housing and Urban Affairs, 3 May 1990, p. 39.

32   Remarks before the Federal Reserve Bank of Atlanta, Georgia, 8 January 1987, pp. 8–9. It should be added that Mr Robert Clarke is one of the most vigorous opponents of the Glass–Steagall Act. He has argued that Glass–Steagall prohibitions have: (1) caused banks to lose a significant share of their high-quality borrowers to the securities markets; (2) prevented banks from achieving needed liquidity through loan sales; and (3) made it difficult for banks to diversify their assets and sources of income — causing the level of risk in the banking system to increase. According to Mr Clarke 'there are few, if any, business activities that cannot safely be combined with banking'. See Statement before the Senate Committee on Banking, Housing and Urban Affairs, 21 January 1987, p. 12.

33   See Statement by Emory Rushton, Deputy Comptroller of the Currency for Multinational Banking, before the Subcommittee on Oversight and Investigations of the Committee on Energy and Commerce, House of Representatives, 3 February 1988.

# 4

# The US Glass–Steagall Act

The previous chapter identified some of the major policy issues arising from the co-mingling of banking and securities business. The present chapter describes the separation provisions of the US Glass–Steagall Act, which represents the US Congress's response to the domestic banking upheavals of 1929–33, and traces recent US regulatory initiatives aimed at liberalizing banks' involvement in securities markets.

The US Banking Act of 1933 includes four provisions, Sections 16, 20, 21 and 32, which mandate substantial separation of commercial and invest-ment banking (see appendix I to this chapter). These four provisions, known collectively as the Glass–Steagall Act, have governed the relationship between US commercial and investment banking for nearly sixty years.[1]

Section 16 of the Act imposes three constraints on banks' securities activities. Firstly, a bank[2] may only purchase equity securities for the account of customers and not for its own account. Secondly, bank authority to invest in debt securities is limited expressly to such marketable obliga-tions as may be prescribed by regulations issued by the Comptroller of the Currency.[3] Thirdly, the underwriting and dealing activities of banks is specifically restricted to US Treasury and agency obligations, and general obligations of state and local governments.

Under Section 20 of the Act, banks are prohibited from affiliating with organizations 'engaged principally' in the underwriting or distribution of securities. The wording here is important, regulatory attention having recently focused on the scale of business that can be undertaken by a bank affiliate without breaching the 'principally engaged' limitation.

Section 21 prohibits any person or organization from engaging both in securities business (except as the section permits) and the banking business of deposit-taking. This section does not contain the principally engaged language of Section 20 and it is not clear at what point a person or organization becomes engaged in securities business for this purpose.

Finally, Section 32 prohibits management and employee interlocks between banks and firms 'primarily engaged' in the securities business. The purpose of this section is to limit conflicts of interest that could adversely affect the impartiality of both lending decisions and investment advice.

In 1971 the Supreme Court, in *Investment Co. Institute v. Camp*, had occasion to reaffirm the legislative policy that lay behind the Glass–Steagall Act:

> The Glass–Steagall Act reflected a determination that policies of competition, convenience, or expertise which might otherwise support the entry of commercial banks into the investment banking business were outweighed by the 'hazards' and 'financial dangers' that arise when commercial banks engage in the activities proscribed by the Act.
>
> The hazards that Congress had in mind were not limited to the obvious danger that a bank might invest its own assets in frozen or otherwise imprudent stock or security investments. ... The legislative history of the Glass–Steagall Act shows that Congress also had in mind and repeatedly focused on the subtle hazards that arise when a commercial bank goes beyond the business of acting as fiduciary or managing agent and enters the investment banking business either directly or by establishing an affiliate to hold and sell particular investments. This course places new promotional and other pressures on the bank which in turn create new temptations. For example, pressures are created because the bank and the affiliate are closely associated in the public mind, and should the affiliate fare badly, public confidence in the bank might be impaired. And since public confidence is essential to the solvency of a bank, there might exist a natural temptation to shore up the affiliate through unsound loans or other aid.[4]

Partly because US commercial banks had little inclination to diversify into securities business, and also because the statutory provisions were viewed as creating an impenetrable barrier between commercial and investment banking, the Glass–Steagall Act attracted little regulatory attention for nearly four decades. However, in the 1970s and 1980s banks increasingly sought to test the limits of Glass–Steagall while the US regulatory authorities, for their part, adopted a progressively more liberal approach to interpreting the Act's restrictive provisions.

The Federal Reserve Board (FRB) has been at the centre of this liberalizing process by virtue of its role as the administering agency for the Bank Holding Company Act (BHCA) of 1956 (as amended in 1970). The BHCA provides that bank holding companies may only engage in non-banking activities that are so closely related to banking as to be considered a proper incident to banking. In determining whether a particular activity is a proper incident to banking, the Board must consider whether its performance by a holding company may reasonably be expected to produce benefits to the public, such as greater convenience, increased competition or gains in efficiency, that outweigh possible adverse effects, such as undue concentration of resources, decreased or unfair competition, conflicts of interest, or unsound banking practices. The Board must also satisfy itself that approved activities are in conformity with the Glass–Steagall Act. Therefore a major responsibility of the Federal Reserve Board has been to define, and then supervise and regulate, the non-banking activities in which bank holding companies may engage.

In exercising the above powers, the FRB has in recent years considerably widened the range of securities-related activities open to bank holding companies. These initiatives have on occasion been challenged by the securities industry but the courts have tended to support the FRB's more liberal interpretation of the statutory wording.

## Investment Advice and Securities Brokerage

In 1972 the FRB amended its regulation Y,[5] which governs permissible non-banking activities, to enable bank holding companies and their non-bank subsidiaries to act as investment advisers to various types of investment company — a decision subsequently upheld by the Supreme Court.[6]

In 1983 the FRB approved the application of BankAmerica Corporation (the bank holding company for Bank of America) to acquire Charles Schwab, the largest US discount brokerage firm, on the grounds that the discount broker would be acting merely as agent, buying and selling securities on the order and for the account of customers.[7] The courts again upheld the FRB's decision, finding that there was no breach of Glass–Steagall since: (1) the agency nature of the brokerage protected the banking institution's own assets; (2) there was no salesman's stake in the success of the investment; and (3) no conflicts of interest or unsound loans were likely to result. Following this ruling, discount brokerage services were added to the FRB's Regulation Y list of permissible bank holding company activities.

In 1986 the FRB broke new regulatory ground when it approved National Westminster Bank's application to offer investment advice and securities brokerage services on a combined basis through its newly formed subsidiary, County Securities Corporation (CSC).[8]

Although the FRB had previously approved the acquisition by Bank-America of discount brokers Charles Schwab, that had been on the basis that Schwab did not provide investment advice. The Board — supported by the Supreme Court — had also previously determined that investment advice per se is permissible for bank holding companies, but, again, this had not been considered in conjunction with brokerage services.

Under the terms of the FRB's approval CSC was subject to the following constraints:

1   Portfolio advice and brokerage services could be given to institutional investors only.
2   CSC could execute a transaction only at the discretion of a customer, and could not exercise discretion with respect to any customer account.
3   CSC could not act as principal or take a position in any securities it brokered or recommended.
4   The subsidiary had to be maintained as a separate and distinct corporate entity, with its own name, premises, books and records. No CSC officer or director could also be an officer or director of any other NatWest subsidiary or of National Westminster Bank plc itself.
5   NatWest had to create a 'Chinese wall' between the bank and CSC to avoid potential conflicts of interest.

In considering NatWest's application, the FRB had to determine: (1) whether CSC's proposed activities were closely related to banking within the meaning of the Bank Holding Company Act; and (2) whether the conduct of such activities by a bank affiliate would violate Glass–Steagall.

On the first issue the FRB determined that the proposal 'represents the combination of two activities, previously determined to be closely related to banking, in such a way that the functional nature and scope of the combined activities conducted would not be altered'.[9]

In reaching this conclusion the FRB rejected an objection raised by the Securities Industry Association to the effect that depositors might lose confidence in CSC's affiliate bank if investments made on CSC's recommendation did poorly. The FRB felt that, so long as CSC maintained a separate corporate identity, 'the public association between NatWest's bank subsidiaries and its securities affiliate will be prevented to a large extent and will not pose an undue risk to the NatWest holding company, its banking and non-banking subsidiaries, or to the soundness of the banking system generally'.[10]

So far as Glass–Steagall is concerned, the crucial issue for the FRB was whether CSC's proposed brokerage activities amounted to a 'public sale or distribution' of securities, which would violate Section 20 of the statute. The FRB relied on the legislative history of the Act and on the Supreme

Court's judgment in the Charles Schwab case in determining that Congress 'did not intend to erect a complete barrier between banking organizations and the conduct of all securities activities'.[11] Rather, the Glass–Steagall Act was intended to prohibit only those situations where a position is taken in the securities traded, or there is a distribution to the public on behalf of an issuer. Hence CSC's proposed activities did not involve the 'public sale' of securities.[12]

# Underwriting Commercial Paper and Other Ineligible Securities

In December 1986 the FRB carried the process of deregulation an important stage further when it approved an application by Bankers Trust New York Corporation to engage in the placing of commercial paper[13] through a commercial lending affiliate. The application was approved as consistent with Section 20 of the Glass–Steagall Act which prohibits a company affiliated with a bank from being 'engaged principally' in underwriting or distributing securities.[14] While acknowledging that commercial paper is a 'security' for purposes of the Act (as earlier determined by the Supreme Court) the FRB held that, so long as it acted only as placing agent and not as principal, Bankers Trust would not be underwriting or distributing commercial paper within the meaning of Section 20. Furthermore, the FRB determined that even if the proposed placement activity were covered under Section 20, Bankers Trust's proposal would still be permissible because the affiliate conducting the activity would not be 'engaged principally' in underwriting securities.

Of major significance was the FRB's rebuttal, in its formal decision, of a number of arguments traditionally used to support the separation of commercial and investment banking. In particular the FRB held that:

- There was little potential for Bankers Trust to make unsound loans to issuers of commercial paper placed by its affiliate in an attempt to strengthen the issuers' financial condition. The reasoning here was that the prospective loss to the bank if such loans were not repaid would greatly exceed the commission payable for placing commercial paper (approx. $\frac{1}{8}$ per cent).
- There was no possibility that Bankers Trust could be tempted to make imprudent loans to its affiliate if the latter were to encounter financial difficulties, because Section 23A of the Federal Reserve Act limits extensions of credit by a bank to its non-bank affiliates (as well as asset purchases from the affiliate).
- There was little possibility that the affiliate would encourage a financially troubled client company to issue CP to enable it to repay loans to Bankers Trust. The reasoning here was that the existence of commercial paper rating

services, as well as disclosure requirements, would make it extremely difficult for a financially troubled company to issue commercial paper.[15]

In April 1987 the FRB went considerably further in removing the barriers between commercial and investment banking when it approved conditionally the applications of Bankers Trust, Citicorp and J. B. Morgan to engage through subsidiaries in underwriting commercial paper, certain mortgage-backed securities and municipal revenue bonds.[16] Because these are 'ineligible' securities that banks themselves may not underwrite or deal in, the FRB had to determine whether the subsidiaries would be 'engaged principally' in underwriting such securities within the meaning of Section 20 of the Glass–Steagall Act.

The FRB concluded that the underwriting subsidiaries would not be 'engaged principally' in ineligible underwriting and dealing activities if:

1   they derived no more than 5 per cent of their total gross revenue from ineligible underwriting and dealing activity on average over any 2-year period;
2   their underwriting activities in connection with each particular type of ineligible security did not account for more than 5 per cent of the total amount of that type of security underwritten domestically by all firms during the previous calendar year; and
3   they limited the amount of each particular type of security held for dealing so as not to exceed the amount of the underwriting market-share limitation in (2).

Under the Bank Holding Company Act the FRB also had to consider whether the proposed activities were 'so closely related to banking ... as to be a proper incident thereto'. This statutory standard requires two separate tests to be met. First, the activity must be closely related to banking; second, the performance of the activity by the applicant bank holding company must reasonably be expected to produce public benefits that outweigh possible adverse effects.

On the first of these tests the FRB had little difficulty in finding that banks already provide services (e.g. underwriting eligible securities) that are functionally and operationally similar to the proposed activities.

So far as the second test is concerned the Board was also readily convinced that the proposed activities would result in substantial public benefits in the form of increased competition, greater convenience and gains in efficiency.

On the other hand, these benefits had to be weighed against any additional financial risks to the affiliated banks as well as conflicts of interest arising from the new activities. The Board's findings on these potentially adverse effects can be summarized as follows:

*Financial risk*   In order to limit the risk of financial loss, the board placed conditions on the types of ineligible securities that may be underwritten and dealt in. Furthermore, various conditions attached to the order (see below) are designed to insulate the underwriting and dealing activities from the applicants' subsidiary banks. Therefore the FRB concluded that even if the securities subsidiaries were to encounter losses, these were not likely to infect the parent institutions or their bank subsidiaries.

*Damage to public confidence*   The FRB required that each underwriting subsidiary provide to each of its customers a statement pointing out that the obligations of the underwriting subsidiary are not obligations of an affiliate bank and that the bank is not responsible for securities sold by the subsidiary. The aim here is to reduce further the association in the public mind between the bank holding company and its underwriting subsidiary. As a further precaution against possible erosion of public confidence in affiliated banks, no bank can engage in marketing activities on behalf of an underwriting subsidiary.

*Conflicts of interest*   In general, the FRB noted that 'there is no evidence that bank underwriting of eligible securities over the past 50 years has produced serious conflicts of interest or other abuses or encouraged imprudent lending practices'.[17] Because the proposed new activities involved securities similar to those already underwritten and dealt in by the banks the FRB believed that 'the potential for significant or new conflicts of interest with respect to the proposed ineligible securities would be manageable'.[18] Specific areas of potential conflict were addressed as follows:

- *Credit to purchasers of securities*   The FRB noted that subsidiary banks might be encouraged to make imprudent loans to depositors for the purchase of securities underwritten by their affiliates. Accordingly, the FRB determined that no lending affiliate of the underwriting subsidiary could extend credit to a customer that is secured by, or for the purpose of, purchasing any ineligible security underwritten or dealt in by the underwriting subsidiary.
- *Credit to issuers of securities*   Banks might be tempted to make imprudent loans to improve the financial condition of companies whose securities are underwritten or dealt in by an affiliated underwriting subsidiary. To prevent this, the FRB determined that a bank should not make loans to issuers of ineligible securities underwritten by the securities subsidiary for the purpose of the payment of principal and interest on such securities. Similarly, banks should not issue or enter into a stand-by letter of credit, asset purchase agreement or other facility that might be viewed as enhancing the creditworthiness or marketability of ineligible securities underwritten or dealt in by the securities subsidiary.

These restrictions reflected the FRB's belief that 'the risk that a bank's credit judgement may be impaired by the existence of an investment banking relationship between a borrower and the bank's affiliate is one of the fundamental hazards at which the Glass–Steagall Act was aimed'.[19]

- *Credit to underwriting subsidiaries*   Banks might be tempted to make imprudent loans to support the underwriting subsidiaries should they encounter financial difficulties. Section 23A of the Federal Reserve Act already limits extension of credit by a bank to its non-bank affiliates to 10 per cent of the bank's capital and requires that any extensions of credit be collateralized. In addition, the applicants agreed to comply with the proposed Section 23B of the Federal Reserve Act (since enacted). This requires that all purchases and sales of assets between a bank and its affiliated underwriting subsidiaries be at arm's length and on terms no less stringent than those applicable to unrelated third parties.

  There is the additional risk that securities dealt in or underwritten by an underwriting subsidiary might be dumped into an affiliated bank's inventory – another major concern underlying Glass–Steagall. To meet this concern the FRB determined that banks should not purchase as principal ineligible securities in which the affiliated securities subsidiary makes a market or, during the underwriting period and 60 days thereafter, ineligible securities underwritten by the securities subsidiary.

- *Biased investment advice*   To meet concern in this area, the FRB required the applicants not to purchase as trustee or in any other fiduciary capacity ineligible securities underwritten or dealt in by their securities subsidiaries unless they are specifically authorized to do so. Under existing fiduciary principles, banks may not express opinions about the advisability of investing in ineligible securities underwritten by the bank or its affiliates without disclosure.

- *Securities issued by affiliates*   The concern here is the conflict that might arise if an underwriting subsidiary underwrites or deals in securities of affiliated entities, particularly those that may be experiencing financial difficulties. Glass–Steagall was designed, inter alia, to prevent this kind of abuse. Accordingly, the FRB required that an underwriting subsidiary must not underwrite or deal in any ineligible securities issued by its affiliates or representing interests in, or secured by, obligations originated or sponsored by its affiliates.

- *Securities to repay loans*   The concern here is that the securities subsidiary might encourage issuers to issue securities the proceeds of which would be used to repay loans made by affiliated banks. The FRB noted that there is a strong economic disincentive to this kind of behaviour (i.e., jeopardizing reputation) and that disclosure requirements and the necessity for objective credit ratings would make it extremely difficult for issuers experiencing financial difficulties to issue securities that would be accepted by the market.

- *Access to confidential information*   The FRB required that no lending affiliate of the underwriting subsidiaries could disclose to the underwriting subsidiaries any non-public customer information consisting of an evaluation of the creditworthiness of an issuer or other customer of the underwriting subsidiary. This was designed to meet the allegation that sharing of confidential information could result in unfair competition. Trading on insider information is already covered by the securities laws.

The conditions attached to the Federal Reserve's approval order, which are designed to meet the financial-risk and conflict-of-interest points described above, are reproduced in appendix II to this chapter.

# Underwriting Corporate Debt and Equity Securities

Following this limited extension of their securities powers conferred by the FRB's April 1987 conditional approval order, the same applicant bank holding companies sought to achieve by the back door what banking industry lobbyists had been trying to attain through statutory reform. On this occasion J. P. Morgan, Chase Manhattan, Bankers Trust, Citicorp and Security Pacific tested the outer limits of Glass–Steagall by applying for FRB approval for their underwriting subsidiaries to underwrite and deal in corporate debt and equity securities — albeit on the same limited basis (including the 5 per cent of revenue ceiling) as required in the earlier approval.

On 18 January 1989 the FRB gave its conditional approval to these new applications, following a comment period during which the securities industry had argued vigorously against the further extension of banks' securities activities. The key passage in the FRB determination reads as follows:

> As the Board has recognized in the past, underwriting and dealing in securities is a natural extension of the activities currently conducted by banks, involving manageable risks and potential conflicts of interest when conducted in an organizational structure that insulates these activities from banking activities supported by the federal safety net of deposit insurance and access to Federal Reserve lending. In the Board's view, bank holding companies, with their existing expertise in securities underwriting, dealing, brokerage and investment advisory activities and their broad financial skills, are particularly well equipped to provide the proposed new services. Moreover, the conduct of these activities, within the prudential framework established in this order, may reasonably be expected to yield significant public benefits in the form of increased competition and convenience, lower costs and a strengthened and more competitive banking and financial system.[20]

However, because of the importance which it attached to adequate operational procedures and risk-management controls, the FRB insisted that the applicants must have in place, at both the underwriting subsidiaries and their affiliates, policies and procedures to ensure compliance with the operating conditions of the order.

The FRB anticipated that this condition could already be satisfied to allow subsidiaries' immediate participation, as underwriter and dealer, in the market for debt securities. But in the case of equity securities the Board believed it appropriate 'to review in one year whether applicants may commence underwriting and dealing in these securities based on a determination by the Board that they have established the managerial and operational infrastructure and other policies and procedures necessary to comply with the requirements of this Order'.[21]

In its detailed reasoning (the determination ran to 84 pages) the FRB referred to one potentially important benefit that could arise from US banks' extended securities powers — namely, an improvement in their international competitiveness. However, the FRB also recognized that unless US banks' enlarged securities powers were very carefully regulated, the activities of underwriting subsidiaries could destabilize their affiliate banks. Accordingly, great emphasis was placed on establishing a tight regulatory framework for underwriting subsidiaries.

In approving the applicant bank holding companies' more limited securities powers in 1987 the Board order had required that the new activities be conducted in a corporation over which the affiliated banks had no ownership, financial, management or operational control (see p. 64). More specifically, the underwriting subsidiaries were required to be capitalized by the holding company from its funds and not from the resources of its bank subsidiaries. The order also imposed restrictions on transactions by an affiliate bank with or for the benefit of an underwriting subsidiary so as to prevent the transfer of risk to federally insured institutions.

The FRB noted, however, that in the present application approval was being sought for underwriting subsidiaries 'to engage in nearly the full range of investment banking activities'.[22] Furthermore, it was noted that the proposed equity and debt securities in which the applicants wished to deal are riskier than those for which approval had previously been given. Accordingly, the FRB decided to impose the following additional safeguards in respect of the newly expanded securities activities:

- Each applicant had to provide the FRB with an acceptable plan to raise additional capital to fund the applicant's equity and debt investment in the underwriting subsidiary or demonstrate that it is strongly capitalized and will remain so after making necessary capital adjustments. In accordance with the new risk-based capital guidelines, applicants had to deduct 50 per cent of the amount of their investment in an underwriting subsidiary from Tier 1 capital and 50 per cent from Tier 2 capital. But they were also required to deduct from consolidated primary capital the full amount of their investment in an underwriting subsidiary.

- Any funds supplied to the underwriting subsidiaries by the holding company or its non-bank subsidiaries, whether in the form of capital, secured or unsecured loans, or other transfer of assets, was subject to prior notice and approval by the FRB. This limitation on the ability of the underwriting subsidiary to draw upon the resources of the parent holding company 'should help to ensure that the market will evaluate the financial standing of the underwriting subsidiary based upon its own resources'.[23]

- There was a prohibition on lending by a bank affiliate to the underwriting subsidiary as well as a prohibition on the purchase and sale of financial assets between these institutions for their own account, subject to a limited exception for clearing US government and agency securities and the purchase and sale of US Treasury securities. 'The Board believes these prohibitions are necessary to limit the transfer of risk of the securities activities to the federal safety net and would serve more effectively to insulate federally insured banks ... from the underwriting subsidiaries'.[24]

- The FRB was concerned that approval of the proposed expanded securities activities would allow bank holding companies to engage to a greater extent than hitherto in leveraged buyout (LBO) and other types of highly leveraged corporate transactions. Furthermore, it noted that because both the underwriting subsidiary and the affiliate bank might receive fees from such transactions, objective risk assessment could be impaired. However, rather than prohibit altogether lending by a bank undertaken in connection with financing transactions underwritten or arranged by an underwriting subsidiary, the FRB required affiliate banks to: (1) control concentrations of credit and overall exposure to individual underwriting clients of the underwriting subsidiary as well as limits on aggregate exposure to all such borrowers; (2) secure approval for all such lending at the highest level of management; and (3) maintain detailed credit and collateral documentation so that examiners might determine that a thorough and objective credit assessment had been undertaken.

In September 1989 the FRB raised the limit on underwriting of all 'bank-ineligible' securities by bank holding company subsidiaries from 5 per cent to 10 per cent of the subsidiary's gross revenue. These higher limits were, however, available only for subsidiaries which had already been permitted by the FRB to engage in this type of activity.

Finally, in September 1990 the FRB made the historic decision to allow J. P. Morgan to underwrite corporate equities through its securities subsidiary, subject to the same conditions as those already applicable to the underwriting of corporate debt securities.[25] In January 1991 equivalent powers were granted to three more banks — Bankers Trust, Royal Bank of Canada and Canadian Imperial Bank of Commerce. These moves may well mark the final stage of the FRB's liberalization process within the confines of the Glass–Steagall Act, with attention now focusing on statutory reforms incorporating the repeal of Glass–Steagall (below).

# US Banks' Foreign Operations

As described above, the FRB has greatly extended the range of securities-related activities that bank holding companies may engage in through their subsidiaries. This willingness to pare down the constraints imposed by Glass–Steagall reflects, among other considerations, the US regulatory authorities' concern to maintain the international competitiveness of the US banking system. That concern has been expressed even more forcefully in relation to US banks' operations abroad. Furthermore, since the Glass–Steagall Act applies only to US domestic banking operations, the regulatory authorities have allowed US banks much greater latitude in their overseas business.

The FRB has a broad discretion to determine the kinds of activities that US banks may undertake in overseas markets. This discretion has been exercised consistently with a view to ensuring that, so far as possible, US banks are not placed at a competitive disadvantage in their international operations.

Thus, foreign branches of US banks, in addition to exercising the normal banking powers they enjoy domestically, may exercise certain additional powers to the extent that such powers are 'usual in connection with the business of banking in the foreign countries where those branches transact their business'.[26] Such additional powers include underwriting debt securities of the national and local governments where the branch is located. However, equity underwriting is not permitted.

In the case of foreign subsidiaries of US banks or bank holding companies, the regulatory concessions are more substantial. The FRB specifies the range of permissible activities open to such subsidiaries in its Regulation K, one of the main objectives underlying the scope of this regulation being 'to keep US banks competitive with their foreign counterparts'.[27] Therefore, to enable US bank subsidiaries to compete with foreign financial institutions in universal banking centres such as London and Frankfurt, the FRB has permitted such subsidiaries to underwrite both corporate debt and equity securities — subject, in the latter case, to strict quantitative limits.[28] Accordingly, foreign investment bank subsidiaries of

US commercial banks have established a large role in underwriting corporate debt, particularly in the London-based Eurobond market. Furthermore, several US banking organizations (including Security Pacific, Citicorp and Chase Manhattan) acquired controlling interests in UK securities firms following the Big Bang restructuring of London's financial markets.

In September 1988 the US General Accounting Office (GAO) severely criticized the way in which US banks managed their securities underwriting and trading activities in the London market during 1986 and 1987.[29] The GAO noted that in several cases the losses suffered by the London securities subsidiaries of US banks during this period were large enough to require capital infusions from the US parent in order to bring capital up to minimum UK standards – although losses were relatively small in relation to parent banks' total capital resources. According to the report the London experience, underlines the need for tight regulation of US banks' securities activities in the event that the Glass–Steagall Act is repealed. The GAO also concluded that US banks should be required to use the bank holding company form of operation for their foreign securities subsidiaries as a means of ensuring adequate separation of banking and securities business – there being at present no firewall arrangements for US banks' overseas securities activities.

## Proposed Statutory Reforms: Repealing Glass–Steagall

The competitive pressures which induced the FRB to allow US banks to expand their securities-related activities both domestically and abroad, have also prompted a number of legislative initiatives aimed at repealing or amending the Glass–Steagall Act. One of the most important of these, which had the support not only of the US Administration, but also of the three US bank regulatory agencies – the Federal Reserve Board, the Comptroller of the Currency and the Federal Deposit Insurance Corporation – was the Proxmire-Garn Bill, otherwise known as 'The Financial Modernization Act of 1988'.[30]

On 19 November 1987 Senators William Proxmire and Jake Garn introduced a Bill repealing key sections of the Glass–Steagall Act and permitting bank holding companies (but not banks themselves) to engage in securities underwriting and other securities activities through separately capitalized securities affiliates. The detailed provisions of the Proxmire-Garn Bill were designed to ensure that any losses incurred by a securities affiliate did not infect its sister bank. In order to achieve this objective certain restrictive terms of the Glass–Steagall Act were in effect 'internalized' — that is to say, the separation of commercial from investment banking was maintained through restrictions on banks' dealings with their securities affiliates. Specifically, a bank would not be permitted to lend to its securities affiliates; it could not make loans or guarantees to a company in order to enhance the marketability of the company's securities that are being underwritten by the bank's securities affiliate; it could not make loans to a person for the purpose of paying the principal or interest on securities underwritten by its securities affiliate. Furthermore, the securities affiliate could not sell securities to the bank or its trust accounts during the underwriting period or for 30 days thereafter, there could be no director or officer interlocks between a bank and its securities affiliate and, crucially, the securities affiliate would have to disclose publicly that its obligations were in no way backed by its affiliate bank or insured by the FDIC.

The purpose of these proposed restrictions was to ensure, as far as possible, that banks are financially insulated from the risks incurred by their securities affiliates and that the lender of last resort and deposit insurance functions need not be extended beyond the banking sector to securities firms. At the same time, securities affiliates of banks were to be regulated by the Securities and Exchange Commission as separate entities and the assets and liabilities of such affiliates were not to be consolidated with the bank holding company for purposes of regulation by the Federal Reserve Board. In other words, the principle of separation embodied in the Glass–Steagall Act would continue to be reflected in the operational, financial and regulatory independence of banks and their related securities firms.

In the event the Proxmire-Garn Bill was approved by the Senate, but not by the House of Representatives, and it did not therefore reach the statute book. However, the separation principles embodied in the bill received widespread support and are indicative of congressional and policymakers' concerns about needed safeguards for banks' securities business.

The next major legislative initiative came in February 1991 when the US Administration published its proposals for restructuring the domestic banking system in a far-reaching policy document entitled 'Modernizing the financial services system: recommendations for safer, more competitive banks'. Subsequently, the Treasury Department published a draft bill, 'The Financial Institutions Safety and Consumer Choice Act of 1991', which provides the legislative basis for implementing these proposals.

Two key factors have given impetus to the Administration's fundamental review of US banking law. First, there is the extraordinarily high bank failure rate of recent years, which is widely blamed on excessive protection of depositors and the fact that present regulatory arrangements do not focus sufficiently on the adequacy of bank's capital resources. Second, the competitiveness of the US banking industry has been declining, both at home, where banks account for a steadily shrinking share of total credit flows, and abroad where US banks have been losing market share to their foreign counterparts. These trends are attributed in part to excessive regulatory constraints on US banks' activities.

In order to address the problem of excessive bank failures, the Administration proposes to limit deposit insurance coverage and to strengthen the regulatory role of capital. At the same time, two major initiatives are planned to improve US banks' competitive position: legislative changes will allow banks to (1) operate nationwide through interstate branching; and (2) engage in a broader range of financial services, including securities underwriting and distribution. Finally, the regulatory structure will itself be simplified by establishing a new federal banking agency — the Office of Depository Institution Supervision — which will have exclusive regulatory responsibility for national banks.

The discussion that follows will focus on only one aspect of the Administration's proposed reforms — the plan to amend those provisions of the Glass–Steagall Act of 1933 that prohibit banks from engaging in securities activities.

Under the Administration's proposals the prohibition on banks' direct involvement in securities activities would be maintained. However, banking groups would be able to establish financial services holding companies (FSHCs) which in turn would be authorized to engage in a broad range of financial activities through separate holding company subsidiaries (see figure 4.1). Furthermore, the legal separation of commerce and banking, mandated by the Bank Holding Company Act of 1956, would be reversed by permitting commercial (i.e., non-financial) firms to own FSHCs — although FSHCs would not themselves be able to engage in commercial activities. Through the FSHC structure, therefore, a wide range of commercial and financial activities could be combined, albeit within separately capitalized entities.

By using the FSHC as a vehicle for financial diversification the Administration hopes to be able to contain risks within the individual financial affiliates and, in combination with appropriate firewalls (see below), to prevent any financial difficulties originating in a non-bank affiliate from overflowing into the related bank entity. Non-bank financial activities are to be carried out in affiliates rather than subsidiaries of the bank 'because

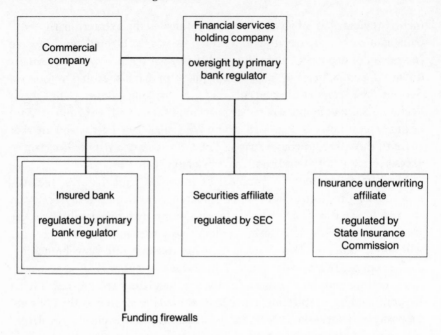

**Figure 4.1** Proposed US financial structure

*Source*: *Modernizing the Financial System* (Department of the Treasury, Washington DC, February 1991), p. 55

of the perception of greater distance from the bank'.[31] Quite simply, the idea is that affiliates could fail without affecting the capital of the bank, and without adversely affecting the confidence of bank depositors.

By allowing commercial firms to own banks through FSHCs, the Administration hopes to attract more capital into banks from outside the industry. However, because commercial firms are not regulated in the same way as financial companies, the proposal is to allow only indirect commercial ownership of a bank through an FSHC, rather than direct ownership. The official view is that indirect ownership should help to establish stronger firewalls between a bank and its commercial parent than between a bank and its financial affiliates.

A key feature of the above scheme for permitting financial diversification within a conglomerate structure is the regulatory role accorded to bank capital. Under the Administration's proposals on capital-based supervision, banks would be categorized into five different 'zones', according to their levels of capital, those with the strongest capital ratios being categorized as Zone 1. Only Zone 1 banks would be permitted to engage in a broad range of non-bank financial activities through FSHCs. Similarly, securities, insurance and mutual fund companies would be permitted to affiliate (through the FSHC structure) only with Zone 1 banks.

Under Section 251 of the draft legislation a Zone 1 bank is defined as one which:

1 'maintains a risk-based capital ratio that is significantly in excess of the required minimum ratio and Tier 1 capital that is significantly in excess of the required minimum for Tier 1 capital'; or
2 'meets the required minimum risk-based capital ratio and maintains Tier 1 capital that is substantially in excess of the required minimum for Tier 1 capital; and maintains capital that meets or exceeds the required minimum ratio for each other relevant capital measure'.

If an FSHC owned a bank which fell from Zone 1 to Zone 2 it would either have to inject capital into the bank so as to restore it to Zone 1 within one year, or else it would have to divest the newly authorized non-bank financial affiliates. This regime is intended to provide further protection to the banking system by ensuring that only well capitalized banks can diversify into securities and other newly authorized non-bank activities.

There already exists a fundamental safeguard designed to prevent US banks from being adversely affected by the activities of their non-bank affiliates. This protection takes the form of 'funding firewalls', which have been incorporated in statute law as sections 23A and 23B of the Federal Reserve Act.[32] Section 23A limits loans to, and guarantees or purchases of obligations of, non-bank affiliates by the bank. In general, loans to a non-bank affiliate must be collateralized; the sale of low-quality assets to the bank is prohibited; and transactions with affiliates must be on terms and conditions 'consistent with safe and sound banking practices'.

Section 23B of the Federal Reserve Act (introduced by the Competitive Equality Banking Act of 1987) requires that transactions with affiliates be on terms and conditions substantially the same as those with non-affiliated companies, and prohibits bank trust departments from purchasing the securities of an affiliate. The section also places stringent restrictions on the acquisition of securities by the bank during any period in which the affiliate is acting as an underwriter of such securities.

Under the Administration's proposals for broader banking powers the above restrictions would continue to apply to transactions between a bank and its non-bank affiliates, including the new securities affiliates. Indeed, Section 23A would be strengthened to include non-credit transactions such as fees and management contracts. In addition, an FSHC would be required to provide prior notice to the bank regulators of unusually large transfers of funds between a bank and any affiliate; while dividend restrictions on undercapitalized banks would help to prevent FSHCs from draining assets from their subsidiary banks.

Finally, the bank regulator would have discretionary authority to prohibit or restrict certain transactions between the bank and its securities affiliate or certain customers of the securities affiliate. Such discretionary authority is already exercised by the US Federal Reserve Board in cases where, under Section 20 of the Glass–Steagall Act, bank holding companies are permitted to establish non-bank subsidiaries that derive up to 10 per cent of their revenue from otherwise prohibited securities activities. The Administration is evidently anxious that these Section 20 firewalls should not now be incorporated in statute law as part of its reform programme, because it would like to see them phased out – or at least substantially relaxed – over time.

In order to ensure that banks can exploit the economic benefits of financial diversification the Administration does not plan to impose any restrictions on shared management, employees, officers, or directors. Furthermore, there will be no general limitation on the ability of a bank and its affiliates to market each other's products. However, under Section 224 of the draft legislation a bank must disclose in writing to its customers that securities recommended or sold by the bank 'are not deposits, are not insured by the Federal Deposit Insurance Corporation, are not guaranteed by [the bank] and are not otherwise an obligation of [a bank] unless such is the case'.

The regulatory regime governing the new US financial conglomerates is to be functional rather than institutional. That is to say, banking activities would be regulated by the banking regulator, securities activities by the SEC and insurance activities by the state insurance commission. This approach is made possible because different activities would be conducted through separate FSHC subsidiaries.

On the other hand, there would be a residual element of institutional regulation in the form of 'umbrella oversight' of the FSHC by the bank regulator. The purpose here is to protect the bank from group risks by enabling the bank regulator to identify and address problems within the FSHC or its non-bank affiliates that could jeopardize the financial position of the bank entity. In the extreme, the bank regulator could require the sale of a non-bank affiliate that posed a threat to the bank, while an FSHC could be subject to bank capital standards applied to the whole group on a consolidated basis. Such umbrella oversight would, however, fall well short of full consolidated supervision and would in no way imply federal protection for the group as a whole. Indeed, it is a central principle of the

Administration's proposals that the official safety net, in the form of FDIC insurance and the Federal Reserve's discount window, would be confined to the bank and that 'creditors of the FSHC or [non-bank] financial affiliates should receive no federal protection in the event of FSHC insolvency'.[33]

## Conclusion

In response to international competitive pressures, the securitization of financial markets and persistent lobbying by the banking industry, the US Federal Reserve Board has chosen to broaden banks' securities powers piecemeal through a liberal interpretation of the Glass–Steagall Act. This process culminated in 1990 with the authorization given to selected bank holding companies to underwrite corporate equities through Section 20 subsidiaries — albeit subject to numerous safeguards and strict quantitative limits.

Attention has now shifted to proposals for statutory reform which would remove altogether the legal barriers between the banking and securities industries. However, it remains a central feature of these proposals — as it does of the Federal Reserve's piecemeal reforms — that banks themselves should be insulated from the risks incurred by their securities affiliates. This approach, which is in direct contrast to that adopted by the European Community, is open to the objection that attempts to segregate risks within diversified banking groups, while imposing costs on the banking industry, are unlikely to work in practice — a point taken up again in chapters 10 and 11.

## Appendix I

### *US Glass–Steagall provisions*

Sections 16, 20, 21 and 32 of the Banking Act of 1933 are collectively known as the Glass–Steagall Act. These provisions are reproduced below:

1.  23 USC Section 24. Section 16 states in relevant part:

[A] national banking association ... shall have power — To exercise by its board of directors or duly authorized officers or agents, subject to law, all such incidental powers as shall be necessary to carry on the business of banking; by discounting and negotiating promissory notes, drafts, bills of exchange, and other evidences of debt; by receiving deposits; by buying and selling exchange, coin and bullion; by loaning money on personal security; and by obtaining, issuing and circulating notes according to the provisions of this chapter.

The business of dealing in securities and stock by the association shall be limited to purchasing and selling such securities and stock without recourse, solely upon the order, and for the account of customers, and in no case for its own account, and the association shall not underwrite any issue of securities or stock: Provided, That the association may purchase for its own account investment securities under such limitations and restrictions as the Comptroller of the Currency may by regulation prescribe. In no event shall the total amount of the investment securities of any one obligor or maker, held by the association for its own account, exceed at any time ten per centum of its capital stock actually paid in and unimpaired and ten per centum of its unimpaired surplus fund, except that this limitation shall not require any association to dispose of any securities lawfully held by it on 23 August 1935. As used in this section the term 'investment securities' shall mean marketable obligations, evidencing indebtedness of any person, copartnership, association, or corporation in the form of bonds, notes and/or debentures commonly known as investment securities under such further definition of the term 'investment securities' as may by regulation be prescribed by the Comptroller of the Currency.

Except as hereinafter provided or otherwise permitted by law, nothing herein contained shall authorize the purchase by the association for its own account of any shares of stock of any corporation. The limitations and restrictions herein contained as to dealing in, underwriting and purchasing for its own account, investment securities shall not apply to obligations of the United States, or general obligations of any State or of any political subdivision thereof ...

2.   12 USC Section 377. Section 20 states in relevant part:

After one year from June 16, 1933, no member bank shall be affiliated in any manner with any corporation, association, business trust or any similar organization engaged principally in the issue, flotation, underwriting, public sale, or distribution at wholesale or retail or through syndicate participation of stocks, bonds, debentures, notes, or other securities ...

3.   12 USC Section 378. Section 21 states in relevant part:

After the expiration of one year after June 16, 1933, it shall be unlawful − (1) For any person, firm, corporation, association, business trust or other similar organization to engage in the business of issuing, underwriting, selling, or distributing, at wholesale or retail, or through syndicate participation, stocks, bonds, debentures, notes or other securities, to engage at the same time to any extent whatever in the business of receiving deposits subject to check or to repayment upon presentation of a passbook, a certificate of deposit or other evidence of debt or upon request of the depositor:

Provided, That the provisions of this paragraph shall not prohibit national banks or State banks or trust companies (whether or not members of the Federal Reserve System) or other financial institutions, or foreign bankers from dealing in, underwriting, purchasing and selling investment securities, or issuing securities, to the extent permitted to national banking associations by the provisions of Section 24 of this title: Provided further, That nothing in this paragraph shall be construed as affecting in any way such right as any bank, banking association, savings bank, trust company, or other banking institution, may otherwise possess to sell, without recourse or agreement to repurchase obligations evidencing loans on real estate ...

4.   12 USC Section 78. Section 32 states in relevant part:

No officer, director, or employee of any corporation or unincorporated association, no partner or employee of any partnership, and no individual, primarily engaged in the issue, flotation, underwriting, public sale, or distribution, at wholesale or retail, or through syndicate participation, of stocks, bonds, or other similar securities, shall serve the same time as an officer, director or employee of any member bank except in limited classes of cases in which the Board of Governors of the Federal Reserve System may allow such service by general regulations when in the judgement of said Board it would not unduly influence the investment policies of such member bank or the advice it gives its customers regarding investments.

# Appendix II

*Firewalls and other restrictions applicable to US banks' Section 20 Subsidiaries (April 1987)*

*A   Types of securities to be underwritten*
1   The underwriting subsidiaries shall limit their underwriting and dealing in ineligible securities to the following:

(a)   *Municipal revenue bonds* that are rated as investment quality (i.e., in one of the top four categories) by a nationally recognized rating agency, except that industrial development bonds in these categories shall be limited to 'public ownership' industrial development bonds (i.e., those tax exempt bonds where the issuer, or the governmental unit on behalf of which the bonds are issued, is the sole owner, for federal income tax purposes, of the financed facility (such as airports and mass commuting facilities)).

(b)   *Mortgage-related securities* (obligations secured by or representing an interest in 1–4 family residential real estate), rated as investment quality (i.e., in one of the top four categories) by a nationally recognized rating agency.

(c)   *Commercial paper* that is exempt from the registration and prospectus requirements of the SEC pursuant to the Securities Act of 1933 and that is short-term, of prime quality, and issued in denominations no smaller than $100,000.

*B   Capital investment*
2   Each Applicant's investment in an underwriting subsidiary and the assets of the underwriting subsidiary shall be excluded in determining the holding company's consolidated primary capital under the Board's Capital Adequacy Guidelines.

*C   Capital adequacy*
3   The underwriting subsidiary shall maintain at all times capital adequate to support its activity and cover reasonably expected expenses and losses in accordance with industry norms.

4   Applicants shall submit quarterly to the Federal Reserve Bank of New York FOCUS reports filed with the NASD or other self-regulatory organizations, and detailed information breaking down the underwriting subsidiaries' business with respect to eligible and ineligible securities, in order to permit monitoring of the underwriting subsidiaries' compliance with the provisions of this Order.

*D   Credit extensions by lending affiliates to customers of the underwriting subsidiary*
5   No Applicant or subsidiary shall extend credit, issue or enter into a stand-by letter of credit, asset purchase agreement, indemnity, insurance or other facility that might be viewed as enhancing the creditworthiness or marketability of an ineligible securities issue underwritten by an affiliated underwriting subsidiary.

6   No lending affiliate of an underwriting subsidiary shall knowingly extend credit to a customer secured by, or for the purpose of purchasing, any ineligible security that an affiliated underwriting subsidiary underwrites during the period of the underwriting, or to purchase from the underwriting subsidiary any ineligible security in which the underwriting subsidiary makes a market. This limitation extends to all customers of lending affiliates, including broker-dealers, and unaffiliated banks, but does not include lending to a broker-dealer for the purchase of securities where an affiliated bank is the clearing bank for such broker-dealer.

7   No Applicant or any of its subsidiaries may make loans to issuers of ineligible securities underwritten by an affiliated underwriting subsidiary for the purpose of the payment of principal and interest on such securities. To assure compliance with the foregoing, any credit lines extended to an issuer by any lending subsidiary of the bank holding company shall provide for substantially different timing, terms, conditions and maturities from the ineligible securities being underwritten. It would be clear, for example, that a credit has substantially different terms and timing if it is for a documented special purpose (other than the payment of principal and interest) or there is substantial participation by other lenders.

8   Each applicant shall adopt appropriate procedures, including maintenance of necessary documentary records, to assure that any extension of credit to issuers of ineligible securities underwritten or dealt in by an underwriting subsidiary are on an arm's length basis for purposes other than payment of principal and interest

on the issuer's ineligible securities being underwritten or dealt in by the subsidiary. An extension of credit is considered to be on an arm's length basis if the terms and conditions are substantially the same as those prevailing at the time for comparable transactions with issuers whose securities are not underwritten or dealt in by the underwriting subsidiaries.

9   The requirements relating to credit extensions to issuers noted in paragraphs 5–8 above shall also apply to extensions of credit to parties that are major users of projects that are financed by industrial revenue bonds.

*E   Limitations to maintain separateness of an underwriting affiliate's activity*
10   There will be no officer, director, or employee interlocks between an underwriting subsidiary and any of the holding company's bank or thrift subsidiaries. The underwriting subsidiary will have separate offices from any affiliated bank.

*F   Disclosure by the underwriting subsidiary*
11   An underwriting subsidiary will provide each of its customers with a special disclosure statement describing the difference between the underwriting subsidiary and its banking affiliates and pointing out an affiliated bank could be a lender to an issuer and referring the customer to the disclosure documents for details. The statement shall also indicate that the obligations of the underwriting subsidiary are not those of any affiliated bank and that the bank is not responsible for securities sold by the underwriting subsidiary. The underwriting subsidiary should disclose any material lending relationship between the issuer and a bank or lending affiliate of the underwriting subsidiary as required under the securities laws and in every case where the proceeds of the issue will be used to repay outstanding indebtedness to affiliates.

12   No underwriting subsidiary nor any affiliated bank or thrift institution will engage in advertising or enter into an agreement stating or suggesting that an affiliated bank is responsible in any way for the underwriting subsidiary's obligations.

13   No bank or thrift affiliate of the underwriting subsidiary will act as agent for, or engage in marketing activities on behalf of, the underwriting subsidiaries. In this regard, prospectuses and sales literature of an underwriting subsidiary may not be distributed by a bank or thrift affiliate; nor should any such literature be made available to the public at any offices of any such affiliate, unless specifically requested by a customer.

*G   Investment advice by bank/thrift affiliates*
14   An affiliated bank or thrift institution may not express an opinion with respect to the advisability of the purchase of ineligible securities underwritten or dealt in by an underwriting subsidiary unless the bank or thrift affiliate notifies the customer that its affiliated underwriting subsidiary is underwriting or making a market in the security.

*H   Conflicts of interest*
15   No Applicant nor any of its subsidiaries, other than the underwriting subsidiary, shall purchase, as principal, ineligible securities that are underwritten by the underwriting subsidiary during the period of the underwriting and for 60 days after the close of the underwriting period, or shall purchase from the underwriting subsidiary any ineligible security in which the underwriting subsidiary makes a market.

16   No Applicant nor any of its bank, thrift, or trust or investment advisory company subsidiaries shall purchase, as a trustee or in any other fiduciary capacity, for accounts over which they have investment discretion ineligible securities (i) underwritten by the underwriting subsidiary as lead underwriter or syndicate member during the period of any underwriting or selling syndicate, and for a period of 60 days after the termination thereof, and (ii) from the underwriting subsidiary if it makes a market in that security, unless, in either case, such purchase is specifically authorized under the instrument creating the fiduciary relationship, by court order, or by the law of the jurisdiction under which the trust is administered.

17   An underwriting subsidiary may not underwrite or deal in any ineligible securities issued by its affiliates or representing interest in, or secured by, obligations originated or sponsored by its affiliate (except for grantor trusts or special purpose corporations created to facilitate underwriting of securities backed by residential mortgages originated by a non-affiliated lender).

18   All purchases and sales of assets between bank (or thrift) affiliates and an underwriting subsidiary (or third parties in which the underwriting subsidiary is a participant or has a financial interest or acts as agent or broker or receives a fee for its services) will be arm's length and on terms no less stringent than those applicable to unrelated third parties, and will not involve low-quality securities, as defined in Section 23A of the Federal Reserve Act.

*I   Limitations to address possible unfair competition*
19   No lending affiliate of an underwriting subsidiary may disclose to the underwriting subsidiary any nonpublic customer information consisting of an evaluation of the creditworthiness of an issuer or other customer of the underwriting subsidiary (other than as required by securities laws and with the issuer's consent) and no officers or employees of the underwriting subsidiary may disclose such information to its affiliates.

*J   Formation of subsidiaries of an underwriting subsidiary to engage in underwriting and dealing*
20   Pursuant to Regulation Y, no corporate reorganization of an underwriting subsidiary, such as the establishment of subsidiaries of the underwriting subsidiary to conduct the activities, may be consummated without prior Board approval.

*Source*: Order Approving Applications to Engage in Limited Underwriting and Dealing in Certain Securities, Federal Reserve Board, April 30 1987.

# Notes

1 For an excellent review of the operation of this Act see Joseph Norton, 'Up against "the wall": Glass–Steagall and the dilemma of a deregulated ("Reregulated") banking environment', *Business Lawyer*, 42, 2, February (1987), pp. 327–68.
2 For simplicity, the word 'bank' has been used throughout this chapter, although the Glass–Steagall provisions do not apply equally to all US banks. For example, Section 16 applies only to national banks and State Federal Reserve System member banks; Section 20 in addition includes corporate affiliates of such banks; while Section 21 covers any institution that is simultaneously and directly engaged in both securities business and deposit-taking.
3 The Comptroller of the Currency has determined that national banks may, for this purpose, invest in investment grade debt securities. US regulatory authorities have jointly defined investment securities to include securities rated in the four highest rating categories by a rating service.
4 401 US 617 (1971) pp. 630–3.
5 See FRB Interpretive Ruling on Investment Adviser Activities, 37 Fed. Reg. 1,464 (1972).
6 See *Board of Governors of the Federal Reserve System v. Investment Co. Institute*, 450 US 46 (1981).
7 Order Approving Acquisition of Retail Discount Brokerage Firm, 69 *Federal Reserve Bulletin* 105 (1983).
8 Order Approving Application to Engage in Combined Investment Advisory and Securities Execution Services, 13 June 1986.
9 Ibid., p. 9.
10 Ibid., p. 20.
11 Ibid., p. 33.
12 Ibid., p. 29.
13 Commercial paper refers to prime quality, short-term unsecured promissory notes (maturities not exceeding nine months) issued by large financial, industrial and commercial companies to finance seasonal or other current needs. Issuers do not have to register the paper under the Securities Act of 1933.
14 See Order Approving Application to Engage in Commercial Paper Placement to a Limited Extent, 24 December 1986.
15 Ibid., pp. 38–50.
16 See Order Approving Applications to Engage in Limited Underwriting and Dealing in Certain Securities, 30 April 1987.
17 Ibid., p. 84.
18 Id.
19 Ibid., p. 92.

20    See Order Conditionally Approving Applications to Engage, to a Limited Extent, in Underwriting and Dealing in Certain Securities, 18 January 1989, pp. 7–8.

21    Ibid., p. 9.

22    Ibid., p. 39.

23    Ibid., p. 49.

24    Ibid., p. 50.

25    On 20 September 1990 the FRB wrote to J. P. Morgan as follows:

> The Board of Governors has reviewed the report of the Federal Reserve Bank of New York relating to the operational and managerial infrastructure of J. P. Morgan Securities, Inc. (JPMS), New York, New York, a wholly-owned subsidiary of J. P. Morgan & Co. Incorporated (Morgan), New York, New York, in accordance with the terms of the Board's Order of 18 January 1989, and letter of 14 February 1990.
>
> On the basis of this review, the Board has determined that Morgan and JPMS have complied with the requirements of the Board's Order, and that JPMS may commence underwriting and dealing in equity securities as permitted by, and subject to the conditions of, that Order. In this regard, the Board has relied upon Morgan's statement that it recognizes its commitment to maintain the capital of JPMS at levels necessary to support its activities and commensurate with industry standards, and that, accordingly, it will increase the capital of JPMS, consistent with the standards in condition four of the Board's Order, as JPMS's business grows.

26    See Appendices to the Statement by Paul Volcker, Chairman of Governors of the Federal Reserve System, before the Subcommittee on Commerce, Consumer and Monetary Affairs of the Committee of Government Operations of the US House of Representatives, June 1986, pp. 13–16.

27    Ibid., pp. 13–14. See also Peter Mortimer and David Slade, 'Foreign securities activities of US banks', *International Financial Law Review*, June (1987), pp. 15–21.

28    Under Regulation K subsidiaries can underwrite no more than $2mn or 20 per cent of an issuers' shares. Several subsidiaries of a banking organization, however, may each underwrite up to $2mn of the same issue — subject to an aggregate limit for the consolidated banking organisation of $15mn. In July 1990 the FRB proposed a major liberalization of Regulation K: this would raise the limit on underwriting equity securities abroad, on a consolidated basis, to the lesser of $60mn or 25 per cent of the banking organisation's Tier 1 capital. Within these limits a subsidiary would be able to underwrite up to 100 per cent of an issuer's shares. See Proposed Revisions of Regulation K, 10 July 1990, pp. 28–31. The proposed amendments to Regulation K were formally adopted in March 1991.

29   See 'International finance: US commercial banks' securities activities in London', 8 September 1988.
30   Senate Resolution 1886, 100th Congress, 2nd Session, 1988.
31   *Modernizing the Financial System* (US Treasury Department, February 1991), pp. 58–9.
32   For an analysis of statutory funding walls see John Rose and Samuel Talley, 'The Banking Affiliates Act of 1982: amendments to Section 23A', *Federal Reserve Bulletin*, November (1982), pp. 693–9.
33   *Modernizing the Financial System*, p. 58.

# 5

# Reforming Japan's Financial System

Since World War Two the Japanese financial system has been characterized by a variety of specialist institutions undertaking distinct activities,
and separated by rigid demarcation rules. Under this regime banks are
classified as ordinary banks, long-term credit banks, trust banks and
specialized foreign exchange banks (a status at present accorded only to the
Bank of Tokyo), while banking is strictly separated from securities business
by statute.

The present chapter examines the existing legal and regulatory
constraints on Japanese banks' securities activities, the increasing pressures
for relaxation of such constraints and the various options open to the
authorities now that it has been decided to adopt a more permissive
approach to the mixing of banking and securities business.

## Introduction of Glass–Steagall Act Provisions

Prior to World War Two there was no prohibition on Japanese banks'
securities activities, although the securities markets themselves were then
relatively underdeveloped. During the 1920s there were widespread bank
failures in Japan but, in contrast to the US experience, banks' securities
operations did not play a part in the disturbances. Accordingly the Banking
Act of 1927 incorporated a number of safeguards, such as more stringent
minimum capital requirements, but did not attempt to separate commercial
from investment banking.[1] In addition, the so-called 'clean bond'
campaign, launched in 1933, sought to strengthen financial market stability
by requiring collateral for all corporate bond issues.[2]

In contrast, the operations of US banks' securities affiliates were blamed
for the US banking collapse of 1929–33. This led to passage of the

Glass–Steagall Act in 1933 which established a formal barrier between banking and securities business.

After World War Two, the USA, as occupying power, imported the main restrictions of the Glass–Steagall Act into Japan (relevant provisions of Japan's Securities and Exchange Law and Banking Law are reproduced as an appendix to this chapter). The key provision is contained in Article 65 of Japan's Securities and Exchange Law of 1948 which in effect states that no bank may engage in securities business. Such business is defined by Article 2 of the Act to include any of the following:

1  Buying and selling securities.
2  Acting as an intermediary, broker or agent with respect to buying and selling of securities.
3  Acting as an intermediary, broker or agent with respect to entrustment of transactions on securities markets.
4  Underwriting securities.
5  Affecting the secondary distribution of securities.
6  Handling the public offering of new or outstanding securities.

Article 65 also contains three exemptions to the restriction on banks' securities activities. First, any bank 'may purchase and sell securities upon the written order of and solely for the accounts of clients'. Second, any bank 'may purchase and sell securities for its own investment purpose'. Finally, the prohibition does not apply to 'national bonds, local government bonds, corporate debentures and other debt issues with respect to which principal redemptions and interest are guaranteed by the Government'. However, the scope of banks' permissible dealing in national (that is, Government) bonds remained unclear and in 1981 a new Article 65(2) was added which in effect provides that banks can engage in the underwriting and public distribution of national bonds subject to authorization from the Ministry of Finance. At the same time, the Banking Law was amended in May 1981 (with effect from April 1982) and this, too, clarified the scope of banks' securities business. Article 10 of the revised Banking Law states that banks may 'underwrite Government bonds, local government bonds and Government guaranteed debentures and offer for subscription those Government bonds etc. so underwritten'. More generally, Article 11 of the same law states that 'a bank may engage in the business of underwriting, offering for subscription or sale, selling, purchasing, and otherwise dealing in Government bonds', although a supplementary provision also states that a bank wishing to engage in such business 'shall have to obtain, for the time being, the approval of the Ministry of Finance in regard to such business as to be conducted'.

Following this clarification of the law Japanese banks were permitted by the Ministry of Finance to engage in sales of long-term Government bonds from April 1983; from October of the same year they began over the counter sales of medium-term Government bonds and from June 1984 they were allowed to deal in public bonds.[3] With effect from August 1987 banks have been permitted to sell public bonds on the same basis as security houses.[4]

## The Glass–Steagall Act and Article 65

A comparison between the US Glass–Steagall Act and Article 65 of the Japanese Securities and Exchange Law points up a number of important differences. The US law, like Article 65, provides an exemption for public sector bonds: the US restrictions on banks' securities activities do not apply to 'obligations of the United States, or general obligations of any state or of any political sub-division thereof'. Similarly, US banks are permitted to act as agency brokers: 'The business of dealing in securities and stock [by banks] shall be limited to purchasing and selling such securities and stock without recourse, solely upon the order and for the account of customers, and in no case for its own account.' However, in practice, Japanese banks cannot exploit their statutory power to buy and sell securities (including equities) for the account of customers because the existing rules of the stock exchanges prevent securities houses from dealing directly with banks other than trust banks. This is one area, therefore, where US banks can engage in a broader range of securities activities than their Japanese counterparts, despite the similarity of the statutory framework.

On the other hand, the Glass–Steagall Act differs from Article 65 in two crucial respects, both of which impose restrictions on US banks that do not exist in Japan. First, the US law prohibits banks from purchasing for their own account shares or stocks of any corporation, whether or not for the banks' own investment purposes. In contrast, Article 65 explicitly authorizes banks to undertake such purchases for their own investment accounts. The US law does permit a bank to 'purchase for its own account investment securities under such limitations and restrictions as the Comptroller of the Currency may by regulation prescribe' but investment securities are defined to include only marketable debt instruments and to exclude stocks and shares. Therefore, Japanese banks may acquire without legal limit equity holdings in companies, whereas US banks are prohibited altogether from such purchases. This contrasting legal position is reflected in the balance sheets of US and Japanese banks, the latter having major equity holdings which have been acquired over many years.

Second, the Glass–Steagall Act provides that 'no member bank shall be affiliated in any manner with any corporation ... engaged principally in the issue, flotation, underwriting, public sale, or distribution at wholesale or retail or through syndicate participation of stocks, bonds, debentures, notes or other securities'. This is a key provision because it was widely supposed that US banks' securities affiliates had played a major part in the financial upheaval of the 1930s. However, there is no equivalent provision in either Japan's Securities and Exchange Law or its Banking Law. Article 11 of Japan's Anti-Monopoly Law does prevent financial institutions from acquiring a shareholding of more than 5 per cent in another company, which thereby effectively prohibits the establishment of directly held securities subsidiaries. Nevertheless, through cross-shareholdings in related companies Japanese banking groups can and do acquire controlling interests in securities affiliates — a point elaborated on below.

There is one other area in which US and Japanese practice differs markedly. Both US and Japanese law specifically prohibit the underwriting of corporate bonds by banks. Yet despite this restriction, Japanese banks are able to participate in underwriting business in a way that is not open to banks in the USA. There are two explanations for this apparent paradox. First, under Japan's 'commissioned underwriting' system banks act as 'commissioned companies' in the bond market while securities companies act as underwriters.[5] A commissioned company serves as financial adviser to the issuer on methods of flotation, timing and terms of issue; as agent for the execution of such necessary procedures as the preparation of related contracts and forms, the receipt and delivery of proceeds etc; and as a trustee whose responsibility, inter alia, is to ensure that any security remains in a good and proper state until the bonds are redeemed. In the event of default by the issuer the position of the commissioned bank has been described as follows:

> in the case of an actual default ... it is the commissioned bank which has protected the investor by purchasing such outstanding bonds at par value. The commissioned bank is not bound by law to carry out such purchases, but (a) as all issues carry collateral, it is possible for the commissioned bank to recover such bond purchases; (b) they have a certain moral obligation as the main bank; and (c) they do so in order to maintain confidence in the bond system.[6]

# Banks and Securities Markets:
# the Pressures for Liberalization

From the above it may be concluded that despite the prohibition of bank underwriting Japanese banks have continued to perform investment banking functions except for underwriting in the strictest sense. Furthermore, because banks can purchase corporate securities for their own investment portfolios they have tended to purchase the new issues of companies with which they have a strong business relationship. For instance, in 1983, 33 per cent of new industrial bond issues were purchased by banks with which the issuing company had a close business relationship (a figure which had been as high as 65 per cent in 1965).[7] It is clear, therefore, that in contrast to the impact of the Glass–Steagall Act in the USA, Article 65 has not prevented Japanese banks from engaging in securities business closely related to underwriting.

Nevertheless, Japanese banks are resentful at being excluded from market-making in and public distribution of corporate securities, and the Japanese authorities are under growing pressure to remove the remaining barriers between banking and securities markets. In the first place, there is an increasing competitive tension between banks and securities houses arising from the marked shift in recent years from indirect financing, involving the intermediation of banks, to direct financing, largely through corporate bond issues, that by-passes the banking system altogether. For instance, the corporate sector's dependence on bank financing virtually halved from 88 to 85 per cent in the early 1970s to little more than 40 per cent in the mid 1980s, while over the same period the share of total domestic credit provided by banks fell from over 80 per cent to below 60 per cent.[8] This shift has major implications for Japan's financial system which has in the past been characterized by its heavy dependence on bank sources of finance.[9] Clearly, banks are concerned that they are losing business to the securities markets.

Second, it is anomalous that whereas Japanese financial institutions can combine banking and securities business in foreign financial centres they are denied this privilege in their home market. Japanese banks have, for instance, established securities operations in London and Frankfurt, while the major Japanese securities houses have similarly secured banking licences in London and other financial centres. Indeed, Japanese banks, as well as securities firms, have been major underwriters of international bond issues.

Third, as part of the process of reciprocal access to national financial markets, Japan has been obliged to permit foreign banks to establish securities operations in Japan. In the past, Japanese practice has been to refuse branch licences to foreign securities firms which are subsidiaries of banks. However, in 1986 the Ministry of Finance began to grant branch licences to securities affiliates of foreign banks, provided that the parent bank holds no more than 50 per cent of the equity of the affiliate. The thinking behind this concession is that such securities affiliates are independent entities and that the arrangements do not therefore breach Article 65.[10] On the other hand, the Ministry of Finance may require letters of comfort from the parent bank on a case-by-case basis to the effect that the bank will support its securities operation in Japan — a practice which, though understandable from a prudential standpoint, cuts across the idea of a truly independent securities affiliate. To begin with, only banks from universal banking countries were permitted to establish securities operations in this way but in March 1987 the Ministry of Finance indicated that the same privilege would be accorded to American banks.[11]

In a parallel move, the Ministry of Finance, with effect from March 1991, granted the banking subsidiaries of three US-based securities houses — Salomon Brothers, Morgan Stanley and Goldman Sachs — licences to open Tokyo branches. This marks the first occasion on which any securities firm has been allowed to operate a bank in Japan.[12]

As a result of these initiatives Japanese banks are objecting, with some justification, that Article 65 is preventing them from undertaking securities business in Japan which is now open to their foreign bank competitors and which, in the US case, cannot be undertaken in the foreign banks' home market. At the same time domestic banks are now facing local competition from the banking units of foreign securities firms.

# A Policy of Piecemeal Reform

Apart from these pressures for liberalization there is the fact that Article 65 of the Securities and Exchange Law is an alien provision imposed on Japan after World War Two, having no basis in Japanese financial policies. Nevertheless, the legal separation of banking and securities markets, while far from complete, has created strongly entrenched vested interests, with the securities houses vigorously resisting any incursions into what they have come to regard as their own exclusive business territory. Given the Japanese preference for consensus solutions, this has greatly complicated the task of reform. Until now the authorities have therefore adopted a gradualist policy of piecemeal reform based on reciprocal concessions by both banks and securities firms, leading to a progressively greater degree of overlap in their respective business activities.

There have been a number of initiatives of this kind. In 1979 an understanding was reached whereby the Ministry of Finance agreed to allow securities houses to establish medium-term bond (*chukoku*) funds while at the same time permitting banks to issue and deal in negotiable certificates of deposit so as to enable them to compete with the *gensaki* (repurchase) market (in retrospect this deal seems to have favoured the securities houses, *chukoku* funds having grown to Yen 6.4 trillion by mid 1987). More recently a compromise has been reached over the contentious question of commercial paper which security houses argued should be classified as a form of 'security' falling within their own exclusive preserve. In October 1986 (prior to the establishment of a commercial paper market in Tokyo) the Ministry of Finance authorized overseas securities subsidiaries of Japanese banks to underwrite and deal in commercial paper issued abroad, although in conformity with Article 65 the authorization was denied to foreign branches of Japanese banks.[13] Subsequently, when formulating the conditions under which a domestic commercial paper market was to operate with effect from December 1987, the Ministry of Finance, after prolonged lobbying from banks and securities houses, decided to classify commercial paper as a promissory note rather than a security. Accordingly, both banks and securities houses are allowed to deal in the new instrument.[14] Similarly, when an organized market in mortgage-backed securities was established in November 1988, banks, as well as securities firms, were authorized to participate.

So far as their overseas securities operations are concerned, Japanese banks are subject to few constraints. However, in order to protect securities houses' domestic client base, the Ministry of Finance still applies administrative guidance to the effect that Japanese banks' foreign securities subsidiaries must not act as lead managers of publicly offered foreign bonds issued by Japanese companies. The banks evidently hope that this remaining restriction may shortly be lifted.

Finally, the new regulatory regime for Japan's futures markets, which was finalized in 1988, reflects a careful application of Article 65.[15] Japanese banks and securities firms have been able to trade government bond futures on the Tokyo stock exchange since 1985. However, under the new scheme the Tokyo exchange is able to offer contracts in foreign government bonds and stock-index futures and a new financial futures market has been established to trade futures and options in interest rates and currencies. Banks have unlimited access to the financial futures exchange, both on their own account and as brokers; but on the stock exchange they are limited to trading government bond futures. Securities firms are permitted to trade freely in stock exchange futures as well as on the financial futures exchange, *except* for spot currency options (foreign exchange being the traditional preserve of the banks).

## Japan and the USA: Substantial Differences in Attitudes to Reform

The process of piecemeal liberalization which is eroding the separation of commercial and investment banking in Japan is very different from the parallel convergence taking place in the USA. As explained above, Article 65, unlike the Glass–Steagall Act, fulfils no domestic policy purpose and exists only by virtue of historical accident. Accordingly, departures from the separation principle embodied in Article 65 have been introduced largely on the basis of what is considered to be 'fair' as between the banking and securities industries – and not in accordance with stated policy goals. Senior bankers in Tokyo describe this process as no more than 'horse-trading'. In contrast the arguments adduced by the US Federal Reserve in interpreting and applying the Glass–Steagall Act under powers conferred by the Bank Holding Company Act are expressed in terms of policy goals.[16] Apart from this, the process of reform in Japan is dictated by the Ministry of Finance exercising its informal powers of interpretation and administrative guidance, without the involvement of the judicature. In the US, on the other hand, the Federal Reserve's decisions on banks' permissible activities are open to challenge and periodically tested in the courts. More generally, the gradual fusion between banking and securities markets that is taking place in Japan can be viewed as a political process that seeks to resolve the conflicting interests of banks and securities houses. In contrast, the review of the Glass–Steagall Act that is underway in the USA is occurring against the background of a vigorous policy debate focusing on such questions as conflicts of interest, financial stability and concentrations of economic power.

## Banks' Securities Affiliates

While piecemeal regulatory concessions are one route by which banks have increased their involvement in securities markets, they have also sought to achieve the same objective less directly by strengthening their relationships with securities affiliates. As pointed out above, Article 11 of the Anti-

Monopoly Law prevents banks from acquiring more than 5 per cent of a non-bank's equity. However, for financial groups majority control can be secured by arranging for non-bank entities within the group to acquire shareholdings in the securities affiliate. The following banks have established semi-captive affiliates by this means:

| Bank | Semi-captive securities house |
|------|-------------------------------|
| Fuji Bank | Daito Securities |
| Mitsubishi Bank | Ryoko Securities |
| Sumitomo Bank | Meiko Securities* |
| Sanwa Bank | Towa Securities* |
| Tokai Bank | Maruman Securities* |
| Longterm Credit Bank | Daiichi Securities* |

*Full securities licence

In addition to the above controlling interests, somewhat looser relationships have been established between the Industrial Bank of Japan and Wako Securities, Taiyo-Kobe Bank and Shinei-Ishino Securities and Daiwa Bank and Cosmo Securities.

In the mid 1980s banks strengthened their ties with securities affiliates, both by increasing group shareholdings and by arranging transfers of staff between the affiliates and by their related banks. However, in 1988 the authorities acted decisively to block this attempt to circumvent Article 65. The Ministry of Finance instructed banks to limit their groups' percentage ownership of securities firms to less than 50 per cent which, in the case of Mitsubishi group, for instance, meant a reduction in its ownership of Ryoko Securities from 75 per cent to under 50 per cent with effect from June 1988.[17] Subsequently, the Ministry of Finance insisted that the number of staff seconded by banks to their securities affiliates should be strictly limited; and that the management of securities affiliates should be kept completely separate from that of the parent banks.[18]

On the face of it, these restrictions looked like a serious setback for the banks in their efforts to broaden their securities activities. But it is probably the price they had to pay for their access to a widening range of securities-type assets such as commercial paper and mortgage loans.

Another possible route to liberalization has been suggested by the banks. The idea here is that the overseas securities subsidiaries of Japanese banks should be permitted by the Ministry of Finance to engage in securities business in Japan in much the same way that foreign banks have been able to establish indirectly held securities branches in Tokyo. The banks have indicated that in return for this authorization they would be prepared to support a parallel arrangement under which securities houses could obtain Japanese banking licences via their overseas banking subsidiaries.[19] In other words the separation of banking and securities business would be eroded within the existing legal framework by a process of 'roundtripping', with banks and securities firms diversifying into each other's home territory by routing business through their overseas operations. The Ministry of Finance's approval in 1987 of a Tokyo representative office for Aubrey Lanston, a US Government securities primary dealer affiliated with the Industrial Bank of Japan, has been cited by some as a precedent for allowing Japanese banks to conduct domestic securities activities via their overseas securities subsidiaries. However, Ministry of Finance officials have argued that Lanston, being a specialized dealer in US Government securities, is not classifiable as a securities company under Japanese law. In any event, Lanston's representative office status in Japan allows it only to provide advice and information, with executions being transacted through the New York office.[20]

Finally, the banks have requested that they should be able to deal directly with the securities houses and to receive commission on stock exchange transactions, as trust banks already do.[21] Such an arrangement would be permissible under the existing law which expressly permits banks to purchase and sell securities on an agency basis. However, it is difficult to envisage a unilateral concession of this kind by the securities houses, except as part of a broader package that would protect their interests.

## Commercial and Investment Banking Integration

As an alternative to the above non-statutory reforms the Japanese authorities are now prepared to consider major changes in the law — particularly if the US Glass–Steagall Act is amended. Article 65 of the Securities and Exchange Law might itself be repealed/amended or banks might be permitted, through appropriate amendments to the Anti-Monopoly Law, to establish wholly owned securities subsidiaries bearing the name of their parent institutions. Another possibility under consideration is the authorization of bank holding companies which could be permitted to own both banks and securities subsidiaries. At present, Article 9 of the Anti-Monopoly Law prohibits the establishment of any bank or non-bank holding company — defined as a company whose main business is to control the business activities of companies whose shares it holds. However, the Anti-Monopoly Law is under review and the introduction of

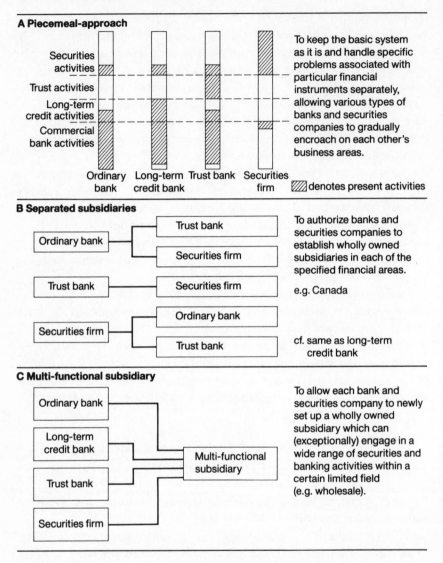

**A Piecemeal-approach**

Securities activities
Trust activities
Long-term credit activities
Commercial bank activities

Ordinary bank    Long-term credit bank    Trust bank    Securities firm

To keep the basic system as it is and handle specific problems associated with particular financial instruments separately, allowing various types of banks and securities companies to gradually encroach on each other's business areas.

 denotes present activities

**B Separated subsidiaries**

Ordinary bank — Trust bank
             — Securities firm

Trust bank — Securities firm

Securities firm — Ordinary bank
              — Trust bank

To authorize banks and securities companies to establish wholly owned subsidiaries in each of the specified financial areas.

e.g. Canada

cf. same as long-term credit bank

**C Multi-functional subsidiary**

Ordinary bank
Long-term credit bank    — Multi-functional subsidiary
Trust bank
Securities firm

To allow each bank and securities company to newly set up a wholly owned subsidiary which can (exceptionally) engage in a wide range of securities and banking activities within a certain limited field (e.g. wholesale).

**Figure 5.1** Continued

the holding company structure as a means of permitting greater financial diversification by banks is evidently favoured in some quarters.

The pressure for more fundamental reform of Japan's fragmented financial system has led to a broad-based policy assessment initiated by the Ministry of Finance. In March 1989 the Second Financial System Committee of the Financial System Research Council, an advisory body to

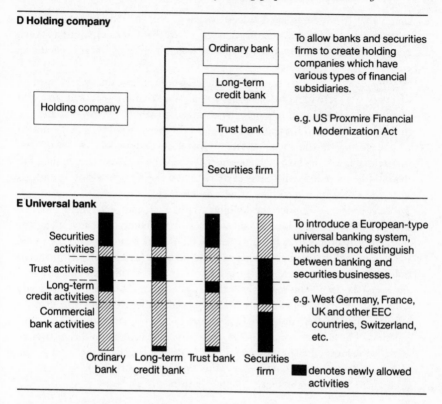

**Figure 5.1** Japan's five policy alternatives

*Source*: Interim Report by the Second Financial System Committee of the Financial Systems Research Council, May (1989), p. 51.

the Ministry, published an interim report 'On a new Japanese financial system'.[22] After acknowledging the case for allowing greater co-mingling of banking and securities business the report identified five possible routes to liberalization (see figure 5.1):

1 *The piecemeal approach.* This would involve a continuation of the existing process of reciprocal concessions by the banking and securities industries. However, the report noted that such an approach can easily degenerate into mere haggling between interested parties that loses sight of national policy objectives. Accordingly, the piecemeal solution was rejected.
2 *Separated subsidiaries.* Under this scheme the parent company would still have to operate within its original area of business but it would be able to diversify into other areas through specially constituted and wholly owned subsidiaries. The authors of the report viewed this option favourably, partly on the grounds

that 'banks would be isolated at least partially from the risks of securities and other business'.[23] On the other hand, it was noted that the incorporation of each new line of activity in a separate subsidiary would impose significant operational costs.

3   *Multifunctional subsidiaries*. This formula would allow the parent firm to diversify its activities by establishing a single multifunctional financial institution. Diversification would be confined to wholesale markets and the multifunctional subsidiary (unlike its parent company) would not be permitted to engage in retail financial services. Operating costs would be lower, and managerial flexibility greater, than under the separated subsidiaries option, but it would be more difficult to segregate risks and there might also be problems in trying to separate retail and wholesale business.

4   *Holding companies*. Under the holding company option diversified financial services would be provided by subsidiaries of a holding company, along the lines recently proposed in the US (see chapter 4). The main difficulty identified in relation to this option is that the prohibition of *all* (and not merely financial) holding companies is a central principle of Japan's Antimonopoly Law.

5   *Universal banking*. The report uses the term 'universal banking' to designate a financial regime in which the bank entity itself, rather than any subsidiary or affiliate, undertakes diversified financial activities, including securities business. The authors conclude that while universal banking in this restrictive sense is the most efficient means of diversification it is also the most risky ('the sight of banks pushing out in every direction in the pursuit of high returns, even at high risk, might shake peoples' faith in them').[24]

In June 1990 the Second Financial System Committee published a second interim report which emphasized the urgency of the case for liberalization and appeared to give preference to the separate subsidiaries option — although it was suggested that special concessions might have to be made to some institutions for whom the subsidiary approach could be prohibitively costly. While the need to segregate activities, so as to prevent bank deposits being exposed to the risks associated with securities business, was acknowledged, it was suggested that this should not be done in such a way as to erode the synergistic benefits of multifunctional financial groups.

Simultaneously, a sub-committee of the Securities and Exchange Council, a Government advisory body on which the views of the securities industry are strongly represented, issued its own report on restructuring Japan's capital market.[25] While accepting that banks should be allowed to conduct securities business according to the separate subsidiaries formula, the report proposed that such activities should be confined to underwriting bonds and equities, selling newly issued stock and own account dealing, while stockbroking on behalf of clients should be specifically excluded. The report also advocated the imposition of strict firewalls between banks and their non-bank operating arms.

These views were reinforced in May–June 1991 by two further subcommittee reports from the Financial System Research Council and the Securities and Exchange Council, which pointed to broad agreement on reform along the following lines:[26]

1 Banks and securities firms would be permitted to establish subsidiaries to enter each other's businesses.
2 Banks' securities subsidiaries would be able to underwrite corporate debt and equity securities but would be excluded from secondary market broking.
3 City banks, with their large branch networks, would be required to phase in their securities activities over a period of time.
4 Certain securities activities, such as private bond placements, could be undertaken within the bank entity itself.
5 The 'Three Bureaux Agreement', which prevents Japanese banks from lead managing overseas bond issues by Japanese firms, should be abolished.

The key question which these reports leave unanswered is whether the proposed corporate structure, involving separate subsidiaries, is to be buttressed by strict firewalls that would be designed to segregate securities market risks within securities firms. It is also rather remarkable that the proposed liberalization of banks securities activities includes primary market underwriting – a high-risk activity – but excludes secondary market broking which involves relatively little risk. The implication is that the emerging consensus on financial reform is based more on Japanese concepts of territorial equity than on considerations of the broader public interest. This interpretation is also supported by the subcommittee's view that City banks should not be allowed to take 'unfair' advantage of their branch networks in expanding their securities operations (point 3 above).

The debate over reform of Japan's financial system has therefore narrowed in so far as all parties accept the need for something more radical than the present piecemeal approach to reallocating financial institutions' business functions. There remains a territorial dispute over retail broking, in particular; the precise legal machinery for achieving the goal of financial diversification has still to be settled; and the key policy issue of firewalls is still a matter of controversy. Nevertheless, there can be little doubt that Japan, like the USA, will shortly bow to international and domestic pressures in favour of allowing much closer integration than hitherto of commercial and investment banking.

One important question for the authorities is whether this development could adversely affect domestic financial stability and therefore require other changes in the regulatory framework. After all, one of the main reasons for enactment of the Glass–Steagall Act in the USA was to prevent banks from becoming exposed to major swings in the prices of securities.

In an important sense, Japanese banks are already exposed to this kind of risk, since Article 65 has not prevented them from acquiring large investment holdings of corporate bonds and equities. Japan's accounting rules allow banks to value their investments securities *either* at cost *or* at the lower of cost or market value, so that fluctuating market prices for securities are not reflected in balance sheet values. This approach to valuation gives rise to very large 'hidden reserves', consisting of unrealized gains on securities holdings which are available to absorb unexpected losses. The treatment of unrealized securities profits for capital adequacy purposes was a matter of controversy during the course of negotiations leading up to the 1988 Basle accord on minimum capital standards. The compromise finally agreed permits banks to treat as supplementary or Tier 2 capital the difference between the book value and market value of their securities holdings — subject to a discount of 55 per cent designed to reflect potential capital gains tax as well as stock market volatility.

The dangers of relying, even to this limited extent, on equity holdings as a source of capital was demonstrated during the first eight months of 1990 when the Tokyo stock market, as measured by the Nikkei Stock Average, fell by over one-third (or 15,000 points). As a rough rule-of-thumb it has been estimated that for every 1,000-point drop in the Nikkei Average the capital ratios of Japanese banks decline by 0.1 per cent, so that banks quite suddenly found themselves with a serious shortfall in regulatory capital. To relieve the situation the Ministry of Finance permitted banks to issue subordinated debt (also allowable under the Basle rules as Tier 2 capital) but the weight of new issues quickly saturated the market, thereby forcing up banks' cost of borrowing. The financial tensions created by this situation led the London *Financial Times* to refer in an editorial to 'the dangerous practice of counting unrealised capital gains on equity holdings in bank capital'.[27] Against this background it may reasonably be argued that if, as has been suggested, all banks were required to adopt a mark-to-market valuation of their securities holdings, the fluctuations in Japanese banks' published net worth ratios could have damaging confidence effects. And if, at the same time, Japanese banks were to expand their securities activities (including equity holdings) in response to amendment or repeal of Article 65, the banking system would become still more vulnerable to stock market volatility.

# Conclusion

The statutory separation of Japan's banking and securities industries is an accident of history rather than the legislature's response to a felt policy need. Nevertheless, the fact of separation has itself created strong vested interests. Accordingly, piecemeal reform has proceeded slowly on the basis of reciprocal concessions negotiated by the banking and securities lobbies. Repeal of Article 65 of the Securities and Exchange Law is now in prospect but, here too, the shape of the new regulatory framework is being determined by questions of business territory rather than those of safety and soundness and economies of scope — the most notable example being the proposal that banks should be free to engage in underwriting of corporate securities but excluded from broking.

While the record might suggest that the Japanese authorities have little to fear, on prudential grounds, from the mixing of banking and securities business, it has to be recognized that the market environment in which these changes are taking place is itself being transformed by the deregulation of domestic interest rates (increasing banks' cost of funds) and intensified competition between financial institutions of all kinds, both Japanese and foreign. Against this background discarding Article 65 in favour of the reunification of banking and securities business would inevitably involve additional risks for the financial system. As one senior Bank of Japan official has warned, in the present wave of financial deregulation 'prevention of the domino–effect of bank failures has become the key issue'.[28]

# Appendix I

### *Relevant provisions of Japan's Securities and Exchange Law of 1948*

*Article 65*
No bank, trust corporation or such other financial institution as may be designated by Cabinet Order shall engage in any of the business enumerated in Paragraph 8 of Article 2; Provided, that any bank may purchase and sell the securities upon the written order of and solely for the accounts of clients, and any bank, trust corporation or such other financial institution as may be designated by Cabinet Order may purchase and sell the securities for its own investment purpose and/or on the basis of trust contracts for its trustors accounts under the provisions of other laws.

  2   the provisions of the foregoing Paragraph shall not apply to national and

local government bonds, corporate debentures and other debt issues with respect to which principal redemptions and interests are guaranteed by the Government.

### Article 65.2

In case any bank, trust corporation or such other financial institutions as may be designated by Cabinet Order intends to engage in, as business, any of the acts set forth in the Items of Paragraph 8, Article 2 hereof in respect of national and local government bonds, and corporate debentures and other debt issues with respect to which principal redemptions and interests are guaranteed by the Government (which do not include the acts falling within the purview of the proviso to Paragraph 1 of the preceding Article, and, in the case of acts referred to in Item 4, Paragraph 8 of Article 2 hereof, include only those to be effected for the purpose of public distribution of these securities on their own account), such bank, trust corporation or such other financial institutions shall obtain a validation from the Minister of Finance by describing the nature and method of business it intends to engage in pursuant to the procedures prescribed by Cabinet Order.

### Article 2.8

The term 'securities business' referred to in the present Law shall mean the business by any person other than banks, trust corporations or such other financial institutions as may be designated by Cabinet Order to do one of the following acts:

1  To buy and sell securities.
2  To act as an intermediary, broker or agent with respect to buying and selling of securities.
3  To act as an intermediary, broker or agent with respect to entrustment of transactions on a securities market (including securities markets, comparable thereto, which are located in foreign countries; the same shall apply in Paragraph 2 of Article 28 and Paragraph 1 of Article 62).
4  To underwrite securities.
5  To engage in public offering of new or outstanding securities.
6  To handle the public offering of new or outstanding securities.

### Relevant provisions of Japan's Banking Law of 1981

### Article 10

A bank may engage in the following lines of business:

1  To accept deposits and instalment deposits;
2  To lend money, and discount bills and notes; and
3  To handle exchange transactions.

2  In addition to those mentioned in the preceding Paragraph, a bank may engage in the below-mentioned lines and any other ancillary to banking:

1  To guarantee liabilities, and accept bills;
2  To buy and sell securities (limited to those transactions made for a bank's own

portfolio investment, and those conducted for account of customers upon the latter's written order);

3  To lend securities;

4  To underwrite Government bonds, local government bonds, and Government-guaranteed debentures (hereinafter referred to as 'Government bonds, etc.' in this and the next Articles) (excepting the underwriting made for the purpose of selling those Government bonds, etc., so underwritten), and to offer for subscription those Government bonds etc., so underwritten;

5  To acquire and cede monetary claims (including those embodied in the instruments designated by an Ordinance of the Ministry of Finance, such as negotiable certificates of deposit);

6  To act as a subscription agent for local government bonds, corporate debentures, and other securities;

7  To act as an agent for other banks and those engaging in financial business (limited to those activities determined by an Ordinance of the Ministry of Finance);

8  To receive, pay, and otherwise handle money on behalf of national or local governments, public bodies, companies, and others;

9  To safekeep securities, precious metals, and other articles; and

10  To change money.

3  'Government-guaranteed debentures' provided in Item (4) of the preceding Paragraph shall mean corporate debentures and other debentures whose redemption of principal and interest payment are guaranteed by the Government.

*Article 11*
In addition to the lines of business provided in the preceding Article, and to the extent of not hindering the performance of the business provided in each Item of Paragraph 1 of the said Article, a bank may engage in the business of underwriting, offering for subscription or sale, selling, purchasing, and otherwise dealing in Government bonds, etc. (excepting the business falling under the provisions of Paragraph 2 of the said Article).

*Article 12*
A bank may not engage in any other lines of business than those provided in the preceding two Articles, the Law of Trustee for Secured Bonds (Law No. 52 of 1905), and any other laws.

# Notes

1  For the history of Japan's financial system see Thomas Adams and Iwao Hoshii, *A Financial History of the New Japan*, (Kodansha International Ltd, Tokyo, 1972).

2  See Kiyoshi Udagawa, Managing Director Japan Credit Rating Agency, 'The

credit rating system of Japan', speech delivered to the Business Research International Conference, London, 13 February 1989, p. 2.

3  See *Banking System in Japan*, (Federation of Bankers Associations of Japan, Tokyo, 1984), p. 53.

4  Until this date banks could only sell public bonds during a specified restriction period after issuance, whereas securities houses were free to sell at any time: see 'MOF takes steps to relax trading of government bonds', *Japan Economic Journal*, 22 August (1987). However, banks are still subject to special prudential rules governing their trading of government bonds, including the maintenance of a reserve against trading losses: see *Banking in Japan* (Peat Marwick Minato, Tokyo, 1987), p. 52.

5  For a description of this system, see Yoriyuko Nagao, 'The bond market', in Eisuke Sakakibara and Yoriyuki Nagao, eds, *Study on the Tokyo Capital Markets* (Japan Centre for International Finance, Tokyo, 1985).

6  Ibid., pp. 63–4.

7  Ibid.

8  'Financial market securitization rapidly gaining ground in Japan', *Japan Economic Journal*, 28 December (1985).

9  A careful analysis of Japan's traditional dependence on bank financing is to be found in Yoshio Suzuki, *Money and Banking in Contemporary Japan*, (Yale University Press, New Haven, 1980).

10  See Kevin Rafferty, 'The assault on Article 65', *Institutional Investor*, January (1987), pp. 133–5.

11  See Michael Sesit, 'Japan to allow US banks to form securities units', *Asian Wall Street Journal Weekly*, 16 March (1987).

12  See 'Japan allows brokers into bank industry', *Financial Times*, 25 January 1991.

13  'Overseas underwriting rules are eased', *Japan Economic Journal*, 15 November 1986.

14  Draft Outline of Commercial Paper Market, Ministry of Finance, Tokyo, 1987.

15  See Michael Whitener, 'The steady erosion of Japan's "Glass–Steagall"', *International Financial Law Review*, May (1988), pp. 12–13.

16  For a full discussion of the Federal Reserve's approach to US banks' securities activities see Appendices to the Statement by Paul Volcker before the Subcommittee on Commerce, Consumer and Monetary Affairs of the Committee on Government Operations of the United States House of Representatives, June 1986.

17  See *Financial Times Financial regulation report*, September 1988, pp. 13–14.

18  See *Financial Times Financial regulation report*, November 1988, p. 10.

19  Yoko Shibata, 'Japan's banks try to enter broking overseas', *Financial Times*, 7 October 1986.

20  *Economist*, 13 June 1987, pp. 85–6.

21 'Bankers ask permission to be discount brokers', *Japan Economic Journal*, 28 June 1986. It should be pointed out that the pressure for liberalization of banks' securities business has come largely from the City Bank Forum — an industry association consisting of 12 of Japan's 13 city banks (excluding Bank of Tokyo). Some smaller Japanese banks are not in favour of liberalization, partly because they fear increased domination by their larger rivals.

22 See English translation by the Federation of Bankers Associations of Japan, 26 May 1989.

23 Ibid., p. 48.

24 Ibid., p. 46.

25 See *Financial Times Financial regulation report*, September 1990, p. 12.

26 See Naoyuki Isono, 'Recommendations point to liberalizing financial system', *The Nikkei Weekly*, 15 June 1991, p. 1.

27 'Japan on a tightrope', *Financial Times*, 13 September 1990, p. 20.

28 See Shijuro Ogata, 'Maintaining a sound financial system in Japan', in Richard Portes and Alexander Swoboda, eds, *Threats to International Financial Stability* (Centre for Economic Policy Research, Cambridge, 1987), p. 283.

# 6

# UK Financial Regulation after Big Bang

In considering the safety and soundness policy issues arising from the fusion of banking and securities business, the UK, along with Canada, provides an interesting example of a country which has recently moved from a separationist regime to one more akin to the West German universal banking model. This chapter examines the regulatory problems associated with London's Big Bang financial revolution and the threat to financial stability posed by the UK's new banking conglomerates.

Historically, there has been no statutory separation of banking and securities activities in the UK. However, as a matter of practice, banks circumscribed their activities, and market segmentation was formalized by a Stock Exchange rulebook that prevented outsiders from taking a controlling interest in member firms.[1] Traditionally, such firms had to be partnerships but when in 1969 they were permitted to become limited companies, a 10 per cent ceiling was imposed on shareholdings in a member firm by any single non-member. In 1982 this limit was raised to 19.9 per cent but still did not allow firms to become wholly or even majority-owned subsidiaries of financial conglomerates or banking groups. Exclusion from the Stock Exchange did not prevent banks from becoming active dealers in Eurobonds, but underwriting and dealing in mainstream UK equities was forbidden territory.

All this changed with Big Bang. The combination of fixed commissions, 'single capacity' (the functional separation of market-making and broking) and a closed Stock Exchange membership had, by the mid 1980s, led to a situation in which a number of major UK shares were being more heavily traded in New York than London, due to high dealing costs in the UK. These competitive pressures were forcing the Stock Exchange to review its trading practices.

What brought matters to a head, however, was the UK Government's decision in July 1983 to exempt the Stock Exchange from the Restrictive Trade Practices Act — thereby removing an earlier challenge to the Exchange's rulebook mounted by the Restrictive Practices Court. Crucially, the terms of the Government's exemption were that fixed commissions should be abolished by the end of 1986 and that certain other changes should be made to the Exchange's constitution.[2]

As a result of this initiative there were three key changes in UK stock market practice. First, as of 1 March 1986 the Exchange's ownership rules were amended so as to allow a single non-member to own 100 per cent of a member firm. Second, with effect from 27 October 1986 minimum commissions on security transactions were abolished. And, finally, dual capacity was introduced, thus eliminating the functional separation of jobbing or market-making on the one hand and broking on the other.

The change in ownership rules in particular had a dramatic impact on the structure of UK financial markets. Out of just over 200 original Stock Exchange member firms, more than half had become part of larger financial groupings by the end of 1986. And of the 65 outside institutions acquiring stakes in these firms, more than half were commercial or investment banks, mainly from the USA, the UK and the rest of Europe. In a one-step change banking and securities business was combined within newly established financial conglomerates and the separation of these activities which had characterized the UK financial services industry for three hundred years or more was abandoned.[3]

The interesting point is that the co-mixing of banking and securities business in the UK was *not* the result of a carefully deliberated policy decision, any more than the previous separation had been the product of government edict. Rather, financial conglomeration was an accidental consequence of a change in the competition rules and the scale and suddenness of the ensuing structural revolution was evidently not entirely to the liking of the UK authorities. As one executive director of the Bank of England put it:

> We should, for the time being at least, be prepared to ration ourselves to 'one miracle at a time' in this field ... we must for the future try to avoid getting into a situation where pressure for change is held back and allowed to build up behind a restriction, so that it breaks out with unnecessary disruptive force once the restriction is removed. We should aim, in the financial system generally, to build in sufficient flexibility to enable it to evolve.[4]

Clearly, one major concern for the Bank of England was to ensure that the UK banking system was not destabilized by the move towards financial diversification and the emergence of banking/securities conglomerates. In

October 1986, at the time of Big Bang, the Governor of the Bank of England, Mr Leigh-Pemberton, gave expression to this concern:

> What would be the consequences of the failure of an undercapitalised investment house? Contracts could be reneged upon; stock could be dumped on the market; and these developments alone might well threaten the viability of other intermediaries. Then there will be firms that are part of conglomerate groups; their difficulties could well spill over into other markets. It is unlikely, given the very large sums involved and the position of the banks in the payment system, that the commercial banks could remain wholly immune. Banks may be vulnerable because they have built up large exposures to securities businesses (whether or not associates). *Those with subsidiaries engaged in securities business will also feel a practical obligation (based on market expectations) to their securities subsidiaries far in excess of the amounts of facilities granted. Such considerations may mean that a bank within a financial conglomerate may be particularly exposed to contagion and a loss of confidence.*[5] (emphasis added.)

Faced with this possibility of contagion, the policy issue the UK authorities had to address was whether to put in place elaborate firewalls of the kind imposed on bank security affiliates by the US Federal Reserve Board and described in the previous chapter. In one specific area of financial activity — gilt-edged trading — the Bank of England did indeed seek to introduce a mechanism for insulating firms from risks incurred in other parts of the business. Because gilt-edged trading lies at the heart of the UK monetary system the Bank of England was anxious to minimize the risk of defaults, which could transmit powerful shock waves through financial markets. Accordingly, the regulatory framework devised for this market incorporated several layers of protection:[6]

1   In order to insulate it from problems that might develop in other parts of the group to which it belongs, a gilt-edged market-maker must be separately established as a company or partnership with dedicated sterling capital in the UK. Furthermore, a market-maker may not, without agreement of the Bank of England, have as a partly or wholly owned subsidiary any other entity operating in financial markets. Therefore there can be no infection from adverse developments 'downstream'.

2   The Bank of England seeks assurances from substantial shareholders in gilt-edged market-making entities that they accept ultimate responsibility for the liabilities of the entity. Although not legally binding, these comfort letters are expected to 'be taken very seriously by the controlling board [of the parent company] which will as a result be encouraged to recognise its responsibility towards the gilt-edged market-maker both at the outset and as its business develops'.[7] The parent comfort letter is therefore designed to ensure that there

is upstream support for market-makers, just as downstream risks are to be prevented by the limitation on subsidiary operations.

3   Gilt-edged market-makers have direct access to the Bank of England and are therefore backed by a lender of last resort. This facility gives them a high credit standing and a corresponding ability to borrow from commercial banks on very fine terms. However, access to the lender of last resort further underlines the need to insulate gilt-edged market-makers from the risks incurred by related entities.

4   The final safeguard is the Investors' Compensation Scheme (ICS) which is available to compensate the outside customers of all member firms in case of default (although the rights of market professional counterparties to claim on the ICS are severely restricted).

The protective arrangements governing UK banks' non-gilt-edged securities business are very different. Whereas the regulatory framework for gilt-edged market-makers is designed to ensure that such firms can survive any difficulties that may be encountered in other parts of the financial group to which they belong, the underlying assumption behind the regulation of bank's general securities business appears to be that the risks are indivisible. As a former Deputy Governor of the Bank of England put it:

> There is ... a potential tension between the desire to isolate market-making risks, and the well-established principle that parent banks have a moral obligation to stand behind their subsidiaries to cover losses, even when they exceed their limited liability in law. The involvement of a bank in a group which contains a market-maker [in equities] is therefore likely to have implications for the assessment of its own capital adequacy.[8]

Accordingly the Bank of England formulated the following rules relating to banks' (non-gilt-edged) securities business:[9]

- A banks' securities operations may be conducted in the bank itself or through a subsidiary/affiliate.
- The same risk weightings (for capital adequacy purposes) are applied to banks' arms-length lending to *connected* securities companies as are applied to their lending to unconnected securities companies. However, where such lending is not arms-length (e.g. more in the nature of risk capital) a higher weighting is applied or else the loan deducted from the banks' capital base.
- The Bank assumes that securities companies supervised by the Securities and Investments Board (SIB) are adequately capitalized. However, if the SIB identifies a capital shortfall in such a company, the Bank will deduct this shortfall from the parent bank's capital base. A capital surplus in a securities subsidiary which is not supervised by the Bank cannot be regarded as adding to a bank's capital resources unless it is paid back into the bank.
- Special rules on large exposures are applied to banks' intra-group lending.

These can be summarized as follows:

(a)  Exposures to subsidiaries which by agreement with the Bank are aggregated within the parent bank's *unconsolidated* returns, and which are treated as divisions of the parent bank, are excluded from the large exposure policy.

(b)  Where it is considered appropriate for a bank to undertake a group treasury role, exposures of a maturity up to one year to group non-bank financial companies (including securities firms) are allowed, up to levels agreed on a case-by-case basis.

(c)  Exposures to connected gilt-edged market-makers are, because of the latters' high credit standing, treated in the same way as ordinary interbank exposures.

(d)  Exposures to other group companies are aggregated and considered as an exposure to an individual non-bank counterparty (meaning that aggregated exposure is subject to a 25 per cent of capital pre-notification requirement).

(e)  More generally, the Bank examines closely all exposures to companies or persons connected to a lending bank and deducts them from the bank's capital base 'if they are of the nature of a capital investment or are made on particularly concessionary terms'.[10]

From the above, it is clear that a bank's exposure to its securities arm is treated differently from its exposure to both gilt-edged market-making and non-financial subsidiaries. The gilt-edged market-making entity is insulated from risks incurred in other parts of the group while enjoying open-ended backing from its parent bank. At the other extreme, a bank's exposure to *non-financial* connected companies is strictly limited, the implication being that such entities might be allowed to fail independently of their related bank.[11]

In contrast, the logic of the Bank of England's regulatory arrangements for banks' securities activities is that the risks involved here are indivisible from those incurred by the Bank itself. This is implicit in the option available to banks to conduct their securities business within the bank entity; in the automatic deduction from a bank's regulatory capital when there is a capital shortfall in its securities subsidiary; and in the group funding role allowed to banks — which clearly creates the potential for cross-infection between banks and securities firms within the same group. The one constraint imposed on the co-mingling of banking and securities market risks arises where a bank's lending to its securities operation is on a concessionary, non-arms-length, basis. However, the official concern in such cases is not so much to limit a bank's exposure to its connected securities company as to ensure that the securities business is subject to proper market disciplines — and not expanded aggressively on the basis of soft loans from a related funding source (i.e., cross-subsidization is ruled out).[12]

The Bank of England's approach is in sharp contrast to that adopted by the US authorities, as described in the previous chapter. US policy is designed to compartmentalize risks within bank holding companies so as to prevent cross-infection between the bank and its related entities, using for this purpose elaborate firewalls that restrict a bank's ability to engage in intra-group financial transactions.

The regulation of combined banking/securities businesses also calls for an appropriate allocation of responsibilities between regulatory agencies. In the UK, Parliament chose to divide statutory responsibility for regulating such conglomerates between the SIB and the Bank of England; the SIB being responsible for regulating businesses authorized to conduct securities/investment activities under Section 25 of the Financial Services Act of 1986, while the Bank is responsible for supervising the banking activities of those firms authorized to undertake such business under the Banking Act of 1987.[13] In other words combined banking/securities businesses are subject to functional rather than institutional regulation, with different parts of the same financial group being treated separately for regulatory purposes.

This division of regulatory responsibilities presents serious difficulties given the integrated nature of risks incurred within combined securities/banking businesses and the consequent need for an overall assessment of such businesses' financial condition. The problem here takes different forms, depending on whether the securities activities are conducted through a separate legal entity or within the bank itself. As indicated above, the UK regulatory regime is intended to be neutral as between these two alternative corporate structures, the idea being that banks should not be forced to subsidiarize their non-bank operations in a manner that might impose additional costs on the group as a whole.[14]

Where securities activities are undertaken through separate non-bank legal entities the Bank of England's rules on consolidated supervision of banking groups come into play.[15] For this purpose the Bank draws a distinction between 'consolidated supervision', involving an overall assessment of banking group's strength after taking account of the impact of the various parts of the group on the bank's financial condition, and 'consolidation' in the formal accounting sense, where the banking group's statistical returns are presented on a consolidated basis.

The general principle is that where a bank conducts securities operations through a separate legal entity, these combined banking–securities activities are subject to consolidated supervision. However, in such cases the securities operations are not subject to consolidation in the accounting sense. The Bank of England has explained its policy as follows:

> The presumption must be that the supervisor of, for example, a securities company is the best judge of the adequacy of its capital. The Bank will not generally expect to have to make an independent quantitative assessment of the capital adequacy of group companies which are subject to detailed supervision by other UK supervisory authorities. ... The Bank will not, therefore, normally require group companies undertaking an investment or insurance business and supervised by another UK supervisory body to be included within banks' consolidated statistical returns. ... Nevertheless all such companies will be included within the Bank's consolidated supervision of banking groups.[16]

In other words, banks' securities (and other non-bank financial) activities which are carried on through non-bank UK supervised subsidiaries are not normally included in consolidated returns but are taken into account, qualitatively, during the course of consolidated supervision. However, the fact that different regulatory authorities supervise different financial activities within a group creates a need for regulatory coordination. This is achieved through a 'college of supervisors' for each financial group, chaired by a lead regulator. Under this arrangement each UK supervisor retains statutory responsibility for the institution it authorizes, while the lead regulator promotes exchanges of information between supervisors and coordinates any necessary remedial action.[17]

Where a bank's securities activities are conducted, not through a separate entity but rather within the bank itself, the lead regulator concept is applied in a different way. To meet this case the Bank of England and the SIB have signed a Memorandum of Understanding (MoU) which sets out a framework for assessing the financial soundness of UK entities which are simultaneously authorized by the Bank under the Banking Act of 1987 and by the SIB under the Financial Services Act of 1986.[18] Under this agreement, which does not affect the supervisor's statutory responsibilities, the Bank becomes lead regulator for all mixed banking/securities entities and it is therefore the Bank, applying its own capital adequacy rules which monitors the entities' overall capital position.[19] However, in addition to being subject to all the Bank's prudential requirements, mixed banking/securities entities must also conform to certain of the SIB's requirements regarding, for instance, conduct of business and segregation of client funds.

In the event that the financial condition of a mixed banking/securities entity causes concern, general guidelines for consultation between the SIB and the Bank of England are laid down by the MoU. The procedures to be followed here are complicated first by the respective statutory responsibilities of the two regulatory bodies and second by the banks' concern over the confidentiality of banking information which may be passed between regulators.

The fundamental difficulty with the UK approach to regulating financial conglomerates in general, and mixed banking/securities businesses in particular, is that functional regulation does not coexist easily with a regime in which risks are assumed to flow freely between different parts of the same financial group. Put another way, if risk exposure is viewed as a matter affecting the institution as a whole, how can it make sense to apply prudential rules on a functional basis to individual subsidiaries within the group? Furthermore, bearing in mind that the *objectives* of bank and securities regulators may differ[20] and that their own prudential requirements will reflect any such differences — it would seem impractical to try to resolve this problem by establishing coordinating machinery in the form of a college of regulators. The lead regulator concept does indeed seek to introduce an institutional element into the functional statutory framework, but it cannot hope to deliver the same quality of prudential supervision as would a regime in which all parts of a financial group are subject to consolidated supervision by one overall group supervisor (assuming, of course, that the group supervisor commands the necessary expertise).

It is possible to identify four alternative regulatory regimes that might in principle be applied to UK financial conglomerates:[21]

1   Different financial activities are subject to separate regulation. In this case a bank's securities activities are subject to a securities regulator even though they are conducted within the bank entity. This is functional regulation as originally conceived in the UK under the Financial Services Act, but now modified by the lead regulator concept.

2   Regulatory responsibility for a particular type of financial activity depends on group structure. Here a bank's securities business would be supervised by a bank regulator if conducted by the bank itself, and by a securities regulator if conducted by a separately incorporated securities subsidiary. This is functional regulation as currently practised in the UK, following adoption of the Memorandum of Understanding outlined above.

3   All subsidiaries of a particular financial conglomerate are consolidated for supervisory purposes and subject to a single regulatory authority. This extended form of institutional regulation has evidently been rejected by UK regulators on policy grounds (see below) and is in any event incompatible with the present UK statutory framework.

4   Different types of financial activity are *required* to be conducted through separate entities and are subject to separate regulation. Here, a bank's securities business would be undertaken by a specialized securities subsidiary and

regulated by a securities regulator. This regime — which might be described as 'institutional-cum-functional' regulation — is currently favoured by the USA.

The lead regulator concept has in effect shifted the UK's supervisory approach from regime 1 to regime 2 but logic would surely point to a further move to regime 3. In other words, if it makes sense for the Bank of England to regulate banks' in-house securities activities does it not also make sense for this responsibility to be extended to banks' securities subsidiaries? The opposing view, expressed recently in an OECD study, is that 'concerns might be raised that consolidated supervision of a group (in this sense) would replace expert with possibly less expert supervision, would lump together disparate balance sheets to which different forms of prudential requirements applied ... and could be taken to imply an enhanced degree of official responsibility and support for the whole diverse array of activities conducted by the conglomerate'.[22]

The main argument here seems to be that consolidated supervision in its more formal sense could open the way to a major extension of the lender of last resort function. This issue will be more fully discussed in chapter 10. However, it is difficult to see how fragmented supervisory arrangements for mixed banking/securities businesses can help to contain the lender of last resort function in a situation where banking and securities risks are not themselves segregated. It is also difficult to avoid the conclusion that the underlying UK statutory framework for regulating financial conglomerates is flawed and that regulators' attempts at modification have left the UK regime uncomfortably placed between functional regulation on the one hand and institutional regulation on the other.

Events since the inception of the UK's post Big Bang regulatory regime might suggest that this concern is overstated. In particular, UK financial markets were able to ride out the October 1987 stock market crash in a manner that the Governor of the Bank of England found 'very encouraging',[23] the main official worry being the risk of counterparty default in securities markets arising from the Stock Exchange settlement system. However, it is also true that the 1987 stock market collapse occurred after a prolonged period of unparalleled prosperity for UK securities firms, capital ratios were therefore at relatively comfortable levels and the regulatory system was not tested by the threatened failure of a major financial institution.

Nevertheless, there was one important incident during the market turbulence of 1987 that underlined the dangers confronting mixed banking/securities businesses. As described in chapter 2, during the autumn of 1987

County NatWest Limited (CNW), National Westminster Bank's securities arm, failed to disclose that it had acquired a large shareholding in Blue Arrow, following an unfortunately timed and poorly received rights issue in September 1987. At the time, Blue Arrow's financial advisers UBS Phillips and Drew and CNW, claimed that the shares had been placed successfully — when in fact they had not. The episode, which was the subject of an investigation by the Department of Trade and Industry, raised a number of issues about how banking/securities firms should be expected to behave in the post Big Bang environment. Among these were the failure to disclose a shareholding in excess of 5 per cent (the disclosure threshold under the UK Companies Act), alleged stock market manipulation arising from misleading statements regarding the rights issue, and the role of 'Chinese walls' — the concern here being that the corporate finance and market-making sides of CNW might have been acting in collusion rather than independently. From a prudential standpoint, the most disturbing feature of this affair was the clash of cultures between the traditional clearing bankers at NatWest and the more entrepreneurial style of CNW which in this instance exposed the banking group to total losses of over £80mn.[24]

The clash of commercial and investment banking cultures highlighted by the Blue Arrow affair brings to mind the warnings of the US Comptroller of the Currency over seventy years ago. It may be recalled (see p. 1) that in his annual report for 1920 the Comptroller stated that the securities affiliates of banks had become 'an element of increasing peril to the banks with which they are associated', and that 'it would be difficult if not impossible for the same set of officers to conduct safely, soundly, and successfully the conservative business of the national bank and at the same time direct and manage the speculative returns and promotions of [securities firms]'. It seems that some UK financial institutions have taken this lesson on board, as illustrated by the decision of Barclays Bank in October 1990 to establish a divisional structure explicitly based on the rival cultures of commercial and investment banking — rather than on the basis of geography or function as in the past.[25] Nevertheless, the evidence to date suggests that the post Big Bang fusion of UK securities and banking markets may have increased the banking sector's propensity for risk-taking, while also exposing banking groups to securities market risks.

Big Bang apart, the collapse in 1990 of British and Commonwealth Holdings, a major UK financial services group, has brought into sharp focus the difficulties facing regulators of financial conglomerates. In mid April 1990 BCH revealed severe problems within its computer-leasing subsidiary, Atlantic Computers. This news triggered deposit withdrawals from BCH's banking subsidiary, British and Commonwealth Merchant Bank (BCMB) and on 1 June the SIB removed BCMB from the list of approved banks with which securities firms could deposit client's money. Since this decision could have caused a run on the bank a petition was made to the courts for an administrator to be appointed. The result was that depositors funds were frozen indefinitely, pending a resolution of the bank's future.

It is disturbing that an apparently healthy bank with £90mn of stated capital and a loan book of only £300mn (reported by the administrators to be 'in very good order') should have to close at all. Even more disturbing is the fact that depositors should seek to withdraw funds from this institution simply because of its connection with a troubled affiliate.[26] The implication is that if *any* part of a financial conglomerate receives adverse publicity, a related bank entity can be put out of business in very short order. The worry for regulators in the emerging regime of financial conglomerates is that banks are being exposed to the risks incurred by their non-bank affiliates: in the BCH case it happened to be a computer-leasing entity, but a related securities firm could equally well be the source of infection.

The BCH affair is entirely consistent with the view of UK regulators that risks incurred within the various financial operations of a banking group are integrated and inseparable. However, BCH also underlines the fragility of a regulatory regime which, as under the UK Financial Services Act, seeks to allocate regulatory responsibilities along functional lines, without due regard for the financial interdependence of related entities within the group.

The conclusion to be drawn is that the UK banking system has become more vulnerable than previously to problems originating in the securities markets and that the potential for cross-infection, described so graphically by the Governor of the Bank of England in his October 1986 speech (see p. 108), has been further compounded by a fragmented regulatory framework mandated by the UK Financial Services Act.

# Notes

1  See Bernard Shull, 'The separation of banking and commerce: origin, development and implications for antitrust', *Antitrust Bulletin*, spring (1983).
2  For the background to Big Bang see, for instance: 'Change in the Stock Exchange and regulation of the City', Bank of England *Quarterly Bulletin*, February (1987), pp. 554–60. Charles Goodhart, 'The economics of Big

Bang', *Midland Bank Review*, summer (1987), pp. 6–15; and Richard Dale, ed., *Financial Deregulation*, (Woodhead-Faulkner, Cambridge, 1986).

3  Although banking and securities business is now combined, UK banks, in contrast to German and Japanese banks, do not generally take equity stakes in companies to which they lend. It has been suggested, however, that UK banks may in future wish to take small equity positions when lending to start-up and small businesses in order to compensate for the risks involved. See Lord Alexander, Chairman of National Westminster Bank, 'Banking – the challenge for the 1990s', speech given to the Chartered Association of Certified Accountants, 10 October 1990, pp. 12–13.

4  E. A. J. George, 'The City revolution', Bank of England *Quarterly Bulletin*, September (1985), p. 424.

5  Speech given to the Group of Thirty Symposium on Equity Markets, London, 15 September 1986, p. 3.

6  See E. A. J. George, 'The City revolution', pp. 424–6. More generally, see 'The future structure of the gilt-edged market', Bank of England *Quarterly Bulletin*, June (1985).

7  'The City revolution', p. 425.

8  'Changes in the structure of financial markets: a view from London', Bank of England *Quarterly Bulletin*, March (1985), p. 78.

9  See 'Banks and securities business', Bank of England Consultative Paper, July 1986; 'Large exposures undertaken by institutions authorised under the Banking Act 1979', Bank of England Notice, September 1987; and 'Consolidated supervision of institutions authorised under the Banking Act 1979', Bank of England *Notice*, March (1986).

10  Bank of England, 'Large exposures', p. 9

11  The Bank does not, however, exclude such non-financial connected companies from the supervisory process:

> Although it is normally neither desirable nor appropriate to consolidate non-financial companies, the potential impact of such companies on the viability of a bank within the same group needs to be considered. The Bank will not seek to extend its supervision to such companies, but it must be recognised that a major difficulty elsewhere in a widely diversified group may have some impact on the fortunes of a bank and the Bank must take account of this, 'Consolidated supervision of institutions', p. 3.

12  Given the co-mingling of risks that is permitted within UK financial conglomerates it is not entirely clear why the Bank of England should be so concerned to minimize the risk of counterparty confusion where financial groups have dual dealing operations (i.e. where dealers are allowed to deal for more than one group company). See Bank of England, 'Banks and securities business', p. 4.

13  In practice, the division of regulatory responsibilities is more complex than

this might suggest, given the proliferation of self-regulatory organizations (SROs) that operate within the statutory framework. A UK banking group may thus have to confront the following array of regulators:

- The Bank of England's Banking Supervision Division regulates commercial banking activities.
- The Bank's Wholesale Market Supervision Division regulates wholesale market transactions.
- The Bank's Gilt-Edged Division regulates (separately capitalized) gilt operations.
- The Securities and Futures Authority (SFA) regulates non-wholesale debt/interest rate operations, equity operations and financial and commodity futures and options operations.
- The Investment Management Regulatory Organization (IMRO) regulates fund management operations.

14 Some members of the UK investment community have argued that subsidiarization (i.e. routing different types of financial business through separately capitalized subsidiaries) reduces the ability to allow capital to flow freely according to demand, increases the risks associated with dealing with such subsidiary companies, complicates the regulatory process, and increases costs.

15 See Bank of England, 'Consolidated supervision of institutions'.

16 Ibid., p. 2.

17 See the Bank of England, 'Banking Act Report for 1988–9', pp. 18–19.

18 Negotiation of the MoU between the SIB and the Bank of England proved extremely difficult and the proposed agreement went through several drafts. Because the two authorities cannot delegate their statutory duties to each other, the proposed arrangements are necessarily complex, involving as they do a separate division of responsibilities in respect of authorization, reporting, monitoring and the application of capital adequacy rules. See *Financial Times Financial regulation report*, December 1987, pp. 11–13. Separate MoUs have been agreed between the Bank of England and the various self-regulatory organizations involved in securities market regulation.

19 This arrangement replaces the earlier much more complex 'hybrid test' whereby the Bank of England, on behalf of the securities supervisors, applied a separate capital test to the securities business undertaken by banks. Here the bank had to submit one set of returns to the Bank of England and another set of returns related to its securities business had to be submitted to the securities supervisors.

20 The EEC Commission has, for instance, accepted that the regulatory objectives of bank and securities market supervisors may be quite different. This issue is dealt with in chapter 10.

21 For a discussion of the functional versus institutional approach to regulation see 'A forward look', the Securities and Investments Board, October 1989, pp. 6–8 and 18–21. The SIB points out that an EEC Commission proposal

for an amended Consolidated Supervision Directive seeks to place responsibility for the prudential supervision of banking groups on the bank supervisor. The SIB evidently objects to this external pressure for a move towards 'quantitative' consolidated supervision by the Bank of England, embracing non-bank securities subsidiaries. According to the SIB, such a development 'could result in an awkward degree of duplication and second-guessing of supervision undertaken by SIB ... and probably before long to [sic] strong pressures for a further substantial move in the direction of institutional regulation', ibid., p. 21.

22  *Systemic Risk in Securities Markets*, (OECD, Paris, 1991), p. 42.
23  See 'Convergence of capital standards and the lessons of the market crash', Bank of England *Quarterly Bulletin*, May (1988), pp. 220–4.
24  See Richard Waters, 'County NatWest in Blue Arrow payout', *Financial Times*, London, 15 February 1990.
25  See David Lascelles, 'Operational shake-up at Barclays', *Financial Times*, London, 1 November 1990. The Barclays move may be viewed as part of a more general trend towards a 'federal' banking structure, where the banking group is broken down into a number of specialist units, each conducted as far as possible as an independent business. See Jack Revell, 'Mergers and acquisitions in banking', Conference on 'The new European financial marketplace', Centre for European Policy Studies, Brussels, 29–30 November 1990, pp. 7–9.
26  Another point worth noting in the BCH case is that efforts by creditor banks to put together a £100mn stand-by facility, which would have been sufficient to keep BCMB afloat, failed. Evidently UK banks are no longer predisposed to bail out their competitors, even where there is no insolvency risk. Curiously, the Bank of England also declined to exercise its lender of last resort powers, presumably because BCMB was too small to keep afloat (a variant of the US 'too-big-to fail' doctrine). More puzzling still is the fact that the SIB removed BCMB from its list of approved banks while the Bank of England was still treating it as an appropriate institution to take depositors' money.

# 7

# The New Financial Regulatory Framework in Canada

The global trend towards the co-mixing of banking and securities business is forcing national authorities to address a number of key policy issues relating to potential conflicts of interest, financial safety and soundness, competitive equality, and concentration of economic power. In the UK the process of regulatory reform post-dates the financial restructuring associated with London's Big Bang; in the USA the sequence of events is the other way round, with Congress considering proposals for a new bank regulatory regime as a precondition for removing the Glass–Steagall barriers to banks' involvement in securities markets; while in Canada financial restructuring and regulatory reform are proceeding in tandem as a programme of phased financial liberalization reaches its final stage.

In all the major banking centres policy-makers and bank regulatory authorities are facing the same financial market pressures. Traditional bank lending is being gradually displaced by securities market financing and this development is prompting banks to press for full participation in securities business on equal terms with securities firms. If banks in any particular centre are denied the power to underwrite or deal in securities they stand to lose business to local non-bank institutions, while financial activity may also shift to centres where there are no such restrictions. By the same token, the fusion of banking and securities markets in one major centre such as London may adversely affect the competitive position of rival jurisdictions where the barriers between bank and securities business remain intact. Against this background, the global momentum towards the creation of banking–securities conglomerates has become irresistible.

While national authorities are seeking to accommodate these market pressures they are doing so in very different ways. This chapter will describe and assess Canada's approach to financial liberalization. The main focus is on the 'prudential' or safety and soundness aspects of regulatory policy — that is to say, the constraints imposed on banks' securities operations in the interests of safeguarding the stability of the financial system. The first section of the discussion that follows is concerned with the background to Canada's regulatory reforms; the second section is concerned with the policy debate that preceded the reforms; the third section describes the new regulatory framework as finally proposed; and the final section provides an assessment of Canada's regulatory regime in the context of parallel developments elsewhere.

## Pressures for Structural Reform

Traditionally, Canada's financial system has been based on the so-called 'four pillars': the chartered banks, the trust companies, life insurance companies and securities dealers. These institutions have been separated by cross-pillar ownership restrictions and regulatory constraints on the business open to each category of financial institution. The banks are the only institutions with full freedom in the field of commercial lending, the trust companies have exclusive power to undertake discretionary fiduciary activities, life insurance companies are empowered to underwrite life insurance and issue life-contingent annuities, while only investment dealers may underwrite corporate securities and be members of the stock exchanges. As the Ontario Securities Commission has stated:

> Each of the major participants in Canada's financial system — the securities dealers, banks, the trust companies and the insurance companies — has a core function. Public policy, as reflected in our laws, reserves to each group the performance of its core function. The Canadian financial system may therefore be described as a segregated system and the division of the system into four segments may metaphorically be referred to as the 'four pillar' concept.[1]

The regulatory regime governing the four-pillar system is complicated by the division of regulatory responsibilities between the federal Government and the provinces. The federal Government regulates the banks, the provinces have responsibility for authorizing and regulating securities firms, while insurance and trust companies may have federal or provincial charters.

Banks have been separated from the securities industry at both the federal and provincial levels. Before the latest reforms, federal law prevented any person from owning more than 10 per cent of a domestic bank while the unamended 1980 Bank Act prohibited banks from acquiring more than 10 per cent of the voting shares of a non-banking company (subject to certain exceptions, see below). At the provincial level, the Ontario Securities Act prevented any non-industry investor (including banks) from holding more than 10 per cent of the voting shares of a securities firm. There were, therefore, tight controls on both upstream and downstream linkages between banks and securities dealers.

These restrictions on domestic ownership were closely linked to rules limiting foreign entry to Canada's financial markets. Under federal law the 10 per cent limit on ownership of a domestic bank, a rule originally intended to prevent the acquisition of domestic banks by foreign institutions, was buttressed by a further provision restricting aggregate foreign ownership to 25 per cent of a bank's outstanding shares. In addition, domestic banking was (and still is) protected by a market share limitation on foreign banks' subsidiaries whose combined domestic assets cannot exceed 16 per cent of the total domestic assets of all banks in Canada.[2] At the same time, provincial laws restricted foreign access to domestic securities markets. In particular, the Ontario Securities Act prevented non-residents in the aggregate from holding more than 25 per cent of the shares of a securities firm, while no single non-resident investor could hold more than 10 per cent (the so called '25–10' provision).

Federal law has meanwhile placed direct restrictions on the range of financial services that may be offered by banks. For over a century, between 1876 and 1980, Canadian banks had statutory authority to 'deal in' securities, without further definition as to what this meant. However, the Bank Act of 1980 replaced this general power with more precise rules specifying which securities activities banks may or may not engage in.[3] Under the 1980 Act banks may invest in corporate securities (both debt and equity) for portfolio purposes without formal limit — although they are subject to a 10 per cent voting share limitation on holdings in any one company. Banks are also free to underwrite and distribute Government bonds, to buy and sell securities generally on an agency basis and to distribute corporate securities as members of a selling group.[4] However, section 190(5) of the Act specifically prohibits the underwriting of corporate securities (subject to the selling group exception) and under section 174(2) a bank cannot 'hold itself out as engaging in or engage in portfolio management or investment counselling in Canada'. These restrictions do not apply to securities business carried out by banks through their foreign offices and, indeed, Canadian banks, like their US counterparts, have conducted investment banking operations through their subsidiaries in London and elsewhere.

Section 193(12) of the Bank Act permits the temporary acquisition of securities in excess of the 10 per cent shareholding limit where this is a result of realizing the security for any loan. Section 193(13) also provides a general exemption, subject to ministerial discretion, for the temporary (generally, up to two years) acquisition of shares above the 10 per cent limit in a financial corporation (other than a trust company) that does not accept deposits from the public.[5] This provision provided the original statutory basis for banks' acquisition of securities firms (see below) although, clearly, it was not intended for this purpose.

In summary, before the present regulatory reforms the four pillars of the Canadian financial system were separated both by ownership restrictions and regulatory constraints on permissible activities. The rationale for this separation has never been entirely clear (see note 19, p. 135) but appears to owe much to the division of regulatory responsibilities between the federal and provincial governments. In particular, the fact that the federal government has sole jurisdiction over banks and banking, while the provinces claim exclusive regulatory responsibility for the securities markets (a matter of some controversy) has strengthened the separatist tendencies within the system. At the same time, Canadian financial markets have been insulated to some extent from international competition through overtly protectionist legislation at both provincial and federal levels.

Pressures for a radical restructuring of Canada's financial system have come from a variety of sources.[6] Of particular importance is the fact that in Canada, as elsewhere, there has been a marked shift in recent years from intermediated (bank) finance to direct (non-bank) finance, with inter-mediated borrowing by the non-financial sector falling well below direct borrowing during the period 1981 to 1984.[7] While this trend was encour-aging banks to press for greater securities powers, the securities industry itself, and its regulators, became concerned that Canadian borrowers were raising an increasing proportion of their funds from the Eurobond market. One response to this loss of competitiveness was the abolition of fixed stock exchange commissions in 1983, but it was felt that the problems of the securities industry were more deep-seated and that what was required was greater access to outside capital. Some commentators pointed out that Toronto was in danger of becoming a regional rather than an international financial centre, the Canadian securities industry having lost the bulk of the underwriting and placing of government and corporate bonds to the Euromarket.[8] It was against this background that the Canadian authorities began to consider the possibility of opening up the securities markets to both domestic banks and foreign institutions as part of a more general programme of financial liberalization.

The whole process of regulatory reform was also accelerated by inter-provincial rivalry. Taking advantage of Quebec's move to open its securities market to outsiders and relying for federal authority on section 193(13) of the Bank Act (above), the Bank of Nova Scotia established in 1986 a wholly owned Quebec securities subsidiary, Scotia Securities.[9] The apparent purpose — and effect — of this initiative was to exert further pressure on Ontario and Ottawa to deregulate Canada's financial markets.

## The Debate over Regulatory Reform

Responding to market pressure, the federal government carried out a major review of regulatory arrangements for the financial sector, the results of which were contained in a policy document published in 1985 known as the Green Paper.[10] The policy concerns set out in this paper focused on competition and efficiency, solvency, conflicts of interest and concentration of economic power.[11]

The Government recognized that if Canada was to remain an important locus for international financial activity, financial institutions would have to be allowed to diversify their activities. This was to be achieved by removing restrictions on common ownership of the four pillars, widening the range of permissible financial services provided within each pillar and allowing joint marketing or 'networking' of these services across the four pillars.

On the other hand, the Green Paper acknowledged that within the financial sector 'solvency has historically been, and continues to be, the prime regulatory issue'.[12] In order to safeguard solvency while permitting greater diversity of activities, it was proposed that different categories of financial institution should be commonly owned through a financial holding company structure and that the subsidiary companies and their parent should remain distinct corporate entities with their own board of directors and financial statements. Furthermore, there would be a virtual ban on intra-group financial transactions:

> The strict controls on non-arms length transactions would apply generally to all transactions within the financial holding company group of institutions and between the financial holding company group and affiliated businesses. Thus, there would be no transferring of assets or liabilities or lending or investing back and forth allowed between financial institutions affiliated with the same financial holding company.[13]

In a technical supplement accompanying the Green Paper the rationale for this proposed regulatory framework was clarified:

> In the structure that the government has in mind, the operating financial institutions would be linked to each other solely through a common shareholder which itself would be an 'inactive' holding company ... the

primary purpose of requiring financial holding companies to be inactive as defined above will be to prevent any possibility of 'contagion' of operating financial institutions arising from difficulties that a levered holding company could encounter.[14]

Furthermore, under the Green Paper proposals each institution would be supervised on an individual, as well as on a consolidated, basis. The technical supplement again provides clarification:

> while the holding company will be looked to as a means of support, in the event of the liquidation of one of the related institutions, only the resources of that particular institution will be available to compensate its shareholders and creditors. This would be a particularly important consideration in the case of insured deposit-taking institutions. Each individual institution must, therefore, have sufficient capital to sustain its own operations and supervisors should be able to satisfy themselves that this is indeed the case.[15]

It seems clear from the above that the main purpose of the proposed *regulatory* separation of the four pillars, in the context of common *ownership* through a holding company structure, was to ensure that the risks incurred within each pillar did not overflow into the remaining pillars. In particular, the proposed regime was designed to segregate banking and non-banking risks and to prevent banks from being destabilized by their non-bank affiliates.[16]

In contrast to what it referred to as 'self-dealing' (i.e., related party transactions), the Green Paper stated that 'the problems raised by conflicts of interest do not tend to be of a nature that threaten the solvency of the institution involved'.[17] The paper proposed a combination of disclosure, civil liability and creation of 'Chinese walls' to deal with the increased potential for conflict of interest abuses arising out of common ownership of the four pillars.

So far as concentration of economic power is concerned, the Green Paper did express some concern that the removal of barriers to inter-industry competition might give large institutions competitive advantages. However, no specific policy proposals were developed in this area.

While the federal government was preparing its Green Paper proposals, the Ontario Securities Commission had submitted its own plan for liberalizing the province's securities market with a view to increasing securities firms' access to outside capital.[18] The Commission asserted that there were two overriding policy objectives: (1) 'the government's policy that ownership of securities firms must remain substantially Canadian'; and (2) the continuing functional (but not ownership) separation of the four pillars.[19] In essence, the Commission proposed that domestic financial institutions and non-residents should be permitted to own up to 30 per cent of a domestic securities firm while a new class of registrant, the foreign dealer registrant, would have the same status as Canadian firms but each would be restricted in its capital to 1.5 per cent of the industry capital. At the same time the Commission proposed that the boundaries of regulation should be extended to the so-called 'exempt' or unregulated market in wholesale transactions, which was already open to outsiders — including foreign institutions.

In the event the original proposals for financial liberalization put forward by the federal Government and the Ontario Securities Commission were substantially amended. At the federal level this was due in part to critical comments from industry representatives and two parliamentary reports, one prepared by the House Committee on Finance, Trade and Economic Affairs[20] — the 'Blenkarn Report' — and the other prepared by the Senate Standing Committee on Banking, Trade and Commerce.[21]

The Blenkarn Report criticized two key features of the Green Paper framework. First, it rejected the concept of financial diversification through a mandatory holding company structure on the grounds that this would erode the economic benefits to be derived from financial conglomeration. It was suggested, instead, that financial institutions should be free to diversify through upstream holding companies and affiliated institutions as well as downstream holding companies and subsidiaries. In this connection it was argued that the policy of risk segregation through a financial holding company structure was unrealistic, since in practice financial holding companies and their affiliates would inevitably operate as integrated firms and 'when activities are either strongly influenced or determined by centralized policies it becomes increasingly difficult, if not impossible, to isolate financial institutions from risk-taking in the rest of the conglomerate organization'.[22]

Second, and on the basis of similar reasoning, the Blenkarn Report rejected the idea of a virtual ban on intra-group transactions: 'The overriding concern for self-dealing would eliminate many legitimate transactions which are necessary for appropriate synergy in multi-firm operations, thus sapping internal economies which are often crucial in the early stages of corporate development.'[23]

The Senate Report also objected to the proposed holding company structure partly on the grounds that since the holding company would be federally regulated the new regime would represent an incursion into provincial regulatory authority and would be bitterly opposed by the provinces.[24] This consideration may have weighed heavily in the federal Government's reassessment of its proposals.

# The New Regulatory Framework

## *Federal regulation*

Following the policy debate prompted by publication of its Green Paper, the federal Government, in December 1986, published a final set of proposals known as the Blue Paper,[25] the main elements of which are described below.

The Blue Paper recognized that 'the financial system worldwide is evolving in a manner that will allow financial institutions in any of the traditional four pillars to provide, directly or through affiliates or subsidiaries, a full range of financial services'.[26] Accordingly, the Government proposed to relax existing restrictions on the common ownership of regulatory financial institutions which 'will be allowed to hold financial subsidiaries in other pillars (including securities dealers) or to be affiliated with other financial institutions through a holding company structure'.[27] Specifically, domestically owned banks and financial institutions were to be permitted to acquire 100 per cent of a securities dealer from 30 June 1987, with non-resident controlled institutions limited to acquiring 50 per cent interest as at 30 June 1987, but permitted to purchase 100 per cent interest as at 30 June 1988 (essentially mirroring Ontario's revised proposals, see below). Within this scheme, the original Green Paper requirement for diversification to proceed only through a financial holding company structure was abandoned in favour of structural flexibility.

A limited degree of 'in-house' financial diversification was also to be allowed. In particular, unrestricted commercial lending powers were to be given to larger trust companies, thereby removing the main functional distinction between trust companies and banks.[28] At the same time, banks, trust and insurance companies were to be permitted to provide in-house investment advice and portfolio management services. The Blue Paper also departed from the earlier proposals by allowing greater scope for intragroup financial transactions. The paper states that 'to permit the exploitation of synergies by financial institutions seeking to market financial services, it is proposed that transactions between regulated financial institutions be subject to a less restrictive regime than would apply to self-dealing between regulated financial institutions and related non-financial concerns'.[29] Specifically, it was proposed that the following transactions that would otherwise be banned should be permitted where the related party was a federally regulated financial institution:

1   A general exemption should apply to transactions between a regulated financial

institution and a wholly owned subsidiary all of whose liabilities are guaranteed by the parent.

2 Asset transactions would be permitted provided that assets acquired from related financial institutions do not exceed 20 per cent of the capital of the institution, and provided the following conditions are met:

(a) in the case of securities there must be a well defined market for the security exchanged (i.e., the security is actively traded and there is a well established price), the transaction is conducted at market value and the securities are not in default;

(b) in the case of loans, the assets acquired may not be impaired in any way;

(c) transactions involving low-quality assets, such as non-performing loans, should not be permitted except as part of a restructuring (e.g. with capital injections) where there is pre-notification and supervisory approval;

(d) there must be clear identification of such transactions in returns to the superintendent.

3 Inter-affiliate loans should be permitted without limit in the following cases:

(a) loans fully secured by government securities;

(b) loans that are in the nature of deposits, made at market terms and for purposes ancillary to the business of the depositor.

The abandonment of the financial holding company formula, together with the more permissive approach to intra-group financial transactions suggests that the Government had accepted the impracticality, or at least the very high cost, of trying to segregate risks within the emerging financial conglomerates. On the other hand the authorities evidently remained concerned about the threat to solvency in the form of related party transactions, in particular because the failure of several financial institutions had recently been attributed to incestuous lending.[30] Accordingly the Blue Paper set out various other protective measures designed to discourage self-dealing.

In the first place, complex ownership rules were proposed to prevent domination of larger banks by single shareholders. For existing banks with capital in excess of $750 million the rule prohibiting shareholdings in excess of 10 per cent would continue to apply; smaller banks, on the other hand, could be closely held but, within 5 years of reaching the $750 million capital threshold, at least 35 per cent of the voting shares had to be publicly traded and wisely held. The apparent reasoning here was that a single dominant shareholder could pose a threat to a larger bank. It was assumed that a 35 per cent minority shareholding requirement is sufficient to ensure that a bank is not operated so as to benefit only its controlling shareholder.[31]

Further restrictions were aimed at discouraging ownership linkages between the financial and commercial sectors of the economy. For this purpose a commercial company is a company engaged in: (1) the production and distribution of goods and non-financial services; or (2) the distribution of financial services on an unregulated basis. In the case of banks, not even the smaller institutions were to be allowed to have commercial shareholders who owned more than 10 per cent of the shares of any class. The ownership rules governing trust and insurance companies were more complex (and also more permissive) but the proposals were again designed to 'arrest the industry trend towards more pervasive financial–commercial links'.[32]

The restriction on commercial ownership of financial institutions is broadly in line with US and UK practice as far as banks are concerned.[33] Partly the concern is one of concentration of economic power. However, the perceived potential for damaging self-dealing transactions between a financial institution and a related commercial entity was also a major consideration. As the Governor of the Bank of Canada, Mr John Crow, put it:

> a crucial question is whether a set of regulations can realistically be expected to cope with the potentially solvency-threatening nature of non-arms length transactions between a commercial parent and its closely held financial subsidiary. In my view, to put one's faith solely in regulatory walls to restrict the scope for related-party transactions, without a reinforcing buttress of restrictions on ownership links, would not be prudent. That is why I welcome the emphasis on concerns about ownership in the federal government's December 1986 policy statement [the Blue Paper] on the financial sector.[34]

It is worth noting too, that the restrictions on commercial–financial links are consistent with the Government's apparent scepticism on the question of segregating risks within conglomerate firms. The logical, but highly impractical, alternative would be for the federal regulatory authorities to become involved in the regulation of commercial entities linked to financial, or at least deposit-taking, institutions.

Finally, on the issue of self-dealing, the Blue Paper put forward a scheme for 'enhanced corporate governance' as an additional means of discouraging such transactions. In general, only 15 per cent of the board members of a financial institution could be drawn from among the officers and executives of the firm or its affiliates; at least one-third of the directors had to meet stringent criteria establishing independence from the company (for instance, they must not be officers, employees or significant shareholders of, or have significant business links with, the institution or related companies); and institutions were required to establish a committee of the board, with a majority of independent directors, whose functions included the review of related-party transactions.

In summary, the Blue Paper abandoned the strict rules on financial structure and intra-group dealing proposed in the Green Paper, but introduced a number of other measures designed to discourage related-party transactions that might threaten insolvency.

Implementation of the Blue Paper proposals has been a long drawn-out process. Initially, section 193(13) of the Bank Act was relied on to enable domestic banks and foreign bank subsidiaries to acquire interests in securities firms, following Ontario's decision to open up its securities markets to outsiders. Subsequently, the Bank Act was amended by Bill C-56, which provides that 'a bank may, with the prior approval of the Minister, own more than ten per cent of the shares of any class of shares of ... a Canadian corporation the activities of which are limited to dealing in securities'. More controversially (in view of provincial sensitivities over jurisdiction) the Bill authorizes the Government to issue federal regulations imposing terms and conditions applicable to any bank that holds shares in a securities firm.

As a further stage in the financial liberalization process the Government began in 1987 to prepare a new statutory framework for financial institutions. This initiative was cut short by domestic political developments but legislative proposals were eventually submitted to Parliament towards the end of 1990. These consisted of a draft Trust and Loan Companies Act and a draft Bank Act, with a new Insurance Companies Act to follow.

The draft legislation follows closely the Blue Paper proposals. Banks, trust and loan companies and insurance companies are to be allowed to diversify beyond their traditional areas of business, firstly, through expanded in-house powers and, secondly, by establishing subsidiaries operating in each other's territory — so that, for instance, banks may be owned by non-bank financial institutions.

Within the proposed statutory framework, banks' securities activities will be regulated as follows:

1   Banks may continue to own securities subsidiaries and may themselves engage in securities dealing, except as restricted by regulation (below).
2   Specifically, banks may carry on money market business, activities relating to government and government-guaranteed securities and secondary market trading in corporate debt securities. In addition, banks' in-house powers are expanded to include portfolio management services and investment advice.
3   Under new regulations banks are to be prohibited from participating in the primary distribution of corporate debt and equity securities and other classes of equity securities, such as mutual funds. Banks are also to be prohibited from acting as brokers in secondary market trading of equity securities.

4 According to the Government, 'full flexibility to invest in downstream commercial companies is not appropriate for financial institutions entrusted with the savings of Canadians'.[35] Accordingly, banks are not generally permitted to have a 'substantial' investment (meaning more than 10 per cent of voting rights or 25 per cent of shareholders' equity) in entities outside the financial services area, unless these are acquired indirectly through a financial subsidiary or through a work-out situation.

5 A bank and its subsidiaries may not acquire portfolio investments in equity securities exceeding 70 per cent of the bank's regulatory capital (nor combined equity securities and real estate investments exceeding 100 per cent of regulatory capital).

6 Banks, in common with other financial institutions, are permitted to market financial services offered by affiliates or independent firms, except for retailing insurance.

In one important respect, the legislative proposals depart from the Blue Paper. Under the new statutory regime the various restrictions on self-dealing do *not* apply to a bank's transactions with its subsidiaries, including a securities subsidiary, because the latter are not considered to be 'related parties' for this purpose. Therefore a bank may fund its securities subsidiary without limit and without any requirement that such funding be on an arm's-length basis. Similarly, transactions between a bank and its parent are exempt from the self-dealing restrictions so long as the parent is a domestic (and not foreign) financial institution.

This permissive approach to intra-group financial transactions represents an important change in official thinking. We have seen that the Blue Paper rejected the risk segregation regulatory model adopted by the earlier Green Paper. Accordingly, the Blue Paper abandoned the idea of a virtual ban on intra-group financial transactions in favour of a more liberal regime in which such transactions would be allowed on a regulated basis. The new legislative proposals carry this approach an important stage further by lifting all restrictions on transactions, whether upstream or downstream, between related entities within a financial conglomerate. This liberalization appears to be a response to criticism of the Blue Paper's proposals for residual restrictions on internal risk transfers which could be viewed as redundant unless, being completely watertight (which clearly they were not) the restrictions provided effective financial insulation for each operating unit within a financial conglomerate.

## Provincial Regulation

On 4 December 1986 the Minister of Financial Institutions of Ontario announced a more radical plan for opening up the Ontario securities industry to outsiders than had been foreshadowed in the Ontario Securities Commission's earlier proposals. The Minister stated that from 30 June 1987 there would be no limit on investments in securities firms by Canadian financial institutions, that from this date non-residents would be free to own up to 50 per cent of a securities firm and from 30 June 1988 up to 100 per cent. Direct entry by foreign securities firms would also be permitted from 30 June 1987 without any capital limit.

On the broad question of the timing and scale of outside entry into the securities markets there was agreement between Ontario and Ottawa. However, there remained the sensitive jurisdictional question of how regulatory responsibilities were to be divided between provincial and federal authorities. Clearly, given the shift in the Department of Finance's thinking on risk segregation within financial conglomerates, it was essential that the Office of the Superintendent of Financial Institutions (OSFI), as the federal regulatory agency, should be satisfied that banks were not exposing themselves to unacceptable risks through the operations of their securities subsidiaries. On the other hand, the Ontario Government had no intention of allowing its own exclusive jurisdiction over securities firms to be displaced by Ottawa.

As a first step towards resolving this issue the Ontario Government reached a bilateral accord with the federal Government in April 1987 setting out those securities activities which — subject to necessary legislation — could be carried out directly by federal financial institutions (and would therefore be regulated by the OSFI) and those which could only be carried on in a subsidiary or affiliate (and would accordingly be regulated at a provincial level). In summary the 'in-house' activities included all transactions in Government: debt, money-market activities, secondary-market trading in corporate debt securities, capital-market activities in syndicated or consortium loans, unsolicited participation in secondary trading of equity securities and portfolio management and investment advice.

Securities activities that could only be carried on through a subsidiary or affiliate included all activities relating to the primary distribution of equity and corporate debt securities and secondary-market trading in equity securities.

Following the conclusion of the federal–Ontario accord, regulations under the Ontario Securities Act were amended with effect from 30 June 1987, so as to allow outside entry into the securities markets. However, the provincial–federal jurisdiction issue was not finally settled. For one thing, the other nine Canadian provinces declined to participate. Furthermore, there were problems with the implementation of the accord. Under powers conferred by Bill C-56, the OSFI in August 1987 issued guidelines relating to the operation of the securities subsidiaries of federally regulated financial institutions.[36] These guidelines were rejected by the provinces, including Ontario, as being an incursion into their regulatory jurisdiction over securities firms.

Subsequently, in March 1988, a new and supplementary accord was concluded between the federal Government and the provinces of Quebec and Ontario. This took the form of bilateral agreements,[37] which, in effect, give the OSFI the right to be consulted on regulatory matters affecting the solvency of a securities subsidiary/affiliate. It is implicitly accepted that the present capital adequacy rules are sufficient and the provincial securities regulators undertake not to amend these before giving notice to the OSFI. If there is a disagreement over a proposed amendment then there will be a holding period of 180 days during which time the OSFI may decide to impose its own rules on banks in respect of their securities business. The accord also deals with reciprocal information flows between the federal and provincial authorities in relation to federal financial institutions and their connected securities firms. In this way the OSFI has established its right to ensure that the financial condition of a bank is not jeopardized by its securities subsidiary/affiliate, while at the same time constitutional niceties are preserved.

## Assessment

In assessing Canada's approach to financial deregulation it is necessary to bear in mind that the major policy objectives are to secure the efficiency and competitive benefits of financial diversification, while imposing sufficient regulatory safeguards to ensure financial stability.

A key assumption underlying Canada's new regulatory regime, as indicated above, is that the risks incurred by the various operating units of a financial conglomerate are interdependent. In the context of a bank's acquisition of a securities subsidiary, this means that the parent bank would be free — indeed would generally be expected — to meet any shortfall in the subsidiary's regulatory capital that might arise from losses on securities underwriting or market-making (any such capital infusion would, however, be deducted from the bank's own regulatory capital). The presumed financial linkage between a bank and its securities subsidiary is underlined by the OSFI's guideline to the effect that 'in principle, an investment dealer corporation should have a name that clearly identifies it with its (bank or other financial institution) parent'.[38]

The question that has to be asked is this: If a bank stands behind its securities subsidiary or affiliate what is the purpose of the continuing regulatory separation of banks and securities firms and of the four pillars generally? In particular, why should banks' in-house securities powers be circumscribed and the full range of securities activities have to be conducted through separately capitalized subsidiaries/affiliates? Arguably, the securities and banking business might just as well be freely inter-mingled, thereby securing the maximum benefits from diversification. From this standpoint the Canadian approach represents a somewhat awkward compromise between the fully fledged risk segregation model proposed by the US Administration and total functional integration as, for instance, permitted by the UK's post-Big Bang regulatory framework and traditionally practised in Germany and Switzerland.

## Notes

1   'Report of the implications for Canadian capital markets of the provision by financial institutions of access to discount brokerage services', Ontario Securities Commission (1983). It should, however, be stated that there has been a general tendency for the demarcation lines between the four pillars to become blurred in recent years and that the banks and trust companies, in particular, are no longer functionally distinct.

2   Under the Canada–US Free Trade Agreement, US bank subsidiaries in Canada are exempted from the market share limit. As a quid pro quo Canadian banks in the USA are able to underwrite and deal in securities of Canadian Governments and their agents, and will also receive the same treatment as that accorded to US financial institutions with respect to amendments to the Glass–Steagall Act. The new Canadian Bank Act will reduce the market share limit for non-US bank subsidiaries to 12 per cent of total domestic assets of all Canadian banks.

3   For a review of these powers see 'A regulatory framework for entry into and ownership of the Ontario securities industry', Ontario Securities Commission, February (1985), appendix 10; and the White Paper on the Revision of Canadian Banking Legislation, Department of Finance, August (1976), pp. 34 and 35.

4   The rationale for this selling group exemption was stated in the 1976 White Paper (at p. 35): 'If banks are not permitted a role in the distribution of the new issues of securities as members of the selling group, Canadians purchasing such securities through banks would always have to pay a commission in addition to the issue price. This additional cost would fall particularly on

securities purchasers outside the major urban centres who may not have ready access to investment dealers and brokers.' In practice this exemption has not been actively used.

5  According to the 1976 White Paper (at p. 39) the purpose of this exemption was 'in order to provide for innovations and for joint ventures'.

6  See Charles Freedman, 'Financial restructuring: the Canadian experience', a paper presented to a Symposium on 'Restructuring the financial system', sponsored by the Federal Reserve Bank of Kansas City, August 1987.

7  Data cited in 'The regulation of Canadian financial institutions: proposals for discussion' (the Green Paper), Department of Finance, April (1985), at p. 61.

8  See Thomas Courchene, John Todd and Lawrence Schwartz, *Ontario's Proposals for the Canadian Securities Industry* (CD Howe Institute, Toronto, 1986), at p. 23.

9  For the background to this move, and a general assessment of Quebec's regulatory policies, see 'Reforms of financial institutions in Quebec', Associate Minister for Finance and Privatization, October (1987).

10  See note 6 above.

11  The explicit policy goals set out in the Green Paper (and endorsed in subsequent policy documents) are:

1  improve consumer protection;
2  strictly control self-dealing;
3  guard against abuses of conflicts of interest;
4  promote competition, innovation and efficiency;
5  enhance the convenience and options available to customers in the marketplace;
6  broaden the sources of credit available to individuals and business;
7  ensure the soundness of financial institutions and the stability of the financial system;
8  promote international competitiveness and domestic economic growth;
9  promote the harmonization of federal and provincial regulatory policies.

12  Green Paper, at 11.

13  Ibid., p. 33.

14  'The regulation of financial institutions', Technical Supplement, Department of Finance, June 1985, at p. 13.

15  Ibid., p. 18.

16  In fact the Green Paper did not explicitly address the question of financial diversification by banks, this being left to the 1990 decennial review of the Bank Act. However, there was an implication that the model proposed for the other three pillars would apply also to the banking sector.

17  Green Paper, at p. 37.

18  'A regulatory framework for entry into and ownership of the Ontario securities industry', Ontario Securities Commission, February (1985).

19  'The Commission also accepts for the purposes of this study the premise that

the Canadian financial system should be organized on a segregated basis with each group of financial institutions performing a separate function, the so-called "four-pillars" principle. This principle is accepted, not because of any specific statement of government policy, but because it is generally reflected in the legislation governing financial institutions.' Ibid., p. 13.

20   'Canadian financial institutions', Ottawa, November (1985).
21   'Towards a more competitive financial environment', Ottawa, May (1986).
22   Blenkarn Report, p. 63.
23   Ibid., p. 64.
24   Senate Report, p. 20.
25   'New directions for the financial sector' (the 'Blue Paper'), Department of Finance, 18 December (1986).
26   Blue Paper, at 7.
27   Ibid., at 6.
28   In order to achieve greater competitive equality between banks and trust companies, in the context of functional convergence, the non-interest-bearing reserve requirements imposed on banks are to be phased out. In this context the Bank of Canada has proposed that institutions which are direct clearers should maintain a small positive balance at the Bank (of the order of a quarter per cent). This would represent a target compensating balance rather than a reserve requirement. See 'Discussion paper on the implementation of monetary policy in the absence of reserve requirements', Bank of Canada, 29 September (1987).
29   Blue Paper, p. 27.
30   See Timothy Unwin and David Glennie, 'Conflicts of interest and self-dealing: current reform proposals', Blake, Cassels, and Graydon, 12 March 1987, pp. 2 to 3.
31   These ownership rules have been criticized on the grounds, *inter alia*, that 'as one moves towards wide ownership, the ability/incentive for owner-related self-dealing diminishes while the ability/incentive for management- and director-related self-dealing increases'. Thomas Courchene, 'Re-regulating the Canadian financial sector: the ownership controversy', monograph, April (1987), p. 66.
32   Blue Paper, p. 8.
33   For a policy assessment of the separation of banking and commerce in the US context see Gerald Corrigan, 'Financial market structure: a longer view', Federal Reserve Bank of New York, *Annual Report*, February 1987. In a speech the Governor of the Bank of England, Mr Leigh Pemberton, stated that: 'I have to say that I would need some persuading before an industrial or commercial company is allowed to take control of a bank.' Speech before the Northern Ireland Chamber of Commerce, 13 October 1987.
34   Address to the Investment Dealers' Association of Canada, Ottawa, 9 June 1987.

35 'Reform of federal financial institutions legislation', Department of Finance, Ottawa (1990), p. 6.

36 'Information and guidelines pertaining to a shareholding by a federally incorporated and regulated financial institution in an investment dealer corporation or holding corporation', Office of the Superintendent of Financial Institutions, 20 August (1987).

37 See, for instance, 'Memorandum of understanding', Office of the Superintendent of Financial Institutions and Ontario Securities Commission, 28 March (1988).

38 See 'Information and guidelines', p. 4. As noted in the text, the provincial governments objected to these guidelines which were subsequently withdrawn, but their content nevertheless reflects official thinking at federal level. By way of contrast it is interesting to note that in the US debate on financial deregulation there have been proposals to prohibit banks and their securities subsidiaries/affiliates from trading under the same name.

# 8

# Universal Banking: Germany and Switzerland

Universal banking is the term used to describe a banking tradition found in continental Europe in which banks engage in a full range of securities activities, usually through the bank entity itself rather than through separately incorporated subsidiaries.[1] Universal banking is also associated with close linkages between banking and industry which may be formalized by banks acquiring equity holdings in their client companies and seeking representation on those companies' boards of directors.

This chapter examines the practice of universal banking — a financial model which, under the EEC's new regulatory regime, may be adopted in much of western Europe after 1992. Attention is focused on the banking experience of Germany and Switzerland since these two countries are most often cited as leading examples of the universal banking tradition.

## Universal Banking in Germany

The German banking system embraces three categories of financial institution, each with its own distinctive legal status. First, there are the private commercial banks, consisting of the big three branch banks (Deutsche Bank, Dresdner Bank and Commerzbank), the regional banks and the so-called private banks which were established as single proprietorships or partnerships and specialize mainly in securities business. Second, there are the savings banks and their central giro institution. The savings banks are incorporated by public law and are guaranteed by their respective public authorities (city, town or rural district councils), their traditional business being mortgage finance and lending to local authorities. Third, there are the agricultural and commercial credit cooperatives which accept deposits from and lend mainly to their own membership.

Finally, there also exists a miscellaneous group of specialized banks including, for instance, mortgage banks, instalment credit institutions and the postal savings and giro offices.

Within this heterogeneous structure there has in recent years been a marked convergence of the different sectors' financial activities. On the liabilities side, the savings and cooperative banks have encroached on the commercial banks' traditional business by taking short-term deposits, while the commercial banks have in turn made inroads into the savings market. On the assets side, savings banks have increased their private-sector commercial lending, commercial banks have expanded mortgage lending through their mortgage subsidiaries and the savings and cooperative banks have increased their share of the banking system's security holdings.

At the same time the savings banks have been increasing their involvement in securities trading: the central giro institutions can engage freely in securities business and there is a move among some savings banks to broaden their charters to enable them to do likewise. Meanwhile, the market share of the specialized financial institutions has continued to decline, reflecting business conditions that increasingly favour those offering a broad range of services. On these developments the Bundesbank recently commented: 'The major categories of banks have tended to lose market shares to their competitors in their traditional domains while making up lost ground in those types of funding which used to be less significant. The trend towards an all-purpose banking system has therefore tended to strengthen further in the German banking industry.'[2]

Within this universal banking system the private commercial banks, and particularly the big three, maintain a dominant position in securities business. In describing the involvement of German banks in stock market activity, therefore, attention is here focused particularly on the large commercial banks.

The banks' stock market operations take a variety of forms. First, they hold major equity positions. These holdings may represent long-term investments, trading and market-making activities, or underwriting business. Second, the banks earn commission from brokerage and fund management. Aggregate equity holdings are revealed in published balance sheet data but commission from securities business is not separated from other forms of commission income and must therefore be estimated.

The banks' long-term equity holdings arise in part from corporate restructurings and rescue operations.[3] In the Great Depression banks were compelled to convert loans that were in default into equity and some of these positions are still on their books. More recently, the AEG rescue package in 1979 included a new equity subscription by the banks with a limitation on subsequent resale. And in 1983 Deutsche Bank became a major shareholder in Kloeckner, Germany's largest trading company, as a result of a DM 400mn bail-out operation arising from the latter's losses on oil forward contracts.

In other cases, shares have been acquired with a view to eventual resale to the public: Deutsche Bank's purchase of the Flick Group's 29 per cent holding in Daimler-Benz in 1975 falls within this category, as does the same bank's purchase of 25 per cent of the shares in Nixdorf in 1979 (subsequently placed in the summer of 1984). Finally, long-term equity positions may represent straight investments: for instance Commerzbank has held a large stake in the stores group Karstadt since 1955 which it shows no sign of wishing to dispose of.

Equity holdings arising from underwriting activity come somewhere between long-term investments and short-term trading positions. The balance sheet strength of the big banks enables them to take up major shareholdings and to wait until the market is 'right' before disposing of them, thereby acting as principals rather than underwriters in the conventional sense. The most spectacular example of this kind of transaction was Deutsche Bank's acquisition in December 1985 of the Flick industrial group for a price of DM 5bn. This deal was, in fact, specially structured to comply with regulatory requirements and in the event yielded a substantial profit when the Flick industrial holding company, Feldmuehle Nobel, was finally offered to the public five months later.

Detailed information on German banks' equity holdings has hitherto been scarce, but in recent years some statistics have become available. The German Banking Association has calculated that the shareholdings of its members in non-banks amounted in 1989 to less than 2.8 per cent of the capital of all non-banks, while the comparable figure for its ten largest members was put at only 0.57 per cent, down from 1.3 per cent in 1976 (see table 8.1).[4] These figures have been criticized as too low and the Bundesbank estimates that banks' holdings of equities (portfolio investments and participations) account for around 9 per cent of the total value of shares outstanding in Germany.[5]

In 1989 Deutsche Bank revealed for the first time its major equity holdings when it was obliged to meet the disclosure requirements associated with a public equity offering. Equity stakes of 10 per cent or over are listed overleaf (see table 8.2). By comparison with Japanese banks, whose equity holdings account for some 22 per cent of Tokyo's stock market capitalization German banks' equity investments are relatively modest. Furthermore, they appear to be on the decline. For instance, in 1990 Dresdner Bank reduced its shareholdings in Heidelberger Zement and

**Table 8.1.** Participations of the ten largest private banks in non-banking firms

|  | Nominal capital (DM mn) | | Number of firms | |
|---|---|---|---|---|
|  | 1986 | 1989 | 1986 | 1989 |
| All enterprises | 1,748 | 1,676 | 89 | 101 |
| Participations: | | | | |
| between 10–25% | 430 | 713 | 47 | 63 |
| between 25–50% | 1,277 | 919 | 33 | 29 |
| more than 50% bn | 41 | 44 | 9 | 9 |
| Enterprises listed on a stock exchange | | | | |
| Participations: | 1,503 | 1,380 | 46 | 38 |
| between 10–25% | 287 | 536 | 19 | 23 |
| between 25–50% | 1,204 | 830 | 23 | 12 |
| more than 50% bn | 12 | 14 | 4 | 3 |

*Source*: Bundesverband Deutscher Banken, 1989.

**Table 8.2.** Deutsche Bank's major equity stakes, end June 1989

| Company | Stake (10%) |
|---|---|
| Daimler-Benz | 28.24 |
| Philipp Holzmann | 30 |
| Karstadt | 25.08 |
| Kloeckner-Humboldt-Deutz | 40 |
| Suedzucker | 23.05 |
| Allianz | 10 |
| Muenchener | 10 |
| Rueckversicherung Linde | 10 |
| Heidelberger Zement | 10 |
| Hapag-Lloyd | 12.5 |
| Indirect holdings | |
| Metallgesellschaft | 10.9 |
| Horten | 18.75 |

*Source*: *Financial Times*, 22 October 1989.

Metallgesellschaft as part of a stated long-term policy of reducing its industrial investments. And in the same year, Commerzbank sold its 10 per cent stake in the German construction company, Hochtief. These developments are consistent with the Bundesbank's observation that the equity holdings of the big banks, along with those of the other banks, 'have lost ground considerably since the early seventies'.[6]

Beyond their direct equity holdings, German universal banks may influence the management of non-bank companies by exercising proxy voting rights relating to shares deposited with them and through their representation on supervisory boards. A study undertaken by the Monopolies Commission found that in 1975 only about 5 per cent of the voting rights in the top 100 companies was controlled directly by banks, but that this figure rose to 36 per cent when proxies were added. The same study found that at end-1974 banks held 145 seats on the boards of the top 100 companies (10 per cent of the total), and according to data provided by the Association of German Banks the number of board seats of the top 100 companies held by private banks had fallen to 104 in 1988 (7 per cent of the total) from 114 in 1986.[7]

Since the mid 1970s there have been various proposals to reduce German banks' influence over non-bank companies. For instance, the Monopolies Commission in 1976 recommended that equity stakes be limited to 5 per cent, the Gessler Commission in 1979 proposed a limit of 25 per cent and the Free Democratic Party in 1989 began to press for a 15 per cent limit, together with restrictions on bank membership of supervisory boards.

No doubt it is partly because of such political pressures that banks have been reducing their strategic equity holdings. In addition banks are anticipating implementation of the European Second Banking Directive (Article 11) which restricts individual shareholdings to 15 per cent, and total holdings to 60 per cent, of a bank's regulatory capital.

In contrast to the long-term decline in banks' equity investments their holdings of debt securities has increased markedly. Between 1970 and 1986 the percentage of banks' assets represented by bond holdings (at book values) rose from 8.7 per cent to 11.4 per cent while during this period the big banks' equity investments fell from 40 per cent of their total securities holdings to little more than 20 per cent.[8] At the same time banks earnings from securities business appears to have increased. Figures published by the Bundesbank show that in 1989 net commissions received by the big three banks from all sources amounted to around 40 per cent of their net interest received, compared with just under one-third in 1984 and less than 30 per cent in the late 1970s.[9] For the banking sector as a whole net commissions received as a percentage of net interest received rose from 14 per cent in 1979 to over 20 per cent in 1989. Although it is not possible to identify separately commission from securities business (nor, indeed, profits from own account trading which are categorized as 'other receipts') it would seem from these figures that German banks' securities activities are making an increasingly important contribution to profits, notwithstanding the decline in banks' equity holdings.

It should be noted that German commercial banks do not generally conduct their domestic securities business through separate subsidiaries. Even their individual branches provide a full range of financial services and thereby operate as mini-universal banks. As an exception to this general rule mortgage banks, mutual investment fund companies and insurance companies must be separately incorporated. The integration of banking and non-banking activities is in contrast to the emerging corporate structure for banking conglomerates in the UK and in even greater contrast to the US where German banks are obliged to conduct their banking and securities business through separate entities in order to conform to the Glass–Steagall Act.

The regulation of German banks' securities activities is governed by the Banking Act of 1961, as amended, together with regulations pursuant to that Act ('Principles concerning the capital and liquidity of banks') drawn up by Federal Banking Supervisory Office. Within this regulatory framework, securities business is subject to the following constraints:

1  A bank's investments in property and equipment, plus its shareholdings in other companies, must not in aggregate exceed its regulatory capital (Section 12(1) of the Banking Act). However, all equity stakes of 10 per cent or less are excluded from this restriction, as are shares acquired in 'distress' capital restructurings (subject to a 5-year time limit). This provision, which was introduced in its present form in 1985, penalizes banks' larger strategic equity investments, and adds to the pressures on German banks to dispose of, or reduce, their major shareholdings.

2  All equity stakes over 25 per cent are classified as 'participations' and therefore as loans for the purpose of limiting large exposures to single borrowers (Section 19 (6) of the Banking Act). No individual 'loan' may exceed 50 per cent of a bank's capital and all 'large' loans taken together (a loan is 'large' when it exceeds 15 per cent of the lending bank's capital) must not exceed eight times the bank's capital. These restrictions provide a further disincentive for banks to make large equity investments.

3  A bank's loans and 'participations' must not in aggregate exceed eighteen times its regulatory capital (Principle I of the regulations). This represents a further restriction on banks' equity stakes of over 25 per cent.

4  Certain categories of illiquid assets, including unlisted securities and

'participations', must be backed by long-term funding (Principle II of the regulations). Investments in listed shares which are not participations are subject to less stringent liquidity requirements (Principle III of the regulations).
5  Listed bonds escape altogether the capital adequacy and liquidity requirements of the regulations. In effect, such bonds are classified as 'free of risk' under the standards of the Banking Act.[10]
6  With effect from October 1990 amendments to Principles I and Ia of the regulations have incorporated off-balance sheet transactions, embracing swaps, forward contracts and options, into the capital adequacy requirements.[11]

Paradoxically, the regulatory arrangements described above penalize quite severely those strategic equity investments with which German universal banking is normally associated. At the other extreme, banks' holdings of debt securities are largely exempt from regulatory constraints. Accordingly, when loan demand is weak banks have tended to favour bond purchases as a substitute credit transaction — the result being that the banking sector as a whole has built up its bond holdings over the years.

From a safety and soundness standpoint Germany's universal banking regime appears to have performed well. Franke and Hudson have examined the role of universal banking in three periods of financial upheaval in Germany (1923–4, 1931–2 and the immediate aftermath of World War Two) and conclude that, in general, banks' securities activities were not a contributory factor.[12] Furthermore, in more recent times it seems that no bank failure can be attributed directly to losses arising out of securities business. Such banking problems as have emerged from time to time reflect the mismanagement of conventional banking business. Thus the failure of Herstatt Bank in 1974 was due to foreign exchange speculation; Commerzbank's difficulties in 1980–1, when it became the first major German bank in the post-war period to miss its dividend, were due to large-scale interest-rate mismatching; similar problems afflicted Westdeutsch Landesbank Girozentrale in 1981; and the collapse of Schröder, Münchmeyer, Hengst in 1983 was due entirely to disastrous concentrated lending to a single borrower. There is no indication from this record of enhanced risk-taking in connection with securities business and, indeed, some observers have argued that by diversifying into non-bank activities German banks have been able to reduce their overall risks.[13]

It might be tempting to conclude from Germany's experience that universal banking can be safely adopted as a model by other national banking systems. However, such a judgement would be premature, given that Germany's domestic banking stability has been associated with a number of special factors.

In the first place, banks have used their securities holdings to create hidden reserves which are then used to reduce fluctuations in published profits.[14] Under German accounting principles shares which are held by banks as long-term investments may be valued at cost or market value whereas trading positions must be shown at lower of cost or market value. This corresponds to the distinction between fixed and current assets. On the other hand, bonds can always be designated as long-term holdings/fixed assets and need not then be marked to market. However, bonds held by a bank which are recorded at above market value must be disclosed in the accounts and there is therefore pressure on the banks, evidently reinforced by the supervisory authorities, to mark bonds down to market but not up (in contrast, *schuldscheine* do not have to be disclosed in this manner since they are 'loans', which is perhaps one reason why some financial institutions have been eager buyers of these instruments).

By valuing their long-term equity investments at cost, banks are in a position to accumulate substantial hidden reserves — which indeed they do. In addition, Article 26A of the Banking Act gives banks carte blanche to create hidden reserves out of claims or securities designated as current assets. According to this provision: 'Banks may show claims and securities carried as part of their current assets at a value lower than that prescribed or permitted by Section 115 of the Companies Act in so far as this is necessary in the light of reasonable commercial judgment as a safeguard against the specific risks of the banks' line of business.'

It is clear therefore that banks have considerable discretion over the profits they report. Furthermore, where hidden reserves have been released to bolster published profits this is not evident from the accounts because gains on securities may be directly offset against loan losses. The relevant accounting regulation states that 'receipts from the higher valuation or payment of claims that had been partly or wholly written off and from the higher valuation or sale of securities may be offset against writedowns of and provisions for losses on loans or securities'.[15]

A typical example of profit manipulation through the use of secret reserves occurred in 1989 when falling bond prices forced the banks to write a record DM 11bn off their bond portfolios. According to the Bundesbank, these losses were partially offset by the release of secret reserves. Furthermore, in order to limit such write-offs, banks 'transferred parts of their bond portfolios from current assets to fixed assets, thereby, in accordance with current regulations, avoiding write-downs to the lower market value on the balance sheet date'.[16]

Banks may therefore to an important extent control their profits performance which in practice means smoothing fluctuations in their earnings. Evidently it is felt that financial markets do not see through this so that sudden shocks are avoided and confidence sustained. The active exploitation of hidden reserves is therefore closely linked to the German conception of universal banking, with securities investments reducing rather than amplifying published profit fluctuations.

A second reason for caution when drawing conclusions from Germany's universal banking experience is that the nature and scale of banks' securities business is changing. Reference has already been made to Deutsche Bank's temporary acquisition in December 1985 of the Flick industrial group. The acquisition price of DM 5bn was not far below Deutsche Bank's end-1984 consolidated regulatory capital of DM 5.8bn. The acquisition amounted to a 'participation' and, as such, was subject to the prohibition on large loans but by structuring the transaction as three separate placements involving three distinct businesses (Flick's stakes in Daimler-Benz and in the US company W. K. Grace, as well as its industrial holding company, Feldmuehle Nobel) Deutsche Bank was able to clear this regulatory hurdle.[17] However, the episode illustrates the potential scale (and corresponding risks) involved in bought deals and other large-scale securities transactions.

Changing techniques in securities markets can also lead to unanticipated risk exposures. In 1990 Deutsche Gehossenschaftsbank (DG Bank) disclosed irregularities in connection with DM 6bn of disputed bond-swap transactions with a group of French banks.[18] The estimated potential loss of DM 600mn represented over one-third of DG Bank's DM 1.76bn equity capital. Such transactions were a new departure for DG Bank which in 1986 had decided to move away from its traditional lending business and to expand its securities activities. DG's experience underlines the fact that the risks associated with securities business are constantly changing in line with evolving trading techniques.

A final reason for believing that the past record may be a poor guide to future performance is that the intensity of competition in both banking and securities markets is increasing. In 1979 the Gessler Commission expressed concern that banks' domestic underwriting syndicates represented a constraint on competition;[19] the Bundesbank has noted the very high charges imposed by banks for admission to official trading on the Stock Exchange (which the banks themselves dominate);[20] and the 1988 Price Waterhouse study of prices charged for financial services within the EEC indicated that in general German banking products are priced significantly above a competitive level, leading one analysis to conclude that 'if universal banking enjoyed cost advantages they would seem not to be passed on to consumers'.[21] The implication is that German banks have benefited in the past from some degree of protection in their domestic market, and that as this protection is removed in the context of the EEC's 1992 reforms the profitability of both banking and securities business will be under pressure. The move from a protected to a competitive market regime will provide an important test of the robustness of universal banking in Germany.

## Universal Banking in Switzerland

The Swiss banking system consists of both privately and publicly owned institutions. The publicly owned banks include cantonal and local savings banks which are not involved in securities markets to any great extent. In contrast, the five so-called 'big banks' (Credit Suisse, Swiss Bank Corporation and Union Bank of Switzerland, collectively known as the 'big three', together with Bank Leu and Swiss Volksbank) are universal banks.[22] These five institutions dominate both banking and securities markets, claiming around 50 per cent of total banking assets.

The principle of universality was adopted by Switzerland in 1934 at a time when several other countries, notably the USA, were responding to financial disturbances by imposing restrictions on the kinds of activities banks could undertake.[23] However, in contrast to the legal position in Germany, the Swiss Federal Law on Banks and Savings Banks of 1934 defines banking restrictively to include only those institutions which 'publicly solicit customer deposits' (Article 2 (1)). The statute specifically does *not* apply to 'stock exchange agents and stock exchange firms trading in securities ... provided they do not engage in regular banking business' (Article 1(3)). In practice, only banks are members of the Swiss stock exchanges[24] and the prudential (as distinct from conduct of business) regulation of securities operations is therefore left in the hands of the Federal Banking Commission, the agency charged with responsibility for supervising banks.

The statutory definition of banking has recently been given a broader application by an amendment to the Implementing Ordinance of 1972. With effect from January 1990 companies which fund themselves in substantial volume from the interbank market are considered to be banks, as are companies which are active in the primary securities markets (new Article 2a(c)). These changes mean that the regulatory jurisdiction of the Banking Commission has been expanded to include finance companies which do not solicit deposits from the public but which are otherwise engaged in banking and securities business.

Within this regulatory framework, banks' securities activities are governed by the capital adequacy, large exposure and liquidity provisions of the Implementing Ordinance of 1972 (as amended). Article 13 of the Ordinance requires that banks maintain capital backing for various classes of asset, including 10 per cent for listed shares, 20 per cent for unlisted shares and 40 per cent for non-consolidated 'permanent' equity investments. With effect from 1 January 1990 the capital requirements were amended to take into account the Basle accord on capital adequacy and at this time a new provision was introduced requiring a 1 per cent capital backing for all commitments to underwrite new issues, net of committed sub-participations. Article 21 of the ordinance deals with concentrated risk exposures, the basic rule being that unsecured loans to a single borrower in excess of 20 per cent of the lending bank's equity capital must be notified to the Banking Commission (equity participations being treated in the same way as unsecured loans for this purpose). Finally, Articles 15–20 lay down a number of minimum liquidity ratios, under which securities holdings are treated as illiquid assets.

As in Germany, Swiss banks typically conduct their domestic securities business through the bank entity itself. However, their major overseas securities operations are generally undertaken by separately capitalized subsidiaries or affiliates. Such 'subsidiarization' reflects a combination of foreign regulator requirements, tax considerations and, in the case of Credit Suisse, attempts to distance the bank from its international securities arm with a view to minimising the bank's capital adequacy requirements (see below).

Swiss banks, unlike their German counterparts, do not have a large number of strategic equity investments in non-bank companies, although equity positions, such as UBS' 40 per cent stake in Motor-Columbus, are acquired from time to time when loans to distressed borrowers are converted into equity. In addition, there are some long-established relationships, including Credit Suisse's association with hydro-electric companies which accounts for its parent company's 42 per cent stake in Elektrowatt. In contrast to the position in Germany, Swiss banks do not exercise proxy votes and are not routinely represented on the boards of non-bank companies. All in all, therefore, the linkages between the bank and non-bank sectors are weaker in Switzerland than in Germany.

The Swiss universal banking model, like that of Germany, has been characterized by a high degree of financial stability. However, it is again necessary to underline the role of secret reserves in smoothing banks' profits records and (more so even than in Germany) the extent to which stability has rested on protected markets.

Swiss banks have been permitted to build up secret reserves either through the undervaluation of assets or by making provisions in excess of what ordinary banking prudence requires. Such reserves can be released either by crediting earnings or by adjusting asset values. The resulting manipulation of reported profits was openly encouraged by the authorities who viewed profits smoothing as a means of strengthening confidence in the banking system.[25] Accordingly, the use of secret reserves was formally sanctioned by the Banking Commission in a circular dated December 1975.[26] On the other hand, the Commission has insisted that the release of secret reserves be disclosed in particular circumstances, for instance if in three successive years there is a net dissolution of such reserves, or if release of reserves in one accounting year is used to disguise an extraordinarily high loss. Even so, the potential for masking serious problems was illustrated in 1977 when Credit Suisse was able to absorb a massive loss of around SF 1.7bn incurred at its Chiasso branch, without seriously affecting its reported profits.[27]

Since the mid 1980s the Swiss authorities have been reviewing the whole question of secret reserves in the context of the worldwide trend towards greater transparency in bank accounts. In 1990 the Banking Commission issued a circular prohibiting the creation of secret reserves by means of provisions which are not commercially justifiable, and at the same time required that the release of secret reserves be disclosed, inter alia, where the amount involved exceeds the average of 30 per cent of the bank's equity capital and 30 per cent of the reported net profit for the period in question.[28] These changes, which came into effect at the end of 1990, will limit the scope for traditional profit smoothing and expose Swiss banks' published financial statements to the profit volatility associated with their securities activities.

While secret reserves have hitherto helped to iron out fluctuations in Swiss banks' earnings, price-fixing and other restrictive practices have raised banks' underlying profitability. For instance, during the mid 1980s the fees and commissions on an 8-year SF foreign bond issue were typically in the region of $3\frac{1}{4}$ per cent, against 2 per cent for equivalent Eurodollar bonds (Euro-SF issues are in effect prohibited by the Swiss authorities, thereby protecting the domestic cartel).[29] Similarly, the secondary market spreads for SF bonds were in the $\frac{1}{2}$-1 per cent range, well above the equivalent spreads in other securities markets.[30] Apart from underwriting, cartel pricing embraced a wide range of financial services, including stock exchange brokerage commissions, charges for custodian business and documentary credits, and foreign exchange dealing.

By the late 1980s it had become clear to the Swiss authorities that Switzerland's status as an international financial centre would be jeopardized if Swiss banks continued to adhere to their price-fixing practices.

There was a parallel here with the events preceding the UK's Big Bang, when international business was moving away from London's cartelized stock exchange (see p. 106).

The banks themselves began to respond to intensifying global competition by relaxing some of their restrictive practices. In particular, the big three banks revealed in January 1986 that they were cutting their underwriting commission on SF foreign bonds by an average of $\frac{3}{8}$ per cent. However, the decisive development came in April 1989 when the Swiss Cartel Commission launched a wide-ranging attack on the banking sector's price-fixing arrangements. After investigating 22 agreements the Commission concluded that 16 significantly limited competition and accordingly recommended that these should be revoked in total or in part.[31] Significantly, the Commission's chairman, Mr Pierre Tercier, stated that the Commission wanted its objectives met by the beginning of 1992 — ahead of the completion of the European Community's single market.

The Swiss Bankers' Association, in its response to the Cartel Commission's report, accepted 10 out of 19 recommendations but, crucially, opposed the abolition of fixed securities brokerage commissions and the dismantling of agreements underpinning the big three banks' bond underwriting syndicate. Among other points raised by the Bankers' Association, was the argument that unrestricted price completion could increase risks and destabilize the financial system. These objections were overruled by the Government in September 1990 when it ordered the big bank underwriting syndicate to abandon by the year-end its agreement preventing syndicate members from managing outside issues; and also required the agreement fixing stock exchange commissions to be dismantled by the end of 1992.[32] Subsequently, the big three banks decided to dissolve the issuing syndicate which had dominated the Swiss bond market for forty years. At around the same time the Swiss stock exchanges announced that they would abolish fixed brokerage fees with effect from January 1991. These moves established a competitive financial market regime previously unknown in Switzerland.

Clearly, the new regime means lower profitability and increased risk. Just how much risk it is impossible to say, but it is interesting to note that in their overseas securities operations, where competition is intense, the Swiss banks have had a number of unhappy experiences — with Union Bank of Switzerland and Swiss Banking Corporation both losing money on their London securities business in 1989–90 and Credit Suisse having to face heavy losses on its US investment banking operations, CS First Boston, over the same period.

Credit Suisse's handling of its investment banking interests has particular relevance to the assessment of the risks involved in banks' securities activities. In early 1982 a subsidiary company, CS Holding (CSH) took over Credit Suisse's 49 per cent stake in Financière Credit Suisse First Boston (FCSFB), the leading Eurobond house, and 5,000 shares in Elektrowatt, the electrical engineering concern. The intention was to remove these investments from consolidation and thus reduce Credit Suisse's regulatory capital requirements. However, in March 1983 the Banking Commission ordered Credit Suisse to consolidate its subsidiary CSH into the bank's own financial statements for the purpose of calculating regulatory capital needs — thereby largely defeating the purpose of the restructuring.[33]

Having been thwarted in its earlier move, Credit Suisse in March 1989 announced a further restructuring with a view to minimizing its capital needs. Under this scheme CSH was established as a holding company owning Credit Suisse itself, 44.5 per cent of Credit Suisse First Boston (CSFB), and equity investments in Elektrowatt and Fides, a trust services and information technology company. The effect of the initiative was to convert CSFB from an indirectly held subsidiary of Credit Suisse to a sister company.

However, the Banking Commission once again rejected this attempt at regulatory circumvention. In October 1989 the Commission ruled that the new holding company structure did not exempt Credit Suisse from providing full capital cover for group subsidiaries and that the bank would have to consolidate itself with CSH as if it and not CSH were the group holding company. This meant that Credit Suisse would have to hold capital equivalent to 40 per cent of the book value of the group's non-banking investments (Article 13 of the Implementing Ordinance). The reasoning behind the Commission's decision was that, because of the ties between Credit Suisse and CSH, the bank would be obliged as a matter of commercial self-interest to support CSFB if the latter should get into difficulties, even though there was no legal obligation to do so.[34]

Credit Suisse appealed against the Banking Commission's ruling but in December 1990 the Swiss Federal Supreme Court decided in favour of the Commission. In doing so, the court rejected Credit Suisse's assertion that it had no obligation to support its affiliates in the CSH group with which it dealt on a strictly arm's-length basis. In other words, the court upheld the Commission's view that, in the Swiss context at least, risks incurred within a banking conglomerate could not be segregated by means of a holding company structure.[35]

The critical relevance of this dispute was highlighted in November 1990, just before the court's decision, when CSH felt obliged to acquire majority control of CSFB. The move was prompted by heavy losses at CSFB and

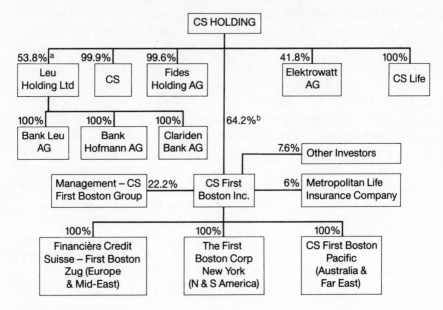

**Figure 8.1** Credit Suisse holding company structure, end 1990

(Percentages shown are capital stakes, not voting rights.)
* CS Holding owns 73.5 per cent of the voting rights.
*Source*: IBCA Ltd

the consequent need to provide a capital injection of some $800mn as well as clear evidence of parental backing. In the absence of such support CSFB's credit-rating would very probably have been lowered, with potentially serious funding implications (bearing in mind that Drexel's terminal liquidity crisis earlier in the same year had been triggered by a credit downgrading). Following the restructuring, CSH's stake in CFSB was raised from 44.5 per cent to over 60 per cent (see figure 8.1). This was also an important step from a US regulatory standpoint because it meant that a foreign bank had taken majority control of a major US securities house — allowable under US law only because Credit Suisse's previous interest in CFSB had been 'grandfathered'.[36]

The Credit Suisse/CFSB affair is indicative of the risks and regulatory problems facing not just the Swiss authorities but all bank supervisors in the newly competitive European market environment. It is clear, too, that, in Switzerland as in Germany, past stability is no guide to future performance where universal banking is concerned and that the robustness of this model which has served both countries so well in the post-World War Two period is going to be severely tested in the aftermath of the EEC's 1992 reforms.

# Notes

1　For recent discussions of universal banking see, George Benston, *The Separation of Commercial and Investment Banking* (Macmillan, London, 1990), pp. 179–214; Richard Herring and Anthony Santomero, 'The corporate structure of financial conglomerates', *Journal of Financial Services Research*, 4, 4, December (1990), pp. 471–97; and Alfred Steinherr and Christian Huveneers, *Universal Banks: the Prototype of Successful Banks in the Integrated European Market* (Centre for European Policy Studies, Brussels, 1989).

2　'The longer-term trend of inflows of funds to banks', Deutsche Bundesbank, *Monthly Report*, October (1985), p. 34. See also 'Longer-term trends in the banking sector and market position of the individual categories of banks', Deutsche Bundesbank, *Monthly Report*, April (1989), p. 14.

3　For an analysis of German banks' equity stakes see Dr W. Guth, Deutsche Bank Foundation paper presented to the Association of Corporate Treasurers on 13 September 1984, pp. 9–14.

4　Data cited in 'Battle over banks' power', *Wall Street Journal/Europe*, 7 December (1989), p. 12.

5　See 'The share market in the Federal Republic of Germany and its development potential', Deutsche Bundesbank, *Monthly Report*, April (1984), p. 16.

6　See 'Longer-term trends in the banks' investments in securities', Deutsche Bundesbank, *Monthly Report*, May (1987), p. 30.

7　Data cited by Steinherr and Huveneers, *Universal Banks*, p. 23.

8　'Longer-term trends in the banks' investments in securities', p. 30.

9　'The profitability of German banks in 1989', Deutsche Bundesbank, *Monthly Report*, August (1990), pp. 14–31

10　See 'Longer-term trends in the banks' investments in securities', p. 26.

11　See 'The new principles I and Ia concerning the capital of banks', Deutsche Bundesbank, *Monthly Report*, August (1990), pp. 37–43.

12　Hans-Hermann Franke and Michael Hudson, *Banking and Finance in West Germany* (St Martin's Press, New York, 1984).

13　See, for instance, H. E. Büschgen, 'The universal banking system in the Federal Republic of Germany', *Journal of Comparative Law and Securities Regulation*, 2 (1979), pp. 1–27.

14　See Richard Dale 'Universal banking: the German model', *The Banker*, July (1986), p. 20. Hidden reserves come from three sources: (1) investments held at historic cost where the market value is now much higher; (2) investments written down to market value where the writedown has not subsequently been reinstated; and (3) 'Section 26A' reserves where current assets are shown at below normal valuation. This is rather different from the UK position where the banks were traditionally allowed to create (and some merchant banks still do create) hidden reserves out of transfers from profits or revaluations which are held in a separate account within 'other liabilities'.

15    Section 4 of Form VO (Ordinance on the Form Sheets for Financial Statements) of 1967.

16    'The profitability of German banks in 1989', p. 18.

17    Richard Dale, 'Universal Banking', p. 18. For details of the Flick transaction, see Jonathan Carr, 'Flick flotation to make winners all round', *Financial Times*, 21 April 1986.

18    For details of DG Bank's problems over bond swaps see Katherine Cambell, 'The lost promise of overseas expansion', *Financial Times*, 7 March 1990.

19    See Report of the Commission of Enquiry, 'Basic banking questions', Summary (English translation), Bonn (1979), p. 11.

20    'The share market in the Federal Republic of Germany', p. 15.

21    Steinherr and Huveneers, *Universal Banks*, p. 10.

22    In 1990, CS Holding, the parent of Credit Suisse, acquired Bank Leu. For an excellent description of the Swiss banking system see *Banking in Switzerland* (KPMG Fides Peat Zurich, 1990).

23    See Benedict Christensen, 'Switzerland's role as an international financial centre', IMF occasional paper No. 45, July (1986), p. 6.

24    According to an OECD study: 'banks are so preponderant throughout the securities sector that, except for some operational functions on the exchange itself, there is no profession of "broker" or similar intermediary in the Swiss market', 'International trade in services: securities', Committee on Financial Markets, OECD, September (1986), p. 88.

25    See Jack Guttentag and Richard Herring, 'Disclosure policy and international banking', Brookings Institution, Washington DC, October (1983), pp. 26–33.

26    For details see Bernhard Müller, 'The supervision of the banks in Switzerland', Federal Banking Commission, May (1981), p. 9.

27    See William Dullforce, 'Swiss crack down on hidden bank reserves', *Financial Times*, 13 April 1989.

28    See 'New treatment of banks' inner reserves', *Financial Times Financial Regulation Report*, October 1990, pp. 21–3.

29    See Benedict Christensen, 'Switzerland's role', p. 14.

30    For instance, in recent years the spread on fixed interest Eurobonds has averaged around $\frac{1}{3}$ per cent. See Peter Gallant, *The Eurobond Market* (Woodhead–Faulkner, Cambridge, 1988), p. 154.

31    See 'Decartelization begins', *Financial Times Financial Regulation Report*, May 1989, pp. 20–1.

32    See 'Swiss Economics Minister orders end to bank cartels', *Wall Street Journal/Europe*, 11 September (1990).

33    See John Wicks, 'Credit Suisse to accept ruling on capital ratio', *Financial Times*, 28 March 1983.

34   See William Dullforce, 'Credit Suisse appeals against ruling on capital', *Financial Times*, 6 October 1989.

35   For a summary of the Court's decision see 'Credit Suisse loses its Supreme Court appeal', IBCA, London, January 1991. It should be noted that because Swiss law gives the Banking Commission regulatory authority only over banks, and not over their holding companies, the Commission had to deal with CSH at one remove via Credit Suisse. Hence the requirement that Credit Suisse consolidate itself with CSH for regulatory purposes.

36   The US International Banking Act of 1978 'grandfathered' the investment banking activities of 15 foreign commercial banks, including Credit Suisse, and permits them, within limits, to conduct both commercial and investment banking in the USA, notwithstanding the Glass–Steagall Act. The US Federal Reserve Board approved CSH's acquisition of majority control over CSFB, evidently because this was viewed as a form of internal expansion, rather than a fresh acquisition, in terms of the statute.

# 9

# The EEC's New Regulatory Regime

The European Commission's Second Banking Coordination Directive, which was formally adopted in December 1989, will allow banks to engage in securities, as well as banking activities, throughout the European Community. The Solvency Ratio Directive and the Own Funds Directive were adopted at the same time in order to provide a common regulatory framework for such cross-border financial activity. The same opportunity for European-wide operations is to be given to non-bank investment firms and in support of this objective the European Commission has proposed a Directive on Investment Services, as well as a Directive on Capital Adequacy of Investment Firms and Credit Institutions.

This chapter assesses the main elements of the EEC's new regulatory regime but in doing so focuses particularly on the different regulatory objectives and techniques applicable to securities firms as compared with banks. From this discussion it appears that the EEC's approach to regulating capital adequacy is not entirely consistent with stated policy objectives and that there are potential systemic risks in the post-1992 European financial market regime that the EEC regulatory framework may not have adequately addressed.

## The EEC Regulatory Regime

The key principle contained in the Second Banking Coordination Directive is that there should be a single licence for both establishment and the range of permissible banking activities. Under this regime a bank wishing to set up a branch in any member state would not have to be separately authorized by the host country supervisory authority; the branch would not have to find 'endowment capital'; it would not be subject to supervision by

# Annex

*List of activities subject to mutual recognition*

1 Acceptance of deposits and other repayable funds from the public.
2 Lending.[a]
3 Financial leasing.
4 Money transmission services.
5 Issuing and administering means of payment (e.g. credit cards, travellers' cheques and bankers' drafts).
6 Guarantees and commitments.
7 Trading for own account or for account of customers in:
   (a)   money market instruments (cheques, bills, CDs, etc.);
   (b)   foreign exchange;
   (c)   financial futures and options;
   (d)   exchange and interest rate instruments;
   (e)   transferable securities;
8 Participation in share issues and the provision of services related to such issues.
9 Advice to undertakings on capital structure, industrial strategy and related questions and advice and services relating to mergers and the purchase of undertakings.
10 Money broking.
11 Portfolio management and advice.
12 Safekeeping and administration of securities.
13 Credit reference services.
14 Safe custody services.

[a] Including inter alia: consumer credit; mortgage credit; factoring, with or without recourse.

**Figure 9.1** Second Banking Coordination Directive

the host country; and the range of permissible financial activities would be determined by the home not the host country.

Article 16 defines the scope of mutual recognition in the banking sector. The financial activities listed in a separate annex (see figure 9.1) are those which are subject to automatic recognition by the host authority, i.e. member states are obliged to accept this range of banking activities, conducted by institutions exercising their intra-EEC branching rights, but need not permit their own domestic banks to engage in all these activities.

The list of permissible banking activities will be updated under special flexible procedures to take account of new banking services.

The list has been drawn up on the universal banking model so that, crucially, it includes own-account trading in securities, securities broking, underwriting and distribution of securities and portfolio management and advice. Any bank authorized in its home country may exercise such activities in the host country through mutual recognition, provided that its licence covers the relevant activities, even if the same activities are not permitted to similar credit institutions in the host country. The far-reaching implication is that national authorities will lose control over the range of activities that banks may undertake within their own territories.

A further major consequence of the proposed Directive is that it will effectively impose the universal banking model on the whole of the Community. Countries like Greece, Spain and Portugal, which have had tight restrictions on the range of financial activities open to banks (see table 9.1), will be faced with inward branching foreign banks that are not subject to these constraints. The competitive pressures arising from this situation will no doubt prompt the host countries concerned to reconsider their own domestic banking rules.

Furthermore, the Directive places no constraints on the kind of corporate structure that diversified financial groups may adopt, so that bank entities are free to engage directly in the full range of permissible 'non-bank' activities.

However, the Commission is concerned that banks' shareholdings in non-banks could endanger financial stability. Accordingly Article 10 imposes two limits on such shareholdings. First, a bank should not have any shareholding in a non-bank that exceeds 10 per cent of the bank's capital; and, second, the total value of such shareholdings should not exceed 50 per cent of capital. These limits do not apply to shares acquired temporarily either during a financial rescue operation or in the normal course of underwriting. This provision is of particular concern to German banks, whose industrial shareholdings are at present not subject to regulatory constraint (see chapter 8).

The companion legislation to the Second Banking Coordination Directive is the proposed Investment Services Directive.[1] This provides for basic standards of authorization of investment firms and sets out the single passport rules whereby an investment firm authorized in one member state may provide investment services into, or establish a branch in, any other member state. In support of the principle of freedom of establishment EEC securities firms are to be given a reciprocal right to membership of stock exchanges in all member states.

**Table 9.1.** Banks' permissible non-bank activities

| | Securities underwriting | Real-estate investment | Insurance business | Financial leasing | Fiduciary business |
|---|---|---|---|---|---|
| Australia | | | | | |
| Austria | | R | | | |
| Belgium | | R | R | | |
| Canada | R | R | F | R | F |
| Denmark | | R | F | | |
| Finland | | R | F | | |
| France | | | F | | R |
| Germany | | S | F | S | |
| Greece | R | F | F | a | |
| Ireland | | R | R | | |
| Italy | | | F | | |
| Japan | R | | F | F | |
| Luxembourg | | S | F | | |
| Netherlands | | S | F | | |
| New Zealand | | | | | |
| Norway | | R | F | | |
| Portugal | | R | R | F | F |
| Spain | | S | F | F | |
| Sweden | | F | F | F | |
| Switzerland | | S | F | | |
| Turkey | R | R | F | R | |
| United Kingdom | | S | | | |
| United States | R | R | R | R | R |

F  Forbidden
R  Legal restrictions or specific authorization requirements
G  Informal guidelines or gentlemen's agreements
S  Limitations arising from comparatively heavy weighting in solvency and/or own-funds/ fixed-asset requirements

[a]  Relevant legal arrangements under consideration.

*Source*: R. M. Pecchioli, *Prudential Supervision in Banking* (OECD, Paris, 1987), p. 59.

Agreement on a final version of the Investment Services Directive has been threatened by a dispute between those (notably the French and Italians) who wish to ensure that all securities transactions are routed through a centralized market within the local jurisdiction, and those (including the UK and Germany) who favour the idea of competing market arrangements, including the option of off-market transactions.

This problem apart, there are two features of the proposed Investment Services Directive which could become a source of serious difficulty: namely, the allocation of regulatory responsibilities between home and host country, and the extent to which further regulatory harmonization may become necessary if there is to be a unified European market in investment services.

Under the proposed Directive, the *home* state will have exclusive competence in the formulation and enforcement of prudential rules. Yet initially at any rate, branches of investment firms will be subject to investor compensation arrangements prevailing in the *host* country — thereby breaching the commonsense principle that the same regulatory jurisdiction should be responsible for both supervising financial soundness and organizing compensation when things go wrong. There would be less room for confusion if prudential regulation and investor compensation arrangements were under one roof.

The potential for confusion is also evident in the distinction between conflict of interest and other conduct of business rules. Under the proposed directive it is the *home* state's responsibility to ensure that an investment firm is organized in such a way that conflicts of interest between the firm and its clients or between one of its clients and another do not result in clients' interests being prejudiced. The generality of this obligation may itself be a cause of difficulty. It does not in any event coexist easily with the *host* state's responsibility for all other conduct of business rules governing the relationship between the firm and the investor (including advertising and marketing).

The problems associated with the division of regulatory responsibilities between home and host states would be greatly reduced if there were a greater measure of regulatory harmonization. This point has been recognized in relation to investor compensation schemes where a draft harmonization directive is awaited. However, it is difficult to envisage a smoothly operating European market in investment services where other arrangements affecting investor protection — Chinese walls, disclosure requirements, advertising and marketing, and general conduct of business rules — vary significantly between member states. Such fragmentation may confuse investors, impede cross-border financial activity, invite regulatory circumvention and impose differential costs, and therefore competitive distortions, on both individual stock exchanges and investment firms based in particular states. Of course, the process of competition will tend to bring about regulatory convergence over time but damage could be caused in the interim and there is no guarantee that the regulatory norms that eventually emerge will be appropriate.

In the key area of capital adequacy there is a proposal for harmonization in the form of a draft Capital Adequacy Directive (CAD).[2] The issues raised by the CAD proposal are so fundamental to the safety and soundness of the financial system as to warrant a detailed policy analysis which is the subject matter of the remainder of this chapter.

# The Need to Regulate Securities Firms

It is possible to identify three separate reasons for regulating securities firms: the protection of retail investors; the protection of counterparties; and the stability of the financial system.

The traditional approach to regulating securities markets has focused primarily on the risk to investors.[3] Broadly, the idea here is that investors should be free to incur whatever risks they choose, provided that they are made fully aware of those risks and provided also that those risks do not include losses arising from the insolvency of the securities firm itself. In order to cover the latter eventuality it has been the practice in many countries to establish an investor protection scheme that compensates investors up to some maximum figure. The proposed EEC Directive on Investment Services follows this practice by requiring that an investment firm 'is either a member of a general compensation scheme designed to protect investors who are prevented from having claims satisfied because of the bankruptcy or default of the investment firm or makes individual arrangements which provide investors with equivalent protection'.[4] This provision is buttressed by the further requirement that investors' securities and cash be held separately from the investment firm's own assets.[5] Given these safeguards it may be doubted whether there is an additional need for capital adequacy requirements simply to protect investors against the risk of default.

There is, however, a second rationale for regulating investment firms — namely, the need to reassure counterparties, including banks and other creditors, who might otherwise be reluctant to deal with such firms. The suggestion here is that the market could not operate efficiently without regulation because the financial condition of investment firms cannot be effectively monitored by market participants. This argument was, for instance, advanced by the Technical Committee of the International Organisation of Securities Commissions in their recent study[6] of the capital adequacy problem. On the other hand, it might reasonably be argued that, in the absence of regulation, investment firms would simply be forced to become less reliant on short-term unsecured borrowing and more dependent on secured and medium-term borrowing. Indeed, it appears that an adjustment of this kind is now taking place within the US investment banking industry in the wake of the collapse of Drexel Burnham Lambert in 1990.[7]

The third and most persuasive case for regulation is based on the view that the default of unregulated securities firms could destabilize the financial system. Official concern over the potential for systemic disturbances of this kind have increased following the global stock market crash of 1987. A recent OECD study expressed these concerns as follows:

> the rising importance of securities markets in the financial systems of OECD countries, the growing concentration in the securities industry, the effects of new technologies, the nature of the risks now being born by securities market intermediaries and the links between the securities market and the banking and payments system all suggest that the occurrence of serious misfunctions in the securities markets would have the potential to destabilize the entire financial system.[8]

It might be objected that the collapse of Drexel Burnham Lambert without any serious financial ripple effects provides contrary evidence. However, it should be recalled that Drexel's failure was very carefully managed by the US regulatory authorities with a view to ensuring that the holding companies' broker-dealer subsidiary was given the opportunity to wind down its business in an orderly manner. The SEC Chairman has since stated in Congressional testimony that by maintaining the broker-dealer's solvency immediately following the parent company's collapse, the authorities were able to protect other broker-dealers and their customers from defaults on trades involving billions of dollars in securities, and that 'a sudden collapse of a major broker-dealer such as Drexel Burnham Lambert could have had extremely adverse consequences on confidence in the marketplace, and on the smooth functioning of our clearance and settlement system'.[9] Of course, it is hardly necessary to emphasize that the failure of a major *bank-related* investment firm in a universal banking country would be a more serious matter still. Suffice it to say here that concerns over financial stability, rather than investor protection, seem to be the main driving force behind recent initiatives to strengthen the regulation of investment firms.

# Differences between Bank Regulation and the Regulation of Securities Firms

Before examining the EEC's approach to regulating securities firms it is helpful to consider the main differences between bank regulation and the regulation of securities activities.[10] In order to make such a comparison it is necessary to identify those key differences between securities and banking business that have implications for regulatory policy.

The most fundamental difference is that securities firms have a much shorter commercial time horizon than banks. Banks typically hold loans on their balance sheet until maturity, whereas securities firms experience rapid asset turnover as a result of their underwriting, market-making and trading activities. The difference in time horizon is reflected in the liquidity characteristics of the assets which the two types of institutions hold. That is to say, a large proportion of bank assets are in the form of unmarketable commercial loans, whereas the assets of securities firms are by definition highly marketable. This means that the main business risk for securities firms is market risk, whereas for banks it is credit risk. Also, because of their differing time horizons, securities firms are evaluated on a liquidation basis and their accounting is mark-to-market whereas banks are evaluated as going concerns and their accounting is based on original cost.

A closely related point is that securities firms can adjust their balance sheets rapidly to changing circumstances whereas the composition of a bank's loan portfolio changes only slowly. Similarly, while the market-risk profile of a securities firm can be adjusted very quickly, the credit risk associated with a bank's commercial lending can be modified only gradually.

Arising out of their ordinary business operations, securities firms also experience large fluctuations in their balance sheet size and in their capital ratios. Banks, on the other hand, have relatively stable balance sheets and their capital ratios change relatively slowly.

Finally, on the liabilities side, securities firms are entirely dependent on wholesale money markets for their non-capital funding whereas for banks an important contribution to funding may come from retail deposits. History suggests that wholesale markets are more fickle than a captive retail deposit base but against this it has to be recognized that a large proportion of securities firm's borrowing is secured. As the recent Drexel collapse demonstrates, it is the *unsecured* component of securities firms borrowing — notably in the form of commercial paper — that is most liable to sudden contraction. Overriding these considerations, however, is the fact that banks' deposit liabilities are uniquely vulnerable to contagious panic withdrawals owing to the illiquid and non-transparent nature of banks' assets and related uncertainties concerning net worth.

These differences in the business characteristics of banks and securities firms have important regulatory consequences. The most important of these concerns is the way in which the two types of institution are expected to respond to financial difficulties. A securities firm with impaired capital is expected to shrink its balance sheet immediately in order to comply with its regulatory capital requirement. This it can do so long as its assets are in readily marketable form. Hence the regulatory emphasis on securities firms' 'liquid capital'. In the extreme, a securities firm is required to wind down its business completely. For instance, the SEC's capital adequacy rules for US broker-dealers are explicitly designed to ensure that such firms can wind down their activities, while protecting their customers, within a time frame of one month. The targeted wind-down period for UK securities firms, under the securities industry's self-regulatory framework, is somewhat longer, at three months.

By way of contrast, a bank is most emphatically not expected to respond to financial problems by going out of business since if it were to do so its non-marketable assets could be sold quickly only at a heavy discount which would leave depositors and other creditors exposed to losses. Therefore, the main objective of bank regulators is to sustain banks as going concerns and in the event of capital impairment to allow them time to raise new capital, strengthen management, and conserve financial resources by, for instance, cutting dividend payments.

Accordingly, regulatory capital fulfils different functions for banks and securities firms. In both cases it is there to absorb losses but for banks the capital should be permanent — to support the institution as a going concern — whereas for a securities firm it may be temporary, reflecting the latter's ability to scale down its activities as well as its fluctuating need for capital resources. It is also worth noting here that because securities firms' business activities fluctuate so much, they typically operate on a capital base far above the regulatory minimum.[11] The excess capital enables such firms to take immediate advantage of business opportunities, such as underwriting, as they arise, and it also advertises to the financial community a firm's ability to serve large customers and to undertake large-scale transactions.

The regulatory emphasis on permanent capital for banks and the more permissive approach to temporary capital for securities firms is therefore the result of divergent regulatory objectives. Because banks are uniquely vulnerable to contagious deposit withdrawals, bank failures involve risks to the financial system as a whole. The capital which a bank must hold is therefore intended to prevent it from going into liquidation. Securities firms, on the other hand, have not generally been vulnerable to 'runs' in the same way as banks: their assets are required to be readily saleable and prompt contraction and liquidation are the regulators' chosen methods of protecting customers and creditors.

One consequence of these differences in regulatory approach is that securities firms are generally entitled to rely heavily on subordinated debt as a source of capital, whereas for banks such financing typically counts only towards secondary capital and is subject to strict limits. Furthermore, to the extent that banks may rely on subordinated debt, it must generally have a minimum term to maturity of several years.[12] In contrast, under SEC rules for broker-dealers, an unusually large underwriting may be capitalized with temporary subordinated debt repayable within 45 days.

Regulatory differences extend also to the role of deposit insurance and the lender of last resort. Within most banking systems deposit insurance plays an important part in maintaining confidence, thereby stabilizing banks' deposit base. At the same time official liquidity assistance is available to sustain solvent banks as going concerns pending any necessary adjustments in their operations or financial structure. But because securities firms can generally contract their way out of trouble, they do not have the same need for a lender of last resort. Moreover, investor protection schemes have the limited purpose of providing protection to retail customers who are not in a position to monitor the financial condition of those with whom they deal.

In a sense, therefore, securities firms are much easier to regulate than banks even though the risks they incur may be as great, or greater.[13] The net worth of securities firms can be more readily ascertained, because their assets are saleable and marked to market; their liabilities are less vulnerable to contagious withdrawal; and the scale of their operations can be rapidly contracted in the event of capital impairment. Indeed, forced contraction and, in extreme cases, shut-down, are the regulators' main weapons in dealing with financially troubled securities firms, whereas troubled banks call for longer-term remedial programmes involving management restructuring, capital infusions and, as final measures, official liquidity support and even nationalization.

The above differences in the regulation of banks and securities firms have led to serious difficulties for EEC policymakers in their attempts to establish an appropriate regulatory framework for the single European financial market. The problems here arise from the prevalence of universal banking in continental Europe, the related fact that the Second Banking Coordination Directive gives a broad definition of banking which includes securities activities, and the perceived need to maintain competitive equality between specialist and bank-related securities firms.

# The EEC's Approach to Regulating Investment Firms

The EEC proposal for a Directive on the Capital Adequacy of Investment Firms and Credit Institutions (CAD) allows alternative definitions of capital for the supervisors of non-bank investment firms. These supervisors may choose either the definition of capital applied to banks in previous EEC Directives, or they can adopt an alternative definition which is 'purpose-built' for securities businesses. In this alternative definition the emphasis is on liquidity rather than solvency, so that: (1) all illiquid assets must be deducted from capital; while (2) subordinated debt with an initial maturity of at least 2 years is allowable as regulatory capital up to a ceiling of $2\frac{1}{2}$ × equity capital. This alternative definition is broadly in line with that currently applied to investment firms by the US, UK and Japan — although the limits on subordinated debt are more restrictive. Under the EEC rules the implied time frame for winding down an investment firm follows the three-month target adopted by the UK so that, for instance, bank deposits repayable within 90 days are included as liquid assets.

Under the CAD rules, supervisors of banks which undertake securities activities are also given alternative definitions of capital. They may continue to apply to *all* of the bank's business the 'bank definition' of capital set out in earlier Directives, or they may permit an alternative definition which allows the risks on the bank's trading book[14] (only) to be covered by additional subordinated debt. This subordinated capital is subject to the same maturity and quantity constraints as under the alternative capital definition for non-bank investment firms, but in addition the use of the alternative definition must not add more than 25 per cent to the regulatory capital that would be allowed under the 'bank definition'. Banks are not required to deduct illiquid assets when applying the alternative definition of capital, since their trading book, by definition, is made up entirely of marketable securities.

These alternative definitions of capital are, of course, intended to meet the policy objective of ensuring a level playing field as between banks and non-bank investment firms. However, the question that must be asked is whether these capital rules can be justified on prudential grounds.

The official thinking behind the proposed definitions of capital was indicated in a speech by the Vice-President of the European Community, Sir Leon Brittan. Sir Leon stated that non-bank investment firms should be allowed a larger amount of subordinated debt than banks since subordinated debt provides adequate protection for investors and counterparties.

However, he went on to say that such debt does not provide adequate protection in the case of banks:

Their buffer [against potential losses] needs to be mainly in the form of equity so that losses may be absorbed without their net worth turning negative. In this way depositors can be confident that their credit institution will remain solvent. If this confidence was lacking, a panic withdrawal of funds would rapidly lead to a liquidity crisis for a bank given the long-term illiquid nature of its assets. Non-banks do not face the same problem, for their assets which are held for short periods are, by contrast, liquid and readily marketable.[15]

According to this line of reasoning the appropriate regulatory goal for bank supervisors is to ensure solvency — hence the emphasis on equity capital. For investment firms, however, the stated regulatory objective is more limited: it is to protect investors and counterparties without necessarily ensuring solvency, a goal that can be achieved with more liberal use of subordinated debt.

Given the way securities markets have developed in recent years, this statement of regulatory objectives may be questioned. In particular, the Drexel episode suggests that investment firms, too, can suffer a collapse in confidence in much the same way as banks. It will be recalled that the Drexel group had over $1bn of short-term unsecured borrowings, mostly in the form of commercial paper, but when the rating on Drexel's paper was downgraded in December 1989 it became impossible to roll over these borrowings.[16] The Chairman of the US Federal Reserve, Mr Alan Greenspan, subsequently referred to this funding collapse as the equivalent of a 'bank run'.[17] The Drexel affair also highlights the importance of a reliable funding base and the interconnections between solvency, asset liquidity[18] and the liquidity of liabilities. Yet the proposed EEC Directive, in common with the SEC's capital rules, says nothing about investment firms' non-capital liabilities.

If one does accept the EEC's divergent regulatory objectives for banks and investment firms, it is difficult to justify the alternative definition of capital available to banks. As explained, the alternative definition allows more liberal use of subordinated debt to support the bank's trading book. But to this extent the burden of absorbing losses on the trading book may have to be borne by the equity capital that supports the rest of the bank's business. The risk of insolvency is therefore increased.[19]

Furthermore, there is a danger that publicized losses on the trading book may trigger deposit withdrawals: if these withdrawals were to exceed the funding needed to support the trading book, the bank itself could be placed in jeopardy. For these reasons it seems inappropriate to try to segment a bank's securities and conventional banking business, and to apply different capital rules to each.

There is also a danger that in its efforts to secure competitive equality within Europe between banks and non-bank investment firms, the proposed CAD Directive will create competitive distortions between European investment firms and those outside. For instance, under the capital rules for UK investment firms subordinated debt qualifies as regulatory capital up to a ceiling of 4 × equity capital so long as it has an initial maturity of at least two years, while the SEC permits subordinated debt repayable within 45 days to be used to capitalize unusually large underwritings. Given the stated objective of ensuring solvency, it is understandable that the proposed EEC Directive applies more stringent capital criteria than these to banks — indeed, as indicated earlier, the proposed rules may already be too permissive on this count. On the other hand, by applying to investment firms similar restrictions on the use of subordinated debt, the EEC proposal arguably deprives the latter of needed flexibility and may place them at a disadvantage vis-à-vis their US counterparts, particularly when competing for large-scale underwriting business.

Of course, problems of this kind are inescapable so long as securities firms are subject to a dual regulatory regime — that is, a European regime designed to accommodate universal banking, and a US regime which separates banking and securities business.

It is necessary to consider also the various categories of risk against which investment firms are required to maintain capital. These are identified by the proposed EEC Directive as position risk — a broad concept, embracing market, credit and liquidity risks — settlement or counterparty risk, foreign exchange risk and 'other' risks. The most important of these, considered below, are position risk and settlement risk.

The risk weights included in the fixed interest position risk requirements differentiate between only three categories of issuer: essentially, central government, other public-sector plus listed-corporate, and the rest. Furthermore, there is no differentiation by currency denomination of the issue. These risk categories are much cruder than those currently applied by the UK Securities and Futures Authority which has identified significantly different price volatility as between, for instance, US Treasuries and Yen Sovereign issues.[20] Similarly the standard 10 per cent risk weighting for qualifying equities proposed by the EEC is much cruder than the present UK arrangements which differentiate between equities on the basis of the volatility of the stock markets where they trade.[21] The difficulty associated with the simplified EEC approach is that it may lead to inefficient use of capital, unacceptably high risks for investment firms specializing in volatile securities, as well as competitive disadvantages for lower-risk markets.

This important consideration apart, the EEC capital requirements for position risk appear to be broadly in line with, albeit somewhat lower than, those currently applied in the USA, UK and Japan. The EEC proposal states that, so far as equities are concerned, the position-risk requirements are intended to cover a firm against a 10 per cent change in the general level of equity prices on its main markets, but it is not clear over what period the movement is to be measured. Put another way, it is unclear how quickly a firm is expected to be able to dispose of its equity position and how long it is therefore assumed to be exposed to market risk. The same uncertainty applies to interest-rate risk in relation to a firm's holdings of fixed-interest securities.

The chief danger for regulators in assessing position risk is that the characteristics of particular securities markets can change dramatically due to unforeseen developments, as happened with the seizure of the markets in junk bonds (see n. 7, p. 172) and perpetual floating-rate notes.[22] That is a risk which cannot easily be guarded against, but there is a case for penalizing investment firms whose activities are focused on a particular sector of the market, even if there is diversification within that sector. After all, it was Drexel's specialization in the junk bond market that led to its downfall.

One other qualification needs to be made. As with the definition of capital, it is difficult to see how interest-rate risk, as captured by the EEC's proposed fixed-interest position requirements, can be usefully applied to a bank's trading book. A bank's interest-rate risk can be viewed only in the context of *all* its assets and *all* its liabilities: it surely cannot make sense to isolate some portion of one side of the balance sheet and use it as a basis for determining the market risk associated with interest-rate movements. This is just one of the many difficulties that may arise when applying the trading book option to banks' capital adequacy requirements.

So far as settlement or counterparty risk is concerned, there are two types of exposure. The first arises where there is 'free' delivery and money is paid away, or securities are delivered, prior to the other party fulfilling its side of the transaction. Here the exposure takes the form of full credit risk. The second type of exposure occurs under a cash against delivery transaction where the counterparty defaults: here the risk is that of replacement cost, which can be measured by the difference between the agreed settlement price for the security and its current market value.

The proposed EEC Directive makes explicit provision only for the second type of risk. This it does by specifying a capital requirement, measured as a percentage of the difference between the settlement and current market price, for transactions which remain unsettled after the due delivery date. The percentage capital requirement increases with the lapse of time, reaching 100 per cent 46 days after due settlement date.

As indicated, no special provision is made for the full credit risk that arises under free delivery. However, this is covered indirectly by the ordinary capital adequacy rules in so far as unsecured receivables are illiquid assets that have to be deducted from capital. Arguably, this is unnecessarily severe, and it might have been better to follow the US Securities and Exchange Commission in allowing routine receivables to count towards capital to an extent based on their age.

# Systemic Risks and 1992

The real difficulty with the EEC proposals for regulating securities activities lies not so much in the way that particular risks are dealt with, but rather in the attempt to establish competitive equality between banks and non-bank investment firms. There is a fundamental policy dilemma here which can only be properly understood by examining the way in which modern banking systems have evolved. For this purpose the USA can serve as an example, simply because the relevant data is more readily available.[23]

In 1840 the average equity-capital-to-total-assets ratio for US banks was around 50 per cent. Over the next 75 years this ratio declined but by the late 1920s the average was still around 12 per cent. These high ratios − as they now seem to us − were the consequence not of any regulatory action but of market forces. That is to say, visibly high equity capital ratios were necessary to maintain depositors' confidence. Yet by 1989 the equity-capital-to-total-assets ratio of the 25 largest US banks was only 5 per cent − despite a decade of regulatory action aimed at strengthening US banks' balance sheets.

The markets have accommodated this dramatic decline in banks' capital ratios mainly because deposit insurance and access to the official discount window have drastically reduced the risks born by depositors. However, because the riskiness of a bank's assets is no longer reflected in the cost or availability of its funding, the propensity for risk-taking by banks has greatly increased. Hence the need for stringent regulation of the banking industry.

Against this background, the mingling of banking and securities activities under the EEC's 1992 regulatory programme presents some formidable policy problems. First, banks may be infected by their securities activities, whether these be conducted within the bank itself or through separate subsidiaries. The issue here is not one of firewalls[24] since, as the Drexel collapse has demonstrated, a well capitalized entity, such as Drexel's government securities subsidiary, can have its funding cut off if questions are raised about the health of its parent company.[25] The same problem was highlighted, albeit on a much smaller scale, by the forced closure of a highly capitalized UK bank, British and Commonwealth Merchant Bank, simply because of its association with a troubled affiliate. The clear message for regulators is that if *any* part of a financial conglomerate gets into difficulties, then any other part that depends on short-term unsecured funding can be put in jeopardy.

More broadly, it is reasonable to concur with the Chairman of the US Federal Reserve Board, Mr Alan Greenspan, that 'as financial institutions engage in more and more similar activities, disruption and pressures in non-banking financial markets may create systemic risk similar to that faced in earlier years in a narrower banking system'.[26] If national authorities respond to these pressures by extending the official safety net to non-bank financial activities, including securities business, then the problem of subsidized, and therefore excessive, risk-taking will be widened beyond the banking sector to securities markets. That development will in turn lead to demands for even more stringent regulation of investment firms.

By focusing its efforts on establishing a level playing field between banks and non-bank investment firms, and failing to address this more fundamental policy dilemma, the proposed EEC approach to regulating investment firms could achieve the worst of all possible worlds. The 'trading book' option allows banks to dilute the quality of their capital, while at the same time the risk of cross-infection from securities activities is increased. On the other hand, the competitive position of European-based investment firms may be weakened by the application of more stringent tests of capital adequacy than would be strictly necessary for self-standing securities houses.

# Conclusion

The intensified competition between financial intermediaries that will inevitably accompany the 1992 liberalization of European financial markets must be viewed against a background of existing surplus capacity in the global financial services industry.[27] The combination of a highly competitive environment, associated declines in lending margins and risk premia, and a European-wide change in regulatory regime could create the kind of conditions after 1992 that in the past have led to financial instability.[28]

It is therefore important that the European Commission's capital adequacy proposals should be designed to ensure that financial institutions can cope with the difficult business climate that is in prospect. Unfortunately, the Commission's task has been made more complicated by a tight time schedule and the absence of any parallel global coordination of securities market regulation of the kind that exists in banking. The proposed capital adequacy rules for investment firms are intended to achieve a number of objectives: namely, to protect investors, counterparties and the stability of the financial system while simultaneously ensuring competitive equality between banks and specialist securities houses and also between European financial institutions and their non-European rivals. The danger is that in giving undue emphasis to establishing a level playing field between banks and securities houses, the Commission's proposals could jeopardize these other objectives.

## Notes

1    For an analysis of the draft Directive see *EC Investment Services Directive: A Consultative Document* (UK Department of Trade and Industry, London, July 1990).

2    See *EC Capital Adequacy Directive: A Consultative Document* (UK Department of Trade and Industry, London, September 1990).

3    See *Arrangements for the Regulation and Supervision of Securities Markets in OECD Countries* (OECD, Paris, 1989), p. 20.

4    Draft article 9 (1).

5    Id.

6    'Capital adequacy standards for securities firms', Report of the International Organization of Securities Commissions, August (1989), p. 6.

7    See 'Morgan Stanley files $1bn shelf registration', *Financial Times*, 9 June 1990, p. 12. Drexel sought protection under Chapter 11 of the federal bankruptcy code in February 1990. The firm faced a liquidity crisis because it had acquired a large portfolio of unmarketable 'junk bonds' financed largely through short-term bank borrowings. Evidently US brokerage houses have been attempting to reduce their reliance on short-term bank borrowing, partly because banks have become much more cautious about lending to such firms since the Drexel collapse.

8    *Arrangements for the Regulation*, p. 20.

9    See statement of Richard Breeden before the Committee on Banking, Housing and Urban Affairs, US Senate, concerning the bankruptcy of Drexel Burnham Lambert Group Inc., February 1990, p. 33.

10 For an excellent analysis, see Gary Haberman, 'Capital requirements of commercial and investment banks: contrasts in regulation', *Federal Reserve Bank of New York Quarterly Review*, autumn (1987), pp. 1–10.

11 For instance, at year-end 1986, 16 US securities firms reported average net capital 7.3 times larger than minimum requirements. See Haberman, 'Capital requirements', p. 6.

12 Under the Basle capital adequacy rules for international banks, subordinated debt is allowable as supplementary capital up to a maximum of 50 per cent of core capital, subject to the condition that it must have a minimum original fixed term to maturity of over five years.

13 Thus the US Securities Investor Protection Corporation, which was set up in 1970 to insure the accounts of customers of broker-dealers, has been able to operate with a low level of reserves on a minimal $100 per firm annual premium (1987): Haberman, 'Capital requirements', p. 6. In comparison the US Federal Deposit Insurance Corporation, which insures bank deposits, has in recent years experienced large claims on its resources, reflecting bank failures running at over 200 per annum.

14 Article 2 of the CAD Directive defines a bank's 'trading book' to include 'its proprietary positions in transferable securities or derivative instruments, which are taken on by the [bank] in order to benefit from actual or expected differences between their buying and selling prices, or in order to hedge other elements of the trading book'. Such a definition, which is based on intention, may lead to some ambiguity in the classification of a bank's securities holdings.

15 Speech to the Overseas Bankers Club, Guildhall, London, 5 February 1990, p. 6.

16 Following the reduction in Standard and Poor's rating on its commercial paper from A-2 to A-3 in December 1989, Drexel's outstanding commercial paper shrank from around $600mn to $180mn. See statement of Richard Breeden, p. 24.

17 See Testimony before the Subcommittee on Economic and Commercial Law, Committee on the Judiciary, US House of Representatives, 1 March 1990, p. 4.

18 The key problem for Drexel was that its approximately $1bn holding of junk bonds became progressively less marketable as the junk bond market collapsed. By early 1990 these bonds could not be readily disposed of, nor could they be used as collateral for bank borrowings. See statement of Richard Breeden, pp. 21–5.

19 This, presumably, explains the additional constraint placed on banks' use of subordinated debt under the alternative definition, i.e. the 25 per cent rule referred to in the text. However, it is surely unwise to accept a higher insolvency risk for one particular group of banks, namely those which undertake securities business and whose supervisors choose to apply the alternative definition of capital.

20   Thus the risk weight applied to 1–2 year US Treasuries is 1.50 per cent and for 1–2 year Yen Sovereign issues only 0.75 per cent. See TSA Financial Regulations, appendix 13, February 1988.

21   For instance, the percentage risk addition (PRA) applicable to equity holdings is 21 per cent for Australia compared with 10 per cent for Switzerland. See TSA Financial Regulations, appendix A, February 1988.

22   The market in perpetual floating rate notes (FRNs), developed rapidly in the mid 1980s, reflecting banks' desire to raise debt capital in this form, and the market's willingness to absorb such paper on a low spread above short-term inter-bank rates. However, in 1986–7 the FRN market suffered a crisis of confidence, prices collapsed and the secondary market seized up.

23   This data was presented by the Chairman of the US Federal Reserve Board, in a recent speech. See Alan Greenspan, 'Remarks before the annual conference on bank structure and competition', Federal Reserve Bank of Chicago, 10 May 1990.

24   Firewalls are a regulatory mechanism designed to insulate one part of a financial group from difficulties experienced in another part. Typically, firewalls consist of strict limits on intra-group financial transactions — as, for instance, applied to US banks and their non-bank affiliates, under the US Federal Reserve Act.

25   See Alan Greenspan, Testimony before the Subcommittee on Economic and Commercial Law, pp. 8–9.

26   Greenspan, 'Remarks', p. 13

27   As one prominent central banker put it recently: 'There is ... undoubted over-capacity in the financial sector which is leading to unrealistic undercutting of fees and margins in much the same way as we saw very low spreads being offered to Third World borrowers in the 1970s.' See Huib Muller, Executive Director, De Nederlandsche Bank 'Risk management', remarks before the International Monetary Conference, San Francisco, 4 June 1990, p. 7.

28   See E. P. Davis, 'Instability in the Euromarkets and the economic theory of financial crisis', Bank of England Discussion Papers, No. 43, October (1989).

# 10

# Weighing the Policy Alternatives:
# Theory and Practice

We have seen in chapter 1 that because banks possess certain characteristics that make them uniquely vulnerable to contagious collapse they are subject to extensive preventive and protective regulation. Furthermore, it was shown in chapter 3 that securities business is potentially riskier than conventional banking and that to the extent banks are permitted to engage in such business the risks to the financial system as a whole may be increased — even though some, even perhaps most, banks may use their securities powers to reduce overall risk. Finally, it was suggested that increased systemic risk arising from financial diversification has implications for the breadth and scale of the lender of last resort function.

Yet if, as has been suggested, there are significant economies of scope to be gained from combining banking and securities activities, the key question for policymakers is whether it is possible to devise a financial structure that will allow these economies to be exploited while insulating banks from securities market risks. That is the central issue to be addressed in this chapter. The first section examines the various policy alternatives, while the second focuses on the regulatory approach adopted in North America, Europe and Japan, drawing on the discussion of earlier chapters.

Essentially, there are three broad approaches to the regulation of banks' securities activities.[1] The first, very simply, is to prohibit the combination of these two businesses within a single organization. At the opposite extreme regulatory authorities may allow banking and securities business to be freely intermingled within the same legal entity, as in the case of universal banks. Finally, by way of compromise, an attempt may be made to construct a financial market regime in which banks undertake securities business on terms which segregate the risks incurred by the bank and its related securities entity.

Separation of the banking and securities industries through the imposition of statutory barriers involves heavy but unquantifiable costs in the form of economies of scope foregone and the apparatus of enforcement. Among other disadvantages of this approach is the difficulty of defining banks' permissible activities in a situation where the distinction between traditional bank lending and securities operations is becoming increasingly blurred. Furthermore, even statutory barriers cannot prevent banks being exposed to securities markets through, for instance, lending to securities firms. Indeed, such exposure was a major concern during the stock market crash of 1987.[2] Nevertheless, a complete prohibition on the riskier types of securities activities, including dealing in and underwriting equities, does limit the scope for risk-taking by banks while confining the lender of last resort function to deposit-taking institutions undertaking conventional banking business. Under this regime, regulation is strictly functional, with bank and securities market regulators having separate, non-overlapping jurisdictions.

The universal banking model lies at the opposite end of the spectrum. Here economies of scope can be maximized and it is left to the bank to decide whether it can conduct its securities business more efficiently through separately capitalized subsidiaries, through a holding company structure, or through the bank entity itself. Whatever the corporate structure there are no regulatory constraints on intra-group financial transactions (though Chinese walls may inhibit transfers of information) and risks are permitted to flow freely from one part of the conglomerate to any other part. In other words, the bank is exposed to all risks incurred within the group. This is so, even if the bank seeks to use a holding company structure to shield itself from its securities affiliate — as the recent Swiss court case involving Credit Suisse has demonstrated (see p. 151–2). Furthermore, any bank that failed to stand behind a securities subsidiary within a universal banking system would be savagely treated by financial markets.[3]

Under a universal banking regime it is clearly essential that the regulatory/supervisory function be organized along institutional lines. Since major problems arising in a bank's securities arm would expose the bank itself to the risk of insolvency, it makes no sense to regulate the two functions separately. Therefore, a single agency should be given regulatory responsibility for the activities of the whole group.

An argument could be made for requiring such mixed banking-securities businesses to adhere to more stringent capital adequacy standards than specialist stand-alone banks and securities firms. The capital 'penalty' would reflect the additional social costs associated with the higher risk of bank failure and the fact that, in the case of banking conglomerates, the lender of last resort function would have to be extended to securities activities since these would be inseparable from the banking function. Indeed, the strongest argument against universal banking, to be set against its undoubted merits in terms of operational efficiency, is that it widens the official safety net to non-bank activities.

Policymakers are therefore faced with a dilemma. On the one hand, formal separation of banking and securities business may involve costly inefficiencies; on the other hand, a permissive regime in which the two businesses can be freely mixed creates risks for the financial system, for the deposit insurance fund and for the lender of last resort. And because neither approach meets the twin policy objectives of efficiency and safety, much attention has been given to devising a third option which might enable banking groups to diversify into securities business while containing securities market risks within the bank's securities unit. Any such scheme which claims to resolve the apparent conflict between efficiency and safety deserves particulary careful consideration.

The first step in seeking to insulate a bank from the risks incurred by its securities operations is to separately incorporate those operations. Whether this should be done through a holding company structure, in which the bank and the securities firm become subsidiaries of the holding company and affiliates of each other, or whether the securities firm should be a subsidiary of the bank, is a matter for debate.[4] The preferred view appears to be that there is less risk of legal separation being overturned by the courts and the bank found liable for the obligations of its related securities firm, if a holding company structure is used. In other words such a structure makes it less likely that the courts will 'pierce the corporate veil'. As one US commentator has put it:

> piercing cross-wide [through the holding company] would be less likely than piercing upward [through the bank]. That is, if a nonbank subsidiary failed, the likelihood that a banking subsidiary would be held liable for its debts is considerably smaller than the (already small) likelihood that the parent holding company would be held liable.[5]

Whatever form of corporate structure is chosen, the next step is to construct firewalls between the bank and its related securities firm to ensure, so far as possible, full legal, economic and market separation. Broadly, these firewalls are of three kinds: they may place restrictions on intra-group financial transactions, they may seek to separate the identity of the bank and securities firm, and they may require separate management.[6] In addition, Chinese walls may be introduced which aim to prevent conflict of interest abuses by restricting information flows within the group.

Restrictions on financial transactions, or 'funding firewalls' are intended to prevent a bank from becoming directly exposed to its securities affiliate/subsidiary through extensions of credit or the acquisition of bad assets.[7] Funding firewalls do, however, have several shortcomings as an insulating device. In the first place, a bank, under the pressure of events, may well breach the walls, in contravention of the law. Several examples have already been cited in chapter 3. Secondly, situations may arise where a securities firm may need the support of its banking affiliate/parent, and where denial of that support could trigger a collapse. The President of the Federal Reserve Bank of New York, Mr Gerald Corrigan, has suggested that in such circumstances funding firewalls could become 'walls of fire'.[8]

Thirdly, while funding firewalls seeks to prevent contagion through the assets side of a bank's balance sheet, the more serious problems are likely to arise on the liabilities side — that is through confidence-induced deposit withdrawals. Even if effective asset insulation were achieved this would not ensure protection on the liabilities side. Finally, funding firewalls involve important costs. They are difficult and expensive to enforce and they deny to diversified financial groups the benefits of a group funding role for the in-house bank.

Firewalls may also be used to separate in the public mind the identity of a bank and its related securities firm. Such separation is intended to prevent contagion via confidence effects in the event that the securities firm should experience publicized financial difficulties. Restrictions under this heading may include (in the extreme) prohibition on joint marketing of bank and securities firm products, separate premises for the two businesses and a ban on the use of similar names. Where joint marketing is permitted, a minimum safeguard would be contractual documentation making it clear that the bank is not liable for the obligations of securities firm products. The major disadvantage of this class of restriction is that it limits economies of scope on the marketing side and, in the case of a separate premises requirement, adds very significantly to operating costs.

Finally, firewalls may require separate management of a bank and its related securities firm, by prohibiting common directors, officers or employees and mandating separate accounts and record-keeping. Such restrictions are aimed primarily at reinforcing legal separation of the two businesses. However, once again the costs may be heavy, since a fragmented management structure is hardly conducive to successful exploitation of economies of scope. Furthermore, in times of crisis — the very contingency for which firewalls are built — it may be too much to expect that management will remain separate.[9]

In addition to these prudential safeguards, it is likely that regulators of banking conglomerates will wish to establish Chinese walls designed to prevent conflict of interest abuses and unfair competition. In particular, a bank may be prevented from disclosing to its related securities firm any non-public customer information relating to the creditworthiness of an issuer or other customer of the securities firm. From the point of view of securing competitive equality, such a restriction may be desirable, but it also erodes the potential benefits to be derived from financial diversification.[10]

In summary, the separate incorporation of securities activities, buttressed by firewalls that seek to insulate the related bank legally and managerially as well as in terms of corporate identity, may go some way towards protecting the bank from non-bank risks. In such a regime the hope would be that the lender of last resort function could be confined to the bank. And to the extent that risks were segregated in this way regulation could be organized along functional lines — although any doubts about the effectiveness of the insulating mechanism would call for some form of institutional supervision.

From this brief review it is obvious that the effectiveness of firewalls in insulating a bank from the risks incurred by a related securities firm will depend on the height of the walls and the rigour with which they are enforced. At the extreme, firewalls may impose such severe constraints on intra-group financial, marketing and managerial relationships as to negate the benefits of diversification — in effect internalizing Glass–Steagall-type barriers within the diversified group and thereby eliminating all economies of scope. Even so, there can be no assurance that a bank will not be adversely affected by any problems experienced within its securities subsidiary/affiliate. Indeed, recent episodes involving, inter alia, Drexel Burnham Lambert and British and Commonwealth Merchant Bank (pp. 115–6), not to mention numerous earlier US cases, suggest that cross-infection on the liabilities side may defeat all efforts to insulate the banking entity. Certainly, this is the view of several leading regulators, as typified by the following comments of Mr Gerald Corrigan:

> what the marketplace tells us with almost unfailing regularity is that in times of stress, some parts of a financial entity cannot safely be insulated from the problems of affiliated entities. Investors, creditors and even managers and directors simply do not generally behave in that fashion and the larger the problem the less likely they are to do so. Because this pattern of behaviour seems so dominant and because the authorities throughout the world generally frame their policies with this in mind, there seems to me little doubt that taken to an extreme, absolute firewalls can aggravate problems and instabilities rather than contain or limit them.[11]

It would seem, then, that attempts to reconcile the conflicting objectives of efficiency and safety through the use of firewalls are unlikely to succeed — and may even be counter-productive. In recognition of this fact, a number of ingenious proposals have been put forward by academic economists in an attempt to square the circle.

One such proposal is based on the idea of the 'narrow bank'.[12] Under this scheme financial holding companies (FHCs) would be free to engage, through separate subsidiaries, in any business activity (including non-financial activities). However, a bank entity within the FHC structure would be required to operate as an *insured* money market mutual fund, accepting insured deposits and investing in highly liquid, safe securities in the form of government obligations. In effect, the deposit-taking function would be separated from the lending function, the latter being conducted by separately incorporated FHC lending subsidiaries wholly funded by uninsured liabilities such as commercial paper. The bank could not, legally, bail out a non-bank affiliate (since its assets would have to consist entirely of government securities), the possibility of contagion would be minimized if not altogether eliminated and deposit insurance, although retained for confidence reasons, would not be strictly necessary.

A variant of the narrow bank proposal is the idea of a 'secure depository'.[13] Here banks would be able to hold only high quality marketable assets traded on well-organized exchanges. Regulatory capital would be calculated daily and subject to immediate corrective action in the event of any shortfall — an approach similar to that currently adopted by securities market regulators. All liabilities of the bank would be insured although, as with the narrow bank, prompt corrective action would make deposit insurance very much a second line of defence. The secure depository could be part of a financial conglomerate whose non-bank activities would not need to be circumscribed in any way. The commercial lending function would have to be undertaken by a separate non-bank affiliate whose obligations would be uninsured. Transactions between a secure depository and an affiliate could not threaten the solvency of the depository since the latter's assets would be marked to market daily. Therefore there would be no need for firewalls.

The authors of the secure depository proposal have also suggested as an alternative the 'secured deposit' approach.[14] Under this scheme banks would be able to conduct any activity they wished but their deposit liabilities would have to be collateralized with marketable assets which would be placed in the legal custody of a third party. Loans that could not be securitized would be funded by uninsured liabilities. Rather than ensuring the safety of the corporate entity that accepts deposits, the purpose here would be to ensure the safety of deposits within a larger corporate entity. The secured deposit scheme would therefore do away with the need for separate incorporation of risky activities and allow financial institutions to function as German-style universal banks, with no activity constraints or firewalls.

The great difficulty with each of these proposals, apart from the fact that they involve a major restructuring of banking as we know it, is their failure to ensure broad-based financial stability.[15] A newly defined core banking system, embracing marketable assets funded by insured deposits, would be protected. But the key problem for bank regulators has always been the funding of non-marketable commercial loans. Under each of these schemes commercial lending would be conducted outside the core banking system but would presumably be funded, as at present, by short-term liabilities. These would be uninsured deposits in all but name. The familiar problems of deposit runs, forced asset disposals and contagious crises of confidence would therefore be merely shifted to other areas of the financial marketplace.

For instance, under the secure depository proposal commercial lending could be undertaken by a finance affiliate whose obligations would not be insured. Such finance companies would be far more vulnerable to funding crises than are present-day banks enjoying the protection of deposit insurance. Furthermore, it is far from clear that a multiple collapse of finance companies would be any less devastating for the financial system and the economy as a whole than would be the multiple failure of conventional banks. Finally, in times of stress it is reasonable to expect that there would be a massive transfer of funds from the uninsured to the insured financial sectors, as lenders sought to safeguard their assets. The potential for such large-scale destabilizing movements of funds would, arguably, increase the fragility of the financial system and defeat the whole purpose of the proposed reforms.

It is difficult to avoid the conclusion that there is a problem here without a solution. Policymakers may give precedence to the safety and soundness of the financial system by separating the banking industry from securities markets — with whatever loss of efficiency and competitiveness that such a division may entail. Alternatively, they can give priority to efficiency and the exploitation of economies of scope by allowing banks to engage freely in securities activities — while accepting a much greater potential for contagious financial disorders and a correspondingly larger role for the lender of last resort. However, attempts to achieve both safety and efficiency by using the apparatus of firewalls, separate legal entities and other risk insulation techniques promise neither safety nor efficiency — and quite possibly achieve the worst of all worlds by combining costly restrictions with hard-to-detect risk 'seepage'.

## National Practice

Having analysed the various policy alternatives for regulating banks' securities activities it is necessary to review national practice in this area. One clear trend to emerge from the discussion that follows is the increasing determination of national authorities to permit banks to participate in securities markets. However, there is no common approach to managing the risks associated with financial diversification, within individual countries policy has tended to shift erratically and the latest moves towards liberalization generally lack a firm analytical base.

### *United States*

The Glass–Steagall Act represented an unequivocal decision by the US Congress to separate the risks associated with commercial and investment banking. However, the statute left an important loophole in overseas markets which US regulatory authorities were happy to tolerate in order to strengthen US banks' competitive position abroad. As described in chapter 4, the strict segregation of domestic banking and securities business was relaxed during the 1980s as a result of a number of decisions by the Federal Reserve Board, exercising its discretionary authority under the Bank Holding Company Act.

These moves culminated in the decision of September 1990 to allow a bank holding company's 'Section 20 subsidiary' to underwrite corporate debt and equity securities on a limited scale and subject to detailed firewall requirements. On the face of it the Federal Reserve Board appeared to be giving its support to a new regulatory regime, in which risk segregation techniques such as separate incorporation and extensive firewalls were to be used as a means of allowing banks expanded securities powers without widening the official safety net.

However, the reality was somewhat different. The quantitative limits imposed on securities business undertaken by Section 20 subsidiaries are designed both to meet the statutory wording of the Glass–Steagall Act and to minimize the overall risks incurred by the securities subsidiary. In other words, bank holding companies are being allowed to engage in potentially risky securities activities but on a scale that would be highly unlikely to jeopardize the solvency of the securities subsidiary, still less the bank. In this situation, firewalls are being employed only as a back-stop, rather than as a central mechanism for segregating risks. The Section 20 subsidiaries therefore represent a hybrid solution to regulating banks' securities activities — involving both costly firewalls and a severe limitation on the extent of banks' participation in securities markets.

The Bush Administration's proposals for repealing Glass–Steagall, introduced in February 1991, rely much more heavily on risk segregation. This is to be achieved through a financial services holding company (FSHC) structure in which the bank and its securities affiliate would be separated by firewalls and the official safety net would be explicitly confined to the bank. In the Treasury's words, 'creditors of the FSHC or [non-bank] financial affiliates should receive no federal protection in the event of FSHC insolvency'. In contrast to the limits currently placed on bank holding companies' Section 20 subsidiaries, a bank's securities affiliate could, under the Administration's scheme, undertake securities business on whatever scale it chose — subject, of course, to the SEC's regulatory capital requirements for securities firms. Consistent with this risk segregation regime, regulatory responsibilities would be allocated on a functional basis.

The authors of the Administration's proposal evidently harbour some doubts about the effectiveness of their attempts to segregate risks. Thus in order to allow for the possibility of cross-infection banks which choose to have securities affiliates will have to maintain especially high capital ratios. Furthermore, the bank regulator is to be given 'umbrella oversight' of the holding company, thereby providing an element of institutional regulation designed to detect and correct problems within non-bank affiliates that could pose a threat to the bank. In short, the apparatus of risk segregation is in this case being combined with other safeguards more properly associated with the universal banking model — with adverse competitive implications for US banks (see below).

However, the main criticism of the Administration's proposal is that the holding company structure and firewalls which lie at the heart of the scheme are likely to prove redundant. There is already ample evidence to suggest that a bank will be quickly infected by a non-bank affiliate's problems, firewalls or no firewalls, one of the most spectacular examples being provided by the collapse of Drexel Burnham Lambert.

On 13 February 1990 Drexel Burnham Lambert Group, Inc. ('Drexel'), the holding company parent of Drexel Burnham Lambert Inc., a major securities firm, and Drexel Burnham Lambert Government Securities Inc., a registered government securities dealer, filed for chapter 11 bankruptcy.[16] Drexel had become increasingly dependent on short-term credit markets, borrowing as much as $1 billion on an unsecured basis, largely through the issuance of commercial paper. In December 1989 Standard and Poor's had reduced its rating on Drexel's commercial paper, with the result that

Drexel's borrowing from this source dried up. But because a large proportion of Drexel's assets were not readily marketable (in particular it had a
large portfolio of 'junk' bonds) its balance sheet could not be contracted in
line with its reduced funding capacity. The result was an acute liquidity
crisis, described by the Chairman of the Federal Reserve Board, Mr Alan
Greenspan, in the following terms:

> As doubts emerged about the ability of Drexel to meet its obligations in a
> timely and predictable way, it suffered what in banking terms would be
> called a 'run'. The run extended across the various units that make up
> Drexel — including both regulated and unregulated affiliates, and including
> affiliates that seemed to be solvent, as well as those whose status was in
> doubt.[17]

Of particular significance was the fact that Drexel's government securities
subsidiary, which was adequately capitalized, stringently regulated and
apparently soundly run, found its access to funds cut off when questions
were raised about the health of the parent company. The unmistakable
implication is that all parts of a financial conglomerate that rely on short-
term borrowing become vulnerable when confidence in *any* part of the
organization is shaken.

This unwelcome message from the markets appears to have had a major
impact on the thinking of at least some regulators. In July 1990 the
Mr Greenspan delivered the following congressional testimony, revealing
his own deep misgivings on the whole risk segregation issue:

> The Board has for some time held the view that strong insulating firewalls
> would both protect banks (and taxpayers) from the risk of new activities and
> limit the extension of the safety net subsidy that would place independent
> competitors at a disadvantage. However, recent events, including the rapid
> spread of market pressures to separately regulated and well-capitalized units
> of Drexel when their holding company was unable to meet its maturing
> commercial paper obligations, have raised serious questions about the ability
> of firewalls to insulate the unit of a holding company from funding problems
> of another. Partially as a result, the Board is in the process of re-evaluating
> both the efficacy and desirability of substantial firewalls between a bank and
> some of its affiliates. It is clear that high and thick firewalls reduce synergies
> and raise costs for financial institutions, a significant problem in increasingly
> competitive financial markets. If they raise costs and may not be effective,
> we must question why we are imposing these kinds of firewalls at all.[18]

Despite the lessons of the Drexel affair and growing official scepticism
about the effectiveness of firewalls, the US Administration has proposed a
new financial structure in which the stability of the US banking system will
depend on the ability of firewalls to insulate banks from securities market

risks. At the same time the requirements that banks with securities affiliates must have additional capital will undermine US banks' competitiveness vis-à-vis their European counterparts without doing anything to neutralize the most potent source of cross-infection — namely, confidence-induced withdrawals of funding.

## Canada

Historically, Canada's banking and securities industries were separated under the 'four pillars' policy which established formal legal barriers between banking, insurance, securities and trust business. These domestic restrictions did not, however, prevent Canadian banks, like their US counterparts, from conducting investment banking operations through their subsidiaries in London and elsewhere. As described in chapter 10, banks have been permitted to acquire domestic securities subsidiaries since 1987 but regulatory policy governing the relationship between a bank and its related securities entity has undergone important changes during the course of this liberalization process.

The Government's 1985 Green Paper setting out its proposals for financial reform followed a risk-segregation approach, utilizing a holding company structure and strict firewalls between a bank and its non-bank affiliates. This was similar to the scheme now adopted by the US Administration. However, in a major policy switch the Government, in its subsequent 1986 Blue Paper, abandoned the risk segregation model in favour of a more permissive regime in which banks would be able to diversify through securities subsidiaries with relatively few restrictions on intra-group financial transactions (in effect low firewalls). The legislation submitted to Parliament in 1990, by lifting these residual restrictions, marked a further shift towards the universal banking model — although the outer shell of risk segregation was retained in the form of a separate incorporation requirement for banks' securities (and other non-bank) business.

Consistent with this approach, the Government has attempted to introduce an institutional element into its supervisory arrangements, in particular by reaching accords with the various provincial authorities that regulate banks' securities subsidiaries. In effect these agreements give the federal bank regulator the right to be consulted on regulatory matters affecting the solvency of a securities subsidiary. Nevertheless, the federal/provincial division of regulatory responsibilities for banks and securities firms makes it very difficult to achieve a satisfactory institutional oversight of banks' securities activities.

## Europe

In launching its single European market programme the EEC Commission at the outset adopted a financial regime based on the Swiss/German universal banking model. That is to say, banking was defined broadly to include securities business, questions of corporate financial structure were left to individual banking organizations to decide as a purely commercial matter, and no attempt was made to segregate banking from non-banking risks within financial conglomerates.

Having prescribed, without much debate or analysis, a universal banking regime the EEC Commission ran into difficulties when it sought to formulate a capital adequacy directive for mixed securities/banking businesses. On the one hand it was recognized that banks, unlike securities firms, are vulnerable to contagious funding crises and should therefore be subject to a stricter definition of regulatory capital than that applied to securities houses. On the other hand, in the interests of competitive equality, it was proposed that a bank should be able to apply the more permissive definition of regulatory capital to its own securities operations. Under the EEC scheme, therefore, banks and their securities activities are fully integrated from the point of view of risk exposure but treated separately for the purposes of capital adequacy assessment. An important — and incongruous — element of functional supervision is thereby introduced into a pooled risk regime that calls for an institutional approach to prudential regulation. The dangers associated with the EEC's ambivalence on this issue are more fully spelt out in chapter 10.

A further difficulty arises from the multifarious arrangements within the EEC for regulating banks' securities business. In general, securities activities carried out by banks on their own balance sheets are regulated by the banking supervisor but this is not necessarily so — for instance UK banking and securities supervisors have overlapping responsibilities in such cases. Furthermore, where banks' securities business is conducted through separately incorporated subsidiaries, the securities subsidiary may be the primary responsibility of the securities supervisor (as in the UK and Spain).[19] In chapter 6 it was shown, in the UK context, how ill-suited such functional regulation is to a universal banking regime.

Quite apart from any shortcomings in their respective regulatory regimes it is clearly unsatisfactory that the EEC and the USA should be moving in opposite directions on the key issue of risk segregation. Within Europe it must be assumed — as the Swiss court did in the Credit Suisse case — that a bank will always stand behind a related securities firm. In the USA the Administration's proposed holding company and firewall structure is explicitly designed to ensure that a troubled securities firm is *not* supported by its bank affiliate. There is a further implication that within Europe the lender of last resort function may have to be extended (directly or indirectly) to bank-related securities firms. In contrast, the US Administration's scheme is intended to confine the official safety net strictly to the banking sector.

The coexistence of these diametrically opposed regulatory structures is fraught with difficulties. In times of global financial stress there may be a temptation, within Europe, for lenders to shift their exposure from stand-alone to bank-related securities firms, on the grounds that the latter are more likely to receive official support. More importantly, in such circumstances there will be a strong inducement for lenders to withdraw funding from US securities firms (whether or not bank-related) in favour of securities firms affiliated to European banks. In the meantime US banks which are part of diversified financial groups will face a competitive disadvantage vis-à-vis their European counterparts because of their mandatory holding company structure, higher capital requirements and restrictive firewalls.[20]

## Japan

We have seen that after the Second World War the USA, as occupying power, imported the main restrictions of the Glass–Steagall Act into Japan. Nevertheless, the separation of banking and securities business has been less complete in Japan, where banks, unlike their US counterparts, are empowered to invest in equity securities, and Japanese banking groups have been able to acquire major interests in securities firms through a complex web of cross-shareholdings. These differences apart, the Japanese authorities have in effect extended the official safety net to major securities houses which typically have direct access to the Bank of Japan's discount window. Paradoxically, therefore, statutory risk segregation has failed to confine the lender of last resort function to the banking sector.

Since the mid 1980s the Japanese authorities have been considering proposals for dismantling the present constraints on banks' securities activities. In June 1991 the Ministry of Finance appeared to be favouring a proposal under which banks would be able to establish separate securities subsidiaries, but the question of what, if any, firewalls might be required remained undecided — as did the more fundamental issue of whether the new structure should continue to segregate bank from non-bank risks. Indeed, in the Japanese context the whole debate about banks' securities powers is linked to concepts of fairness rather than to the more familiar western policy goals of safety and soundness and efficiency. Thus the Ministry of Finance is evidently inclined to limit the pace at which City banks can expand their securities activities because of the marketing advantages they enjoy in the form of extensive branch networks[21] – an approach that turns on its head the traditional case for expanded securities powers based on economies of scope.

# Conclusion

From the above survey it should be apparent that, in addressing the issue of financial diversification, national policymakers and regulators have only one thing in common – a desire to extend the boundaries of banks' permissible securities activities. How this should be done, whether risks should be segregated and what the role of the lender of last resort should be – all these matters are the subject of divergent and often confusing national initiatives. The policy disarray surrounding the key issue of financial market structure has disturbing implications for the stability of the international banking system which are examined in the concluding chapter.

## Notes

1 For general discussions of banking structure see: Financial Structure and Supervision in Germany, Japan and the United Kingdom, Appendix I, in Statement by Gerald Corrigan, President of the Federal Reserve Bank of New York, before the US Senate Committee on Banking, Housing and Urban Affairs, 3 May 1990; Alton Gilbert 'A comparison of proposals to restructure the US financial system', *Federal Reserve Bank of St Louis Review*, July–August (1988) pp. 58–75; Richard Herring and Anthony Santomero, 'The corporate structure of financial conglomerates', *Journal of Financial Services Research*, December (1990) pp. 471–97; Robert Litan, *What Should Banks Do?* (Brookings Institution, Washington DC, 1987); *Systemic Risks in Securities Markets* (OECD, Paris, 1991).

2 See 'The October 1987 market break', US Securities and Exchange Commission, February 1988, pp. 5-24 to 5-30.

3 When Banca Nazionale del Lavoro (BNL) failed to honour the borrowing of Agrifactoring, in which it held a 50 per cent equity stake, several international banks decided to freeze or withdraw their credit and trading lines with BNL. The market's response may also have been influenced by the fact that BNL provided Agrifactoring's management. See Haig Simonian, 'Top banks withdraw BNL credit lines', *Financial Times*, 20 June 1991, p. 26.

4  See, for instance, *Bank Powers: Insulating Banks from the potential risks of expanded activities* (US General Accounting Office, Washington DC, April 1987), pp. 26–41; and *Mandate for Change: restructuring the banking industry*, (Federal Deposit Insurance Corporation, Washington DC, August 1987), pp. 105–25.

5  Samuel Chase, 'The bank holding company – a superior device for expanding activities?', in *Policies for a More Competitive Financial System* (Federal Reserve Bank of Boston, Boston, June 1972), p. 82.

6  For an assessment of firewalls see 'Using "firewalls" in a post-Glass–Steagall banking environment', statement of Richard Fogel, Assistant Comptroller General, before the Subcommittee on Telecommunications and Finance, Committee on Energy and Commerce, US House of Representatives, 13 April 1988.

7  In addition, funding firewalls may be advocated as a means of preventing banks using cheap insured deposits to fund their securities affiliates, thereby allegedly conferring a competitive advantage on bank-related securities firms. However, to the extent that independent securities firms also have access to bank finance this argument for firewalls is unpersuasive.

8  Statement before the Senate Committee on Banking, Housing and Urban Affairs, 3 May 1990, p. 38.

9  See the example of the *Amoco Cadiz* cited on pp. 48–9.

10 An assessment of the information advantages enjoyed by universal banks is provided by Alfred Steinherr and Christian Huveneers, *Universal Banks: the prototype of successful banks in the integrated European market* (Centre for European Policy Studies, Brussels, 1989), pp. 6–7.

11 Gerald Corrigan, Statement before the Senate Committee on Banking, Housing and Urban Affairs, 3 May 1990, p. 39.

12 See Robert Litan, *What Should Banks Do?* (Brookings Institution, Washington DC, 1987) pp. 144–89.

13 See George Benston, Dan Brumbaugh, Jack Guttentag, Richard Herring, George Kaufman, Robert Litan and Kenneth Scott, *Blueprint for restructuring America's depository institutions* (Brookings Institution, Washington DC, 1989), pp. 19–23.

14 Ibid., pp. 23–5.

15 A proposal advanced by Gerald Corrigan is vulnerable to the same criticism. He would distinguish between banks authorized to accept insured transaction deposits and financial holding companies authorized to offer uninsured transaction accounts. Under the proposal commercial activities could be combined with non-bank financial activities and non-bank financial activities could be combined with banking, but commercial activities could not be combined with banking. Commercial-financial conglomerates would not have access to the lender of last resort but since the financial activities of these groups would be integrated with the non-commercial financial-banking sector, there would be every possibility of cross-infection spreading within the financial system

whenever the financial unit of a commercial concern failed. See Gerald Corrigan, Financial Market Structure: A longer view, (Federal Reserve Bank of New York, *Annual Report*, 1986), pp. 3–54.

16  For a full account of Drexel's collapse see Statement of Richard Breeden, Chairman US Securities and Exchange Commission, before the Committee on Banking, Housing and Urban Affairs, US Senate, concerning the Bankruptcy of Drexel Burnham Lambert Group Inc., 1 March 1990.

17  See Testimony before the Subcommittee on Economic and Commercial Law, Committee on the Judiciary, US House of Representatives, 1 March 1990, p. 14.

18  See Testimony before the Committee on Banking, Housing and Urban Affairs, US Senate, 12 July 1990, p. 14.

19  See *Systemic Risks in Securities Markets* (OECD, Paris, 1991), pp. 37–8.

20  Paradoxically, because independent European securities firms are to be subject to a more stringent definition of regulatory capital than stand-alone US securities houses, they may be placed at a competitive disadvantage (see p. 168).

21  See Naoyuki Isono, 'Recommendations point to liberalizing financial system', *Japan Economic Journal*, 15 June (1991), p. 1.

# 11

# A Risky Experiment

This study has focused on one of the most important changes in the structure of international financial markets since World War Two: namely, the merging of banking and securities activities within financial conglomerates.

The case for financial diversification, based on economies of scope and competitive equality, has prevailed over counter-arguments that emphasize potential conflicts of interest and the possible systemic risks associated with securities business undertaken within banking groups. Accordingly, national policymakers have been pressing for removal of the remaining barriers between banking and securities markets. Indeed, the EEC has now adopted the universal banking model as part of its 1992 financial liberalization programme, while Canada, the USA and Japan are either proposing or implementing major initiatives aimed at expanding banks' securities powers. The likelihood is that before long the traditional distinction between commercial and investment banking will have disappeared throughout the industrialized world.

Yet our understanding of financial markets in general, and the behavioural consequences of such structural change in particular, is quite limited. Perhaps one indication of this is the fact that expert opinion has shifted remarkably over time. The great US financial reforms of the 1930s, embracing the separation of commercial and investment banking and the establishment of federal deposit insurance — reforms which at the time and for many years thereafter were hailed as major stabilizing measures — are now being blamed for the increased incidence of US bank failures.

It is also worth emphasizing that the process of change and the transition to a new regulatory regime can itself be destabilizing, especially when it involves a sudden intensification of competition.

It was shown in chapter 1 that banks are, by their very nature, fragile and prone to contagious collapse. It is for this reason that national authorities in all the main industrial countries have introduced elaborate controls designed to prevent banks from failing and to safeguard the financial system when they do. The suggestion was also made that it is becoming more difficult to ensure banking stability, partly because the internationalization of the financial services industry has removed the protective bulkheads separating one banking jurisdiction from another. The implication is that there is increasing potential for cross-border contagion within the global banking system.

At the same time, banks in many countries have been weakened during the past decade or so by a decline in underlying profitability. Partly, this is due to the revolution in information technology which has eroded the value of the banking franchise by making credit information – a bank's traditional stock-in-trade – more generally available to financial markets. One consequence has been the trend towards securitization which has reduced the demand for bank loans from prime borrowers who in the past might have been expected to provide banks' core lending business.

In addition, the dismantling worldwide of barriers to competition in the financial services industry has had the effect of compressing banks' profit margins. The protection afforded by administered or cartelized interest rates has largely disappeared, so that banks are forced to bid for funds against each other – a process that has involved the extension of interest-bearing chequing accounts and a decline in the proportion of 'free' deposits.[1] Meanwhile cross-border competition between banks is continuing to intensify – a trend that will be given further impetus by the inception of the single European financial market.

It is against this background that banks, bank regulators and national governments the world over have launched a determined drive to break down the remaining barriers between banking and securities markets, thereby greatly enlarging banks' involvement in securities business. There is a clear parallel here with US developments in the 1920s when banks were attracted into securities underwriting and trading by the rapid expansion of corporate securities issues and the displacement of bank borrowing by bond financing. Then, too, the debate focused on securitization, the corporate benefits of financial diversification and the advantages to savers and borrowers of having a full range of financial services under one roof.

The move by US banks into securities markets during the 1920s was followed by the greatest financial calamity the world has known. Contemporary opinion blamed the events of 1929–33 squarely on banks' securities activities and the result was passage of the US Glass–Steagall Act. Since then, expert opinion has swung in the opposite direction and there is now a widespread view among academics and policymakers alike that banks' securities business played little or no part in the financial trauma of the 1930s. However, it has been suggested here that the pendulum may have swung too far and that there are legitimate grounds for believing that banks' securities holdings did contribute to financial destabilization during the critical years preceding the financial crash.

Nor can much comfort be taken on this issue from the more recent experience of countries like Germany and Switzerland that have combined banking and securities business within a universal banking framework. These jurisdictions have hitherto enjoyed relative financial stability but the market environment in which universal banks conduct their operations is changing dramatically in response to international competitive pressures and innovative financing techniques. In short, the robustness of the universal banking model has yet to be tested in conditions of intense competition.

It may be argued that securities markets are themselves more effectively regulated than they used to be and therefore pose less of a risk to banks. For instance, US securities legislation dating from the 1930s provides investor protection of a kind that simply did not exist during the 1920s. On the other hand, the behaviour of securities markets has in recent years become a source of concern, particularly since the October 1987 stock market crash. Indeed, the OECD reported in 1991 that 'it would be prudent for securities regulators to work on the assumption that securities markets have become more susceptible to large, precipitous falls which would be rapidly transmitted around the world'.[2] Furthermore, the pace of product innovation in securities markets is proceeding at such a rate that risks in this area are becoming increasingly difficult to assess.

Given all these circumstances the central question that has to be addressed is whether it is desirable from a prudential standpoint for banks to be permitted to engage freely in securities markets as is now happening on a global scale. This study has examined in some detail the arguments about the riskiness of securities operations and the risk characteristics of combined banking/securities businesses. What emerges from the analysis is that securities activities are not inherently riskier or less risky than banking but that they do provide opportunities for additional risk-taking by aggressively managed institutions. Furthermore, it is a disturbing fact that where wider powers have been granted to deposit-taking firms these powers have tended to be used in a risk-enhancing manner — the US savings and loan industry's response to expanded powers introduced in 1982 being a case in point.

Some policymakers believe that banks can be insulated from the risks incurred by their securities operations. However, even if legal and economic separation of the banking and securities units can be achieved, the market perception will be that the credit standing of the two entities is inextricably linked. Time and again we have seen funding withdrawn from financial firms which are sound in their own right but are nevertheless associated in the public mind with problems arising within affiliated institutions — one of the most notable examples being provided by the collapse in 1990 of the Drexel Burnham Lambert group.

Even if one were to accept the case for breaking down the barriers between banking and securities markets, there can be no case at all for carrying out the operation in the present manner. The comparative survey of regulatory arrangements for combined banking and securities businesses demonstrates only too clearly the conflicting approaches adopted by the USA and the EEC, in particular, and the more general policy confusion that exists both within and between the major financial centres. Whether or not an expansion of banks' securities operations is inherently dangerous, it can certainly become so if national policy initiatives in this area are not carefully coordinated within an appropriate regulatory framework.

One must also question the timing of present moves towards financial diversification. As already noted, the banking industry worldwide has been seriously weakened by a number of factors in a situation where financial institutions are also having to adjust to revolutionary changes in information technology and a proliferation of innovative financial instruments. Banks now face the prospect of intensified cross-border competition as a result of the EEC's 1992 financial reforms. The securities industry is meanwhile experiencing similar upheavals. On the principle that for financial markets 'one miracle at a time' is enough, this would seem to be a particularly unsuitable time to be embarking on a further large-scale financial restructuring involving the fusion of banking and securities business.

Finally, if policymakers are to conduct financial experiments it is desirable that they should do so on a limited scale so that any unforeseen destabilizing consequences can be contained. In the present instance, however, competitive pressures are prompting the USA, Japan and Canada (among other countries) to respond to the EEC's financial liberalization programme by allowing their banks to offer a similar range of financial services — including securities business. A principal declared objective of those who are responsible for these reforms is to ensure that financial institutions compete with one another on a level playing field. However, in the light of the arguments presented here there is a serious danger that the level playing surface may be no more than thin ice.

# Notes

1   For large UK banks non-interest-bearing sterling deposits were typically as much as 50 per cent of total deposits in 1970, but by 1990 this proportion had fallen to around 15 per cent. See Bank of England Banking Act Report for 1990–1, p. 9.

2   *Systematic Risks in Securities Markets: financial market trends* (OECD, Paris, June 1991) p. 14.

# 12

# Postscript: The Bank of Credit and Commerce International

As this book was being prepared for publication, news broke of the forced closure of Bank of Credit and Commerce International (BCCI). This was possibly the most important international banking collapse of all time; it was certainly the biggest case of banking fraud; it was the first occasion in recent times that a large European-based bank had been allowed to default on ordinary depositors; and the manner of the collapse illustrated several of the propositions advanced in this study. It was therefore decided to add a postscript chapter in order to clarify some of the policy issues arising out of the BCCI affair.

BCCI was established in 1972 by a group of Pakistani bankers with capital contributions from Bank of America and substantial Middle East investors. Bank of America sold its stake in 1980, leaving prominent Arab financiers, notably the Bin Mahfouz family of Saudi Arabia and the family of Sheikh Zayed Bin-Nahyan, the ruler of Abu Dhabi, as the leading shareholders.

By 1990 BCCI was one of the largest private banks in the world, with stated assets of around $20bn, and branches operating in some seventy countries. This global banking network was managed through an unusual corporate structure, involving a parent holding company in Luxembourg (BCCI Holdings), with the main banking business split between two subsidiaries incorporated in different offshore jurisdictions − BCCI SA in Luxembourg and BCCI Overseas in the Cayman Islands. Since the shareholders were based in the Middle East and the operating headquarters in London, this complex structure was to raise fundamental questions about corporate and regulatory control − as described below.

Despite rapid expansion in the 1970s and 1980s, BCCI had a controversial reputation in financial markets. None of the credit-rating agencies accorded the bank a rating; it had a poor financial record, having incurred a $150mn loss on options trading in 1985, and overall losses of $48mn and $498mn in 1988 and 1989 respectively; while in 1988 its officers were the subject of money-laundering charges in the USA to which BCCI pleaded guilty in 1990.

Reflecting growing concern about BCCI's affairs, a college of regulators was established in 1987 that first met in May 1988. Initially, the college consisted of regulators from the UK, Switzerland, Spain and Luxembourg, but the membership was expanded to include Hong Kong and the Cayman Islands in 1989 and France and the United Arab Emirates (UAE) thereafter. From 1987, too, Price Waterhouse became sole auditor of the group, a function previously shared with Ernst and Whinney: evidently this action was taken in response to pressure from regulators who believed that by engaging different auditors for its two principal banking subsidiaries BCCI was obscuring its global operations.

After BCCI executives had been convicted in the USA of laundering drug money, the Bank of England asked Price Waterhouse to carry out an investigation of BCCI's UK activities under Section 39 of the 1987 UK Banking Act.[1] Price Waterhouse reported that BCCI's systems of control were adequate and no further action was considered necessary. However, in April 1990, Price Waterhouse reported a number of false or deceitful accounting transactions booked in the Caymans and other offshore centres. At the same time it became apparent that BCCI would need a further injection of capital and it was agreed between the bank and its main regulators that a major restructuring of the group was called for. Accordingly, the Abu Dhabi authorities increased their equity stake in the bank from 39 per cent to 77 per cent by buying out Saudi investors, while also providing $600mn of new capital; the operating headquarters of the bank was moved from London to Abu Dhabi; and a reorganization committee was established that later proposed a restructuring of the group, based on separately incorporated units in London (to be named the European Commercial Bank), Hong Kong (Pacific Commercial Bank) and Abu Dhabi (Emirates Commercial Bank) operating under a holding company in Abu Dhabi.

However, the restructuring plan was stopped in its tracks by other developments. In October 1990 Price Waterhouse revealed the need for a further $1.5bn in funds to cover bad loans, but more significantly the auditors reported that 'the previous management may have colluded with major customers to misstate or disguise the underlying purpose of significant transactions'. Immediately after the October report was received, Mr Swaleh Naqvi, the bank's chief executive, and Mr Agha Hasan Abedi, the bank's founder and president, resigned. Then, in early 1991 an executive of BCCI reported the existence of substantial unrecorded deposits, later estimated at around $600mn. At this point the Bank of England ordered Price Waterhouse to carry out an enquiry into BCCI's affairs under Section 41 of the Banking Act. This report, received by the Bank of England on 25 June showed, in the words of the Bank's Governor, 'evidence of massive and widespread fraud, going back over a number of years'. In particular, the report identified some 6,000 files which had been held personally by Mr Naqvi, the former chief executive, and withheld from the auditors.

It was the June 1991 Price Waterhouse report that led directly to the decision to close BCCI. At 1 pm London time on 5 July 1991, regulators in the UK, Luxembourg, the USA, Switzerland, Spain, France and the Cayman Islands acted together in an unprecedented worldwide swoop to close down the BCCI offices in their own jurisdictions. In support of the UK winding-up petition that followed, the Bank of England alleged that BCCI had been involved in massive fraud, that it was insolvent and that its management was both dishonest and incompetent. Subsequently, on 29 July, a New York Grand Jury brought criminal indictments against BCCI, four of its affiliates, as well as Mr Abedi and Mr Naqvi, the charges being described by the Manhattan district attorney as amounting to 'the largest bank fraud in world financial history'. In a separate move the US Federal Reserve Board announced that it was bringing a $200mn civil action against BCCI for secretly and deceitfully acquiring shares in two US banks — First American Bankshares and National Bank of Georgia — as well as the bankrupt US Central Savings Bank.

The BCCI collapse raises fundamental questions about the way in which global banks are regulated by national authorities. Indeed, one is bound to ask whether financial markets have not become so internationalized that the present segmented regulatory regime, loosely coordinated through a central bankers' club in Basle, is any longer appropriate.

This is by no means the first time that regulatory shortcomings have been exposed; indeed, all previous international initiatives in this area have occurred in the wake of financial calamities.[2] The starting point was the collapse of Germany's Herstatt Bank in 1974, which led to the Basle Concordat in December 1975. This agreement, between the central bank governors of the main industrial countries (subsequently endorsed by other financial centres), introduced guidelines for the division of regulatory responsibilities between national authorities, one of the central principles being that the supervision of foreign banks should be the joint responsibility of parent and host authorities.

The collapse of Banco Ambrosiano's Luxembourg subsidiary in 1982 was the occasion of an unedifying dispute between the Luxembourg and Italian authorities, who both disclaimed responsibility for supervising the Luxembourg entity (a holding company as it happens). Following the Ambrosiano affair an amended version of the Basle Concordat was signed in 1983.

The 1983 Concordat introduced two new regulatory principles. First, it sought to ensure the adequacy of supervisory standards within national jurisdictions by adopting a 'dual key' approach in which parent and host authorities assess the quality of each other's supervision. Second, it focused on consolidated supervision, whereby the parent authority must supervise a bank's worldwide operations, including foreign subsidiaries.

Under the dual key approach, if a host country considers that the supervision of parent institutions of foreign banks on its territory is inadequate it should prohibit or discourage the continued operation of such offices or alternatively impose specific conditions on the conduct of their business.

In addition, if the parent authority considers that the host authority's supervision is inadequate it should 'either extend its supervision, to the degree that is practicable, or it should be prepared to discourage the parent bank from continuing to operate the establishment in question'.[3]

In other words, each national supervisory authority must satisfy itself that banks' foreign operations are being conducted in jurisdictions with sound supervisory practices and that foreign banks to which it is host are subject to adequate supervision in their home jurisdiction. The intention was to reverse the tendency for banks to gravitate to the least-regulated jurisdictions with resulting 'competition in regulatory laxity' between financial centres competing for foreign banking business.

This system should in theory ensure that supervisory standards are aligned on those of the most stringently regulated centres rather than vice versa. For that to happen, however, national authorities in the leading banking centres must be prepared to lock out foreign banks originating from permissive jurisdictions and prevent their own banks from conducting international operations in such locations. In the light of BCCI, it must be doubted whether this key element of the Basle framework is working.

The attempt to ensure adequacy of supervision is buttressed by the other significant innovation of the new Concordat — consolidated supervision. The Concordat states that 'banking supervisory authorities cannot be fully satisfied about the soundness of individual banks unless they can examine the totality of each bank's business worldwide through the technique of consolidation'.[4] The idea is that overall supervision should be strengthened by having parent authorities supervise risks on the basis of banks' global operations.

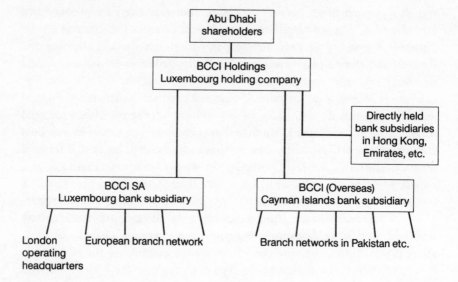

**Figure 12.1** BCCI corporate structure, 1990

Regulatory problems

1   Holding company unregulated.
2   Main operations split between separately located offshore centres.
3   No consolidated supervision.
4   Regulatory responsibilities dispersed within college of regulators: UK, Switzerland, Spain, Luxembourg (May 1988), Hong Kong and Cayman Islands (1989), France and UAE (subsequent).
5   No lender of last resort.
6   Maximum use of secrecy laws.
7   Operating headquarters separated from main shareholders and country of operation.

*Source*: *Financial Times*, 22 July 1991, p. 12

In what may now be viewed as a controversial provision, the Concordat allows for an exception to the consolidation principle. It states that 'where holding companies are at the head of groups that include separately incorporated banks operating in different countries [a precise description of BCCI's corporate structure] the authorities responsible for supervising those banks should endeavour to coordinate their supervision of those banks, taking account of the overall structure of the bank in question'.[5]

BCCI may be viewed as a test case for the Basle Concordat since it appears to have been structured in a way that was intended to minimize regulatory constraints (see figure 12.1). This is an important aspect of the affair because it is precisely those banks that are seeking to avoid regulatory attention that need to be supervised most closely.

In the first place, the parent entity of BCCI was a Luxembourg holding company which escaped regulation under Luxembourg law because it was not classified as a bank. This state of affairs is in itself unsatisfactory, bearing in mind that the collapsed Bank Ambrosiano subsidiary had avoided regulation in Luxembourg for the same reason. Holding companies that own banks should be subject to rigorous supervision – as indeed they are in the USA where the holding company structure is the norm.

Secondly, BCCI's banking operations were split between two main subsidiaries incorporated in different jurisdictions – Luxembourg and the Cayman Islands. This structure ruled out consolidated supervision which was why a college of regulators was established in 1988. However, why was the college not set up earlier? And why was the membership only gradually expanded ultimately to include Hong Kong, the Cayman Islands, France and the UAE? Finally, it is far from clear that a dispersal of regulatory responsibilities among so many national authorities is a safe way of dealing with cases of this kind. Should not *someone* be in charge?

The fact that BCCI was permitted to establish itself and operate for so long within a faulty regulatory framework is surely a central issue in this affair. Once the bank had expanded to become a $20bn multinational institution the regulators faced an awesome choice between a disastrously costly closure and a risky reconstruction.

Furthermore, the closure option was far from straightforward. It was necessary to secure broad agreement among the main regulators since any unilateral action by, say, the UK would have precipitated a disorderly collapse of the whole group. In addition, the Bank of England may have been hampered by the requirements of the 1987 Banking Act. This statute gives the Bank a broad discretion to withdraw authorization from an institution (it is, for instance, unnecessary to prove fraud) but the procedure is cumbersome and includes a requirement to give notice to the institution concerned. That is hardly an appropriate mechanism where fraud is suspected, since the opportunity would be given to remove assets from the jurisdiction, thereby jeopardizing the interests of depositors. The inadequacy of the de-authorization procedure evidently forced the Bank of England to seek liquidation of BCCI, the grounds for which are much narrower and which in this instance required the proof of fraud.

In any event, the decision on whether or not to close a bank is a matter of judgement, and one not lightly taken in a case such as this, where the chief shareholders are apparently willing to make good any capital shortfall.

**Table 12.1.**   Branch network of BCCI SA, Luxembourg, and BCCI (Overseas), Cayman Islands

| BCCI SA branches on 30 June 1991 | | BCCI (Overseas) branches as at 30 June 1991 | |
|---|---|---|---|
| Branch | No. of offices | Branch | No. of offices |
| Luxembourg | 1 | Grand Cayman | 1 |
| Bahrain | 1 | Bahamas | 1 |
| Cyprus | 1 | Bangladesh | 3 |
| Germany | 2 | Barbados | 1 |
| Italy | 1 | China | 1 |
| Japan | 1 | France | 3 |
| Jordan | 3 | Gabon | 3 |
| Mauritius | 1 | India | 1 |
| Netherlands | 1 | Ivory Coast | 2 |
| UAE | 8 | Jamaica | 3 |
| UK | 24 | Kenya | 7 |
| USA | 1 | Korea | 1 |
| Yemen | 2 | Liberia | 1 |
| | | Macau | 1 |
| Total | 47 | Maldives | 1 |
| | | Monaco | 1 |
| | | Oman | 12 |
| | | Pakistan | 3 |
| | | Panama | 2 |
| | | Paraguay | 1 |
| | | Philippines | 1 |
| | | Senegal | 1 |
| | | Seychelles | 1 |
| | | Sierra Leone | 2 |
| | | Sri Lanka | 2 |
| | | Sudan | 3 |
| | | Togo | 1 |
| | | Turkey | 3 |
| | | Total | 63 |

*Source: Financial Times*, 23 July 1991 p. 4.

Indeed, so long as the problems are remediable the interests of depositors are best served by keeping the bank going while ensuring that corrective action is taken. Closure is appropriate only when fraud or other irregularities have infected the whole bank and cannot therefore be cleansed.

On 22 July the UK Prime Minister, Mr John Major, announced that

Lord Justice Bingham would head an enquiry 'into the supervision of BCCI under the Banking Acts; to consider whether the action taken by the UK authorities was appropriate and timely; and to make recommendations'. However, this was a relatively narrow remit and it is important to understand that on the broader question of regulatory reform the problem is one of international rather than specifically UK regulatory weaknesses. The following wider issues need urgently to be addressed:

- Are the informal and broadly-drawn guidelines set out in the Basle Concordat an adequate basis for regulating international banks? Arguably, much tighter rules are needed, particularly as they relate to supervisory standards which vary considerably between financial centres.

  This point is of particular concern with the approach of 1993, when banks incorporated in Luxembourg, for example, will be able to branch automatically into the UK, leaving the UK authorities with no say whatever in the matter. In this context, too, one must question the soundness of a regime in which offshore banking centres compete with one another by offering secrecy, fiscal and regulatory inducements.

- The principle of consolidated supervision that was adopted in 1983 should be more rigorously enforced — particularly in relation to complex multinational banks where the opportunity for regulatory evasion is greatest. There should be no exceptions, even if that means the dismantling of existing structures.

- Every bank operating in international markets should have access to a lender of last resort in its country of origin. In the BCCI case — thanks to a smooth closure operation — this was not a critical factor but it is worth noting that if there had been a disorderly collapse things could have been very different. Because BCCI is largely a dollar-based bank, its sudden failure could have threatened the integrity of the US payments system, possibly forcing the US authorities to provide emergency support.

- The present patchwork-quilt of deposit insurance arrangements around the world should be internationally coordinated if not formally harmonized. Above all, responsibility for making deposit insurance payments (as well as the lender of last resort function) should rest squarely on the national jurisdiction that has primary responsibility for regulating the bank concerned. In this way the costs of a bank failure will to an important extent be borne by those charged with regulating the institution — thereby providing a strong financial incentive for regulators to adopt high supervisory standards.

- The issue of fraud has to be confronted. In the BCCI case the Luxembourg authorities have been quoted as saying that their regulatory arrangements could not cope with fraud. However, fraud and other criminal activity is liable to gravitate to those financial centres which combine stringent secrecy laws with a weak regulatory environment. This is a complex area where there are no ready answers but regulators may have to become involved in regular on-site bank examinations.

- The procedures for closing and liquidating international banks should be examined. The BCCI closure was relatively clean but could have been delayed both by the absence of a lead regulator and by procedural difficulties. The liquidation is likely to take several years and will involve all manner of conflict-of-law problems in many jurisdictions.

So far as the present study is concerned the BCCI affair illustrates a number of arguments advanced in earlier chapters. To begin with, it is clear that large-scale fraud of the kind found at BCCI cannot be effectively monitored by financial markets, which is an important reason why banks lack transparency and are vulnerable to deposit runs. Furthermore, the withdrawal of deposits from second-line UK banks following the BCCI closure underlines the propensity for contagion that may affect banks which are otherwise sound but have no captive retail deposit base. On the supervisory side, too, the regulatory failures at BCCI provide confirmation that the dispersion of supervisory responsibilities over one institution among many regulators is entirely unsatisfactory — a point that has already been stressed in relation to mixed banking/securities businesses.

BCCI was not itself engaged to any great extent in securities activities, and therefore its collapse does not have a direct bearing on the debate about banks' involvement in securities business. Nevertheless, there is an important message here for policymakers. If bank regulators have difficulty in coordinating their responsibilities, this is even truer of securities markets where there is no equivalent of the Basle Committee and the coordinating machinery is still embryonic. For banks to be rapidly expanding their securities operations around the world without the protection of a coherent international regulatory framework is to risk serious trouble of global proportions.

# Notes

1  This account of the investigation into BCCI is based largely on Testimony given by the Governor of the Bank of England to the House of Commons Treasury and Civil Service Committee on 23 July 1991.

2  For a more comprehensive analysis of international regulatory arrangements see Richard Dale *The Regulation of International Banking*, (Woodhead-Faulkner and Prentice Hall, Cambridge and Englewood Cliffs, New Jersey, 1984).

3  See 'Principles of the supervision of banks' foreign establishments' Committee on Banking Regulations and Supervisory Practices', Basle, May 1983, as cited in Dale *The Regulation of International Banking*, p. 190.

4  Ibid., p. 188.

5  Ibid., p. 190.

# Index